Linguistic Variation
Models and Methods

Linguistic Variation
Models and Methods

Edited by
David Sankoff

Center for Mathematical Research
University of Montreal
Montreal, Quebec, Canada

ACADEMIC PRESS   New York   San Francisco   London
A Subsidiary of Harcourt Brace Jovanovich, Publishers

This volume was prepared with the support of National Science Foundation Grant No. SOC70-02316 A04. Any opinions, findings, conclusions, or recommendations expressed herein are those of the authors and do not necessarily reflect the views of the National Science Foundation.

Reproduction, translation, publication, use, and disposal by and for the United States Government and its officers, agents, and employees acting within the scope of their official duties for Government use only, is permitted.

ACADEMIC PRESS, INC.
111 Fifth Avenue, New York, New York 10003

United Kingdom Edition published by
ACADEMIC PRESS, INC. (LONDON) LTD.
24/28 Oval Road, London NW1 7DX

Library of Congress Cataloging in Publication Data

Main entry under title:

Linguistic variation.

Includes bibliographies.
1. Language and languages––Variation.
I. Sankoff, David.
P120.V37L52   301.2'1   77–77244
ISBN 0–12–618850–5

PRINTED IN THE UNITED STATES OF AMERICA

Contents

v

16 Scalar Variation in Comprehension among Aphasics

17 Variation and Change in Patterns of Speaking: Language Shift in Austria

18 The Linguistic Market and the Statistical Explanation of Variability

19 Are the Masses an Inanimate Object?

20 *Quantitative Aspects of Conversational Interaction*

Chet A. Creider   **267**

List of Contributors

Numbers in parentheses indicate the pages on which the authors' contributions begin.

Robert Berdan* (149), Neuropsychiatric Institute, University of California, Los Angeles, Los Angeles, California

Hélène Bérubé (23), Department of Anthropology, University of Montreal, Montreal, Quebec, Canada

Chet A. Creider (267), Department of Anthropology, University of Western Ontario, London, Ontario, Canada

Ralph W. Fasold (85), Department of Linguistics, Georgetown University, Washington, D. C.

Susan Gal (227), Department of Sociology and Anthropology, Rutgers University, New Brunswick, New Jersey

Jackson T. Gandour† (139), Bell Laboratories, Murray Hill, New Jersey

Richard Harshman (139), Department of Psychology, University of Western Ontario, London, Ontario, Canada

Heidelberger Forschungsprojekt "Pidgin-Deutsch" (1), University of Heidelberg, Heidelberg, Germany

Donald Hindle (161), Department of Linguistics, University of Pennsylvania, Philadelphia, Pennsylvania

Paul Kay (71), Department of Anthropology, University of California, Berkeley, Berkeley, California

Kong-On Kim (185), SWRL Educational Research & Development, Los Alamitos, California

Anthony Kroch (45), Department of Linguistics, Temple University, Philadelphia, Pennsylvania

Suzanne Laberge (119, 239), Department of Anthropology, University of Montreal, Montreal, Quebec, Canada

*Present address: SWRL Educational Research & Development, 4665 Lampson Blvd., Los Alamitos, California 90720.

†Present address: Department of Audiology and Speech Sciences, Purdue University, West Lafayette, Indiana 47907.

Stanley E. Legum (185), SWRL Educational Research & Development, Los Alamitos, California

Mark Liberman (127), Bell Laboratories, Murray Hill, New Jersey

John Macnamara (197), Department of Psychology, McGill University, Montreal, Quebec, Canada

Jean Millo (173), Department of Linguistics, University of Montreal, Montreal, Quebec, Canada

Michel Pêcheux (251), C.N.R.S. and University of Paris VII, Paris, France

Harvey Rosenbaum (185), SWRL Educational Research & Development, Los Alamitos, California

Pascale Rousseau (57, 97), Center for Mathematical Research, University of Montreal, Montreal, Quebec, Canada

David Sankoff (23, 57, 97, 119, 239), Center for Mathematical Research, University of Montreal, Montreal, Quebec, Canada

Laurent Santerre (173), Department of Linguistics, University of Montreal, Montreal, Quebec, Canada

Margaret Seguin (211), Department of Anthropology, University of Western Ontario, London, Ontario, Canada

Cathy Small (45), Department of Linguistics, Temple University, Philadelphia, Pennsylvania

Pierrette Thibault (23), Department of Anthropology, University of Montreal, Montreal, Quebec, Canada

Preface

Of the many branches of sociolinguistics, that which is perhaps the most closely intertwined with linguistics stems from Labov's program for redefining the goals, subject matter, and epistemology of the scientific study of language. The investigation of linguistic variation continually provides new insights into current problems of "pure" phonology, syntax, and semantics, while establishing its own solid empirical base, elaborating its own rigorous and reproducible methodology, and erecting its own theoretical framework for understanding the interaction of social and linguistic processes. Most of its practitioners are trained in linguistics. One consequence is that in contrast to other data-oriented interdisciplinary fields—psycholinguistics, acoustic and articulatory phonetics, computational linguistics—it has relied on a relatively restrained inventory of data-analytic procedures. The tabulation of variant token counts classified by linguistic environment, social category of speaker, or both has been basic. The further arrangement of speakers into implicational scales provides a direct way of understanding variation data in terms of the spread of linguistic rules. The fitting of variable rule models has enabled the evaluation of the relative contribution of various linguistic and social factors to the operation of a rule. Beyond this, there has been the occasional analysis of variance, correlation study, or contingency table, but even these elementary statistical tools have not formed part of variationists' standard methodology.

That few statistical techniques have been necessary is also partly a result of the predominance of a single type of data. Labov's development of the linguistic variable provided a uniquely powerful tool for operationalizing notions of variation in all aspects of spoken language. Counting tokens of the two or more variants of a phonological, morphological, or syntactic variable in a number of linguistically distinct environments has been by far the major data collection technique.

A third aspect of the study of variation, which has developed more slowly than its contribution to linguistic theory, is the social science component. Labov's numerous microsociological innovations have not given rise to a coherent approach within variation study, perhaps because they are so difficult to imitate and improve. Their contribution is instead as technically linguistic examples within interaction analysis, ethnography of speaking, and attitude testing. The macrosociological aspect of linguistic variation analysis has remained the geographic or demographic classification of speakers and their ad hoc stratification into superficially defined occupational or income levels.

Within the last few years, much has changed in these three areas, and there is great potential for further development. New types of data, more sophisticated data analysis, and considerations from wider social theory characterize the current direction of the field. The purpose of this volume is to demonstrate the expanding boundaries of linguistic variation study and to indicate possible future directions. Juxtaposed are studies such as those by Fasold and Kay dealing with the more classic problems of variation methodology, variable rules, and implicational scales, and studies employing relatively new statistical techniques, such as in the work of Rousseau and Sankoff or of Gandour and Harshman. The chapters by Fasold and Kay illustrate the resolution of a long-standing, somewhat confused debate within the field, in terms of precise mathematical formulations. Fasold presents what is, in effect, a theorem establishing Labov's early suggestion of "geometric ordering of constraints" for variable rules as a sufficient condition for a one-dimensional scaling of contexts. Kay shows how the "independence of constraints" condition on a variable rule prevents it from accounting for some scales as well as data in which rule frequencies change over time in a single environment. From this we may infer the need to incorporate interaction terms in certain variable rule analyses. The two chapters by Rousseau and Sankoff document the evolution of variable rules from Labov's pencil-and-paper, trial-and-error evaluations of additive constraint effects on rule operation, to a powerful computer-implemented algorithm incorporating modern methods of mathematical programming, capable of handling a wide range of large data sets, testing for significant differences, interaction, and even detecting the existence of qualitatively different grammars within a population of speakers.

This latter capability represents a contribution within the relatively recent field of statistical classification theory. Gandour and Harshman, and Berdan employ multidimensional scaling, a type of method also developed by workers in this field. Berdan uses it to assess the number of independent dimensions inherent in a multidimensional data set, while Gandour and Harshman put to very original and revealing use a refinement called individual difference scaling, in order to analyze the many dimensions of tone perception.

Other original and powerful methodologies are presented by the Heidelberg group, who fit context-free grammars to syntactic data; Hindle, who compares techniques for normalizing phonetic data from many individuals within a population; and Pêcheux, who establishes common structures across a set of similar discourses.

Aside from the traditional variationist data on the output of phonological and syntactic transformations, the chapters in this volume examine a wide range of language data. Although the spoken language still predominates, we present data on lexical choice (Sankoff, Thibault, & Bérubé) and phrase structure (the Heidelberg group), along with more familiar types of phonological (Berdan; Hindle; Santerre & Millo) and syntactic (Kroch & Small; Sankoff & Laberge; Rousseau & Sankoff) data. In addition we have Creider's innovative quantification of conversation-linked body movements as well as a wealth of data types produced in experimental or test conditions, including Pêcheux's ingeniously created paraphrase corpus, the meticulously constructed similarity matrices on tone perception (Gandour & Harshman), Legum, Kim, and Rosenbaum's carefully controlled data on oral and written comprehension among children of different ages, Seguin's results on word comprehension among aphasics, Macnamara's comparisons of babies' vocabularies, Gal's observations on language choice in a bilingual community, and Liberman's reiterant speech data for studying syllable duration.

As for the sociological implications, two trends are visible, both evidence of a decreased reliance on the cut-and-dried categorizations of stratificational sociology. There is an increasing ethnographic component apparent in several of the studies (Creider; the Heidelberg group; Gal), without any attenuation of the variationist approach. A focus on the interrelationships of language, ideology, and class (Kroch & Small; Pêcheux; Sankoff & Laberge; Gal) promises a rapprochement with European tendencies in sociolinguistics, again without any diminution of the specifically variationist understanding.

Many of the chapters derive from psycholinguistic or acoustic interests, but they are studies of linguistic variation nonetheless, and their inclusion is a deliberate effort to compare and promote the exchange of viewpoints and methodologies which already have much in common. For example, variable rules are comparable to multiple regression as used by Liberman. Multidimensional scaling as perfected in conjunction with phonetic studies, and exemplified by Gandour and Harshman's work, has natural applications in linguistic variation, such as in the chapter by Berdan. The work of Macnamara, Hindle, and Legum *et al.* touches on the crucial problem of the psychological significance of variable, or linguistic usage. Not only is it methodologically worthwhile to be aware of the links between traditional linguistic variation study and related areas, but the scientific investigation of linguistic structure can only benefit from an increased interdisciplinarity.

Acknowledgments

Most of the chapters in this volume were presented in draft versions at a conference on linguistic variation at the University of Montreal, March 25–27, 1977. I am grateful to the Mathematical Social Sciences Board for their financial support, to Stan Peters for first suggesting the conference (in 1973), and to Barbara Partee for persevering with this suggestion and for her helpful encouragement. I have been fortunate in having had the opportunity to collaborate with both Bill Labov and Joe Kruskal over the past few years, and their influence can be seen throughout the book. Their guidance in the planning for the conference, as well as their participation in it, was invaluable.

The five chapters from the Montreal French group represent work which has been largely supported by a series of Canada Council and Killam grants and scholarships to G. Sankoff, H. J. Cedergren, S. Laberge, and myself. The statistical developments were also supported in part by National Research Council of Canada grants to P. Rousseau and myself.

I thank Danielle Duquette for arranging for us to hold the conference in the museum of the University of Montreal's Department of Anthropology, a most agreeable locale, and especially my colleague Suzanne Laberge for her tireless help preparing for the conference and for assuring that everything ran smoothly. I thank as well the other members of the Montreal group who helped with the conference and the preparation of the manuscript, particularly Pascale Rousseau, Gillian Sankoff, and Pierrette Thibault.

Linguistic Variation
Models and Methods

1

The Acquisition of German Syntax by Foreign Migrant Workers[1]

Heidelberger Forschungsprojekt "Pidgin-Deutsch"

INTRODUCTION

This chapter deals with the main aims, methods, and some results of a project undertaken at the University of Heidelberg in which we try to analyze the undirected **natural** acquisition of German by Spanish and Italian migrant workers. Their language may be considered as a set of pidginized varieties of German.[2] Because it shows some structural and functional similarities to colonial pidgins, we call it **Pidgin-Deutsch** ('Pidgin-German'), using a term coined by Clyne (1968), the first paper on this topic. The use of this term should not be misinterpreted, however; we

[1]This paper is an extended discussion of the work reported in Heidelberger Forschungsprojekt "Pidgin-Deutsch" (HPD, 1977). See also Becker, Dittmar, and Klein (1977), Dittmar and Rieck (1976, 1977), and HPD (1975a, b, 1976). For the general sociolinguistic background, see Dittmar 1976, Klein 1974. This chapter is based—as are all our papers—on the work of the whole research group: Angelika Becker, Norbert Dittmar, Margit Gutmann, Wolfgang Klein, Bert-Olaf Rieck, Gunter and Ingeborg Senft, Wolfram Steckner, and Elisabeth Thielicke. The present formulation is by Klein and Dittmar. We are very grateful to David Sankoff who carefully corrected the manuscript and made a number of valuable suggestions.

[2]For a discussion of the "pidgin problem" see HPD (1975a, Chapter 2) and the papers in Klein (1975), particularly Meisel (1975).

employ it as a more or less convenient label for a rather complex and unexplored phenomenon. Whether or not the German spoken by foreign migrant workers is a **true** pidgin is a difficult question, requiring a great deal more knowledge both about pidgins in general and about foreign migrant workers' German in particular before it can be answered. One point should be made clear right from the beginning: Pidgin-German is by no means a stable language but is a rather heterogeneous system of varieties. In this respect it does not differ from any other language—if the languages themselves are taken into consideration instead of just regularized descriptions of them.

In the following section something will be said about the project itself, about its aims, and particularly about the process of language acquisition (or, strictly speaking, second language acquisition) and how to model it. In the third section we will explain our descriptive framework as it concerns syntax. We have developed a particular way of describing variation, the central concept of this procedure being that of **variety grammar**. Transitional grammars are particular cases of variety grammars. In the fourth section, a short outline of some empirical aspects of our work will be given, and in the final section, we will informally present some of our major findings.

MODELING THE ACQUISITION PROCESS

In January 1976, the foreign migrant worker population in West Germany amounted to 4.1 million people (including family members), approximately 850,000 of whom come from Italy or Spain. Most of them do not know a word of German when they arrive, but in their daily living, they learn what is most urgently needed, some of them eventually achieving a certain fluency. This is clearly an important problem from both linguistic and social points of view. The miserable social situation of foreign workers is due not only to economic factors, such as insecurity of employment, low-prestige work, and so on, but also in large measure to a rather thorough exclusion from the local social and political life. With some exceptions, they form a class of their own or, strictly speaking, classes of their own, there being often great social distances between nationalities, for example, between Italian and Turkish workers.

The social isolation of foreign migrant workers is closely connected with their linguistic isolation. It would be ridiculous, of course, to posit this as the sole explanation, and it would be even more ridiculous to imagine that their social isolation could be corrected by improving only their language skills. Nevertheless, it seems evident that a reasonable solution to the social problem is impossible without a solution to the language problem. Hence, helping these workers to improve their communicative competence in the widest sense of the term is a necessary though not sufficient condition, and it is to just this task that linguists can contribute—perhaps. It is our opinion that this cannot be done without a careful analysis of the current processes of acquisition of German by foreign workers and of the various social and individual factors governing this natural, undirected kind of language learning. Our research encompasses the phonological, morphological, syntactic, and pragmatic levels, but the following considerations are confined to the role of syntax only within the process of language acquisition.[3]

In the present context, the term **language acquisition** refers only to second language learning in a social environment where the language to be learned is spoken—second language learning without explicit teaching. Language acquisition in this sense is a rather slow process with many intermediate stages, each stage being characterized by a set of grammatical rules the speaker or the group of speakers masters at a given time. These sets may be considered as particular varieties of the second language, varieties that may be correct or ridiculous in the opinion of an average speaker of that language. A highly simplified description of the whole process of language acquisition would then be in terms of a stepwise approximation, passing through a series of intermediate varieties in the direction of a **target variety** (or target varieties, if there is internal variation in the language depending on social environment). In most cases, the target variety is never reached, though the whole process moves in its direction. The specific nature of the different speech varieties, their similarities and differences, and the trajectory of the process are governed by a set of extralinguistic factors such as:

1. Time (i.e., duration of stay)
2. Kind of job
3. Location
4. Origin (i.e., mother tongue or dialect)
5. Degree of social relationship (intensity of contact)
6. Family status
7. Mobility
8. Sex
9. Age (at time of immigration)
10. Education
11. Individual attitudes (e.g., motivation).

[3]Some general aspects of communicative behavior are discussed in HPD (1975a, Chapter 4) and in HPD (1975b).

There are additional factors that might be important, but those listed here will suffice for the present discussion. Taken together, they constitute both a learning context and an individual disposition; correspondingly, they can be subdivided into **environment factors** and **bias factors.** Each learner is characterized by a set of specifications of these factors which determine a complex system of diverse acquisition conditions. Let us neglect for the moment all possible factors but one, namely, duration of stay, and turn to the general problem of how to describe the process of language acquisition along the dimension of time. It should be emphasized, however, that the choice of this factor is for illustrative purposes only. Indeed, we have found that duration of stay is completely overshadowed in explanatory value by other factors after about 2 years.

Let us imagine that each speech variety can be described by a grammar, say, a transformational grammar or a simple context-free grammar. Each of these grammars, which we call **transitional grammars,** characterizes the variety situated at a certain point along the process of language acquisition. This yields a series of grammars along the dimension of time, for example:

Duration of stay: (in months)	6	12	24	48	96
Grammar:	G_1	G_2	G_3	G_4	G_5

The subdivision of time is set by the linguist, who may refine it to be relevant and interesting for current purposes. A key problem becomes how to describe the transition from one grammar to the next. The simplest way to depict the relationships between the grammars is as follows: Form the (set-theoretical) union of all rule sets, i.e., all rules occurring in at least one grammar, and then after each interval of time indicate whether or not the rule in question occurs.

This leads to a presentation such as:

Rule	G_1	G_2	G_3	G_4	G_5
r_1	+	+	+	+	+
r_2	+	+	+	+	+
r_3	-	-	+	+	+
r_4	-	+	+	+	+
r_5	-	-	-	-	+
r_6	+	+	-	+	+
r_7	-	-	-	+	+
r_8	-	-	+	-	+
r_9	-	-	+	-	+
r_{10}	+	+	-	-	-

In this fragmentary (and fictitious) example the transitional grammar G_1 contains the rules r_1, r_2, r_6, and r_{10}; 6 months later, the speaker (or the group of speakers) has learned another rule, r_4; 1 year later, we note that in G_3 four additional rules, r_3, r_7, r_8, and r_9, have been added and two previous rules, r_6 and r_{10}, have been dropped, and so on. This kind of description in terms of rule adding and rule dropping is well known; it suffers from at least two crucial inadequacies:

1. The description of transition in terms of sudden qualitative changes from minus to plus or plus to minus is rather inaccurate. In fact, there is often a long period of time in which rules co-occur and it is only a gradual shift in usage frequency that leads to the replacement of one rule by another. Hence, the description should make use of the whole continuum of real numbers between 0 and 1 instead of just + and −.

2. In the simple model presented above, only one dimension of variation is taken into account, namely, duration of stay. This is clearly inadequate. There is variation, too, according to factors like origin, kind of job, age at the time of immigration, and so on. If we accept that the 11 factors just cited can influence the process of language acquisition, we cannot assume a one-dimensional space of variation. An adequate representation of this variation may well require a multidimensional space.

In developing a model having both of these capacities, we have tried to fulfill one more condition: The model must be simple enough to be operationally applied to a large amount of data.

A DESCRIPTIVE FRAMEWORK FOR VARIATION[4]

Two basic concepts are **space of varieties** and **probabilistic grammars.** Probabilistic grammars, developed mainly by Grenander (1967), Suppes (1972), and Salomaa (1969) are simply formal grammars with an index associated with each rule giving the probability of rule application. The details depend on the type of grammar and whether conditioned probabilities are taken into account; we shall not discuss this here. A space of varieties is an analytic grid sufficient to distinguish all possible speech varieties thought to exist. Suppose in a given domain of investigation there are three relevant factors of variation:

1. Sex, with two possible values s_1 (male) and s_2 (female)
2. Age (at the time of immigration) with, say, four possible values a_1, . . ., a_4, where a_1 = 20 to 30 years, a_2 = 31 to 40 years, etc.
3. Duration of stay, with five possible values d_1, . . ., d_5, where d_1 = from 6 months to 1 year; d_2 = 1 to 2 years, etc.

[4]The concept of variety grammar was introduced and defined in Klein (1974).

This leads to $2 \times 4 \times 5 = 40$ possible varieties, each one defined by a triple of factors; e.g., (s_2, a_2, d_2) is the speech variety of a woman who immigrated a year or two ago between the ages of 30 and 40. This variety may well be identical from a linguistic point of view to some other variety, perhaps to (s_1, a_3, d_2), but whether or not this is the case is an empirical question. The entire set of triples constitutes the space of varieties on which the investigation is based. Of course, one cannot be sure that the space of varieties constructed in this way contains only and all the relevant factors and distinctions. It is simply a hypothesis about the relevant determinants of variation in the domain under study.

Next, representative data must be obtained for each variety within the space of varieties, and a grammar must be written, or part of a grammar, if the interest is only in a particular linguistic problem. This may be a context-free grammar, a context-sensitive grammar, a dependency grammar, a transformational grammar, or whatever, but it must be clearly defined. The result is a set of n grammars, if there are n varieties. The next task is to interrelate these grammars by establishing a **reference grammar** consisting of the union of all rule sets of the particular grammars. This reference grammar describes nothing; it is merely a useful analytical construct. It can generate each variety by the association to each rule of an appropriate number between 0 and 1. This number indicates the probability of application of this rule in the variety in question. A given rule may be applied in a certain variety with probability .9, which means—informally speaking—that it is an important rule in that variety. In another variety, its probability may be .2, that is, it is less probable that it occurs in the derivation of a sentence. In a third variety, its probability may even be 0, that is, it does not occur at all in that variety. The same grammar then is used to describe all varieties in a given space of varieties, and the differences among them are expressed by the differences of rule values.

DATA COLLECTION AND ANALYSIS

Our grammatical description is essentially based on interview material, although in our project we have also made use of participant observation data to study phenomena such as code switching, linguistic expression of social relationship, and so on.

We decided to interview 48 persons and to stratify the sample as follows:

1. 32 men and 16 women (this reflects approximately the actual distribution)
2. 24 Italian and 24 Spanish workers

3. 12 workers from each of the following duration-of-stay categories
   a. Up to 2 years
   b. From 2 to 4 years
   c. From 4 to 6 years
   d. More than 6 years.

(All the other factors mentioned earlier in the second section are also registered.) An informant then may be considered to represent a collection of specified factors, to be representative of a certain variety.

The interview took the form of casual but gently directed conversations which were recorded on a two-track recorder (Uher 210, Lavalière microphones). Special techniques, most of them from Labov, Cohen, Robins and Lewis (1968), were used to avoid communicative disturbances and deviations from usual communicative behavior. From each interview, 15 minutes were transcribed in a simplified phonetic notation. (Excerpts from our transcriptions are published as an appendix to HPD [1975a].)

The next step consisted in developing a reference grammar including all rules applying at least once among our 48 texts. The rules are context-free. A complete syntax would require the addition of word-order transformations, but the treatment of these rules has been postponed to a later phase of our study. The grammar we worked with, after six or seven revisions follows (Figure 1).

In order to facilitate reference and discussion, a list of **categories** was added, but it should be kept in mind that this is a formal grammar, and symbols like AC or PROP have meaning by virtue only of the rules in which they occur. The grammar contains 101 context-free rules in all, grouped into 15 rule clusters. A rule cluster consists of all rules with the same left-hand symbol, the rules within a cluster being alternative ways of rewriting this symbol. For instance, in rule cluster 3, VC may be rewritten as VG or as PVL, where VG leads to sentences with (finite) verb or copula and PVL to sentence without (finite) verb or copula.

This reference grammar was used to parse 100 sentences from each informant's interview, and hence to compile relative frequencies of rule applications within each cluster. The parsing was recorded in the form of labeled bracketing, facilitating the counting of rule applications. We interpret the relative frequencies of rule applications as estimates of the probabilities within the variety the 100 sentences represent. These estimates may not be too accurate in some cases, because the number of occurrences is sometimes too small to ensure that the figures would not significantly change were a larger number of sentences to be considered. Nevertheless, the relative frequencies after 50 sentences and then after 100 sentences per informant were essentially the same.

The result of this procedure may be imagined to be a matrix consisting

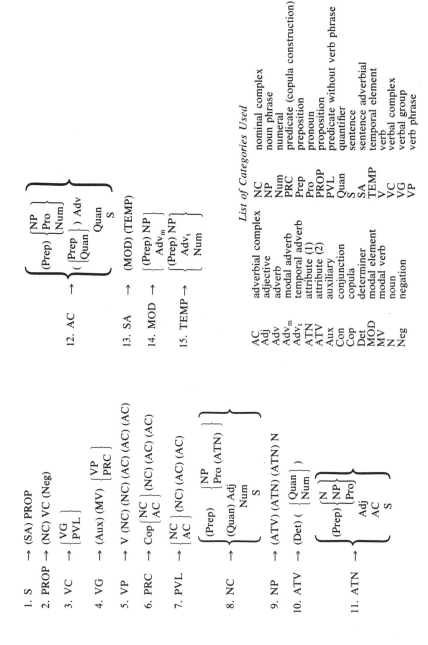

Figure 1. Reference grammar.

of 48 rows and 101 columns, where each row corresponds to an informant, or, strictly speaking, to a variety represented by that informant and each column to a rule of the reference grammar. Each cell of the matrix contains a number between 0 and 1, representing the application probability of the rule in the variety in question.

This basic matrix is a complete description of language variation during the process of language acquisition, insofar as this could be extracted from our data on 48 informants and as it is restricted to syntax and then only a part of syntax. It is not reprinted here because most of the rules show little or no variability, having similar or even identical values in all varieties. In some cases, this lack of variability may be caused by the small numbers of occurrences. Hence, for the next stage of the analysis we excluded (a) all rules with an average of less than 50 occurrences per informant and (b) all rules whose variability ranges over less than 40% of the possible range. (A rule's probability may range from 0 to 1. If it ranges from .3 to .5, it is excluded; if it ranges from 0 to .5, it is taken into account.) This somewhat arbitrary restriction is made to conserve time and effort, and should not materially affect the results. The remaining rules follow (Figure 2). Their probabilities for the 48 informants comprise the reduced matrix in Table 1.

Fine distinctions between different rules of the same cluster are neglected. For instance, the rules from 12.02 to 12.11 are collapsed together (Table 1). This matrix represents the syntax of our informants insofar as it is variable. It allows for a direct and precise study of the variability of particular rules and rule sets. Consider for example the values of rules 2.03 + 2.04 which represent the use of nominal complexes (NC) in subject position, or simply speaking the frequency with which sentence subjects are present. Informant SP-35 uses no subject noun (or pronoun) in more than 70% of all sentences, while Informant IT-01, the speaker closest to the standard dialect, always uses one; he applies the rule with a probability of 1. Or consider rule 3.01 which states one of the two possible ways to construct a simple sentence—with or without a (finite) verb or a copula. Whether a learner uses finite elements is surely an important fact of language acquisition. Informant SP-35 uses no verb (or copula) in most cases; he uses mainly predicative nouns, adverbs, or adjectives (in predicative function) without a copula. IT-01, on the other hand, uses verbs or copulas whenever possible. Between these extreme cases, there is a continuum of intermediate stages as evidenced by the spectrum of values in Table 1.

The values in a given row of the matrix indicate the informants' syntactic performance with respect to a certain set of rules. It seems interesting and useful to compute an overall syntactic index summarizing the infor-

2.01	PROP	→	VC		8.04	NC	→	Prep NP
2.02	PROP	→	VC Neg		8.05	NC	→	Prep Pro
2.03	PROP	→	NC VC		8.06	NC	→	Prep Pro ATN
2.04	PROP	→	NC VC Neg		8.07	NC	→	Adj
					8.08	NC	→	Quan Adj
3.01	VC	→	VG		8.09	NC	→	Num
3.02	VC	→	PVL		8.10	NC	→	S
4.01	VG	→	VP		9.01	NP	→	N
4.02	VG	→	Aux VP		9.02	NP	→	ATV N
4.03	VG	→	MV VP		9.03	NP	→	ATN N
4.04	VG	→	Aux MV VP		9.04	NP	→	ATV ATN N
4.05	VG	→	PRC		9.05	NP	→	ATN ATN N
4.06	VG	→	Aux PRC		9.06	NP	→	ATV ATN ATN N
4.07	VG	→	MV PRC					
4.08	VG	→	Aux MV PRC		10.01	ATV	→	Det
					10.02	ATV	→	Quan
5.01	VP	→	V		10.03	ATV	→	Num
5.02	VP	→	V NC		10.04	ATV	→	Det Quan
5.03	VP	→	V NC NC		10.05	ATV	→	Det Num
5.04	VP	→	V AC					
5.05	VP	→	V AC AC		12.01	AC	→	NP
5.06	VP	→	V AC AC AC		12.02	AC	→	Pro
5.07	VP	→	V NC AC		12.03	AC	→	Num
5.08	VP	→	V NC AC AC		12.04	AC	→	Prep NP
5.09	VP	→	V NC AC AC AC		12.05	AC	→	Prep Pro
5.10	VP	→	V NC NC AC		12.06	AC	→	Prep Num
5.11	VP	→	V NC NC AC AC		12.07	AC	→	Adv
5.12	VP	→	V NC NC AC AC AC		12.08	AC	→	Prep Adv
					12.09	AC	→	Quan Adv
8.01	NC	→	NP		12.10	AC	→	Quan
8.02	NC	→	Pro		12.11	AC	→	S
8.03	NC	→	Pro ATN					

Figure 2.   Phrase structure rules.

mation given by all the individual rule values. There are several possible ways of doing this. For example, we might simply take an informant's average value for all rules, but for several reasons this is not too meaningful a procedure. The way we computed our syntactic index is more complicated and is explained in HPD (1976, Chapters 4 and 6). This index accords well with our intuitions about the syntactic elaborateness of our informants and the highest syntactic index values among them approach those of a group of native speakers we analyzed for the sake of comparison. Nevertheless, for the reasons developed earlier in the second section, we refrain from any theoretical interpretation of such a cumulative index. Here we use it merely to determine the order in which to present the informants.

Table 2 presents the correlation coefficients between some of the subrules used for the construction of the syntactic index (cf. Figures 1 and 2 and Table 1). The pattern which emerges from these values justifies to a

TABLE 1

Different Stages in the Acquisition of German by Migrant Workers: Probabilistic Values for Selected Phrase Structure Rules and Syntactic Index

	Rules								
Informant	2.03 and 2.04	3.01	4.02 to 4.08	5.02 to 5.12	8.02 and 8.03	9.02 to 9.06	10.01	12.02 to 12.11	Syntactic index
IT-01	1.00	1.00	.83	.84	.61	.79	.88	.99	1.602
SP-11	.95	1.00	.89	.91	.60	.68	.82	.97	1.448
IT-31	.95	1.00	.60	.93	.54	.67	.80	.94	1.243
SP-29	.85	.99	.61	.89	.60	.72	.82	.91	1.234
SP-19	.94	1.00	.57	.83	.55	.82	.75	.92	1.233
IT-22	.84	.95	.42	.90	.64	.71	.69	.80	.961
SP-31	.89	.97	.47	.75	.47	.84	.79	.85	.956
IT-02	.74	.88	.47	.85	.55	.73	.79	.96	.934
SP-24	.85	.98	.47	.85	.70	.62	.46	.90	.831
SP-17	.94	.85	.41	.80	.47	.64	.80	.88	.765
IT-10	.73	.92	.45	.89	.48	.62	.72	.91	.709
IT-06	.82	.96	.51	.77	.53	.57	.55	.83	.527
IT-33	.77	.90	.60	.86	.43	.61	.50	.66	.375
IT-20	.70	.91	.24	.76	.52	.60	.58	.96	.374
SP-06	.61	.87	.38	.82	.51	.57	.58	.84	.291
SP-13	.72	.79	.15	.85	.42	.57	.61	.89	.208
IT-15	.63	.82	.27	.87	.35	.55	.67	.88	.200
SP-01	.62	.67	.40	.70	.51	.60	.68	.79	.135
SP-36	.65	.72	.21	.92	.33	.50	.59	.98	.116
IT-26	.57	.78	.12	.81	.49	.51	.69	.92	.112
IT-05	.73	.71	.17	.87	.40	.52	.69	.71	.059
IT-25	.64	.69	.42	.76	.49	.57	.58	.68	.031
IT-32	.64	.73	.07	.82	.40	.63	.57	.77	-.030
IT-18	.63	.65	.20	.81	.31	.76	.64	.62	-.033
SP-30	.72	.70	.07	.74	.35	.59	.62	.81	-.092
IT-16	.50	.75	.13	.71	.32	.67	.63	.92	-.092
SP-18	.61	.72	.04	.90	.43	.44	.67	.72	-.124
SP-26	.67	.66	.18	.75	.30	.46	.81	.81	-.128
IT-28	.55	.66	.11	.73	.41	.60	.67	.72	-.220
IT-07	.60	.68	.15	.80	.46	.42	.69	.66	-.225
SP-15	.66	.86	.16	.86	.41	.34	.35	.87	-.236
IT-29	.55	.69	.06	.57	.49	.52	.83	.74	-.265
SP-14	.62	.74	.05	.85	.34	.52	.59	.63	-.285
SP-12	.65	.65	.02	.67	.25	.73	.64	.73	-.290
IT-12	.56	.51	.18	.76	.45	.53	.50	.80	-.303
SP-09	.58	.76	.00	.76	.48	.58	.32	.68	-.384
IT-13	.65	.46	.02	.61	.35	.42	.71	.79	-.575
IT-09	.68	.43	.05	.82	.40	.41	.41	.66	-.610
SP-04	.55	.57	.00	.82	.26	.45	.57	.62	-.662
IT-23	.53	.41	.08	.69	.38	.60	.46	.56	-.727
IT-24	.52	.45	.13	.78	.24	.45	.59	.57	-.789
IT-08	.53	.21	.00	.95	.10	.52	.53	.64	-.851
SP-08	.45	.61	.15	.83	.33	.36	.26	.64	-.875
SP-02	.56	.42	.05	.70	.37	.48	.47	.33	-.997
SP-21	.42	.36	.00	.72	.23	.70	.52	.31	-1.035
SP-25	.50	.31	.00	.61	.31	.51	.24	.82	-1.064
SP-22	.72	.49	.00	.49	.30	.46	.42	.43	-1.126
SP-35	.29	.16	.00	.33	.15	.33	.05	.43	-2.396
Mean	.67	.71	.24	.78	.42	.57	.60	.76	
Standard Deviation	.15	.22	.23	.12	.13	.12	.17	.17	

TABLE 2

Correlations (Pearson r) between (a) Some Important Subrules, (b) Subrules and Syntactic Index, and (c) Subrules and "Age at Time of Immigration" (A.T.I.) and "Duration of Stay" (D.S.)

Subrules	Subrules						Sociological variables	
	2.03+2.04	3.01	4.02+4.04	8.02	9.02, 9.04 +10.01	12.04, 12.05, 12.06 +12.08	A.T.I.	D.S.
2.03+2.04	-						-.40[+]	.07
3.01	.79[++]	-					-.55[++]	.16
4.02+4.04	.72[++]	.62[++]	-				-.38[+]	.23
8.02	.70[++]	.81[++]	.61[++]	-			-.42[+]	.09
9.02+9.04 +10.01	.72[++]	.65[++]	.63[++]	.50[++]	-		-.48[++]	.26
12.04+12.05 12.06+12.08	.60[++]	.66[++]	.43[+]	.49[++]	.48[++]	-	-.42[+]	-.02
Syntactic index	.88[++]	.92[++]	.73[++]	.80[++]	.81[++]	.65[++]	-.56[++]	.19

+ = significant at .01 level.
++ = significant at .001 level.

certain extent the construction of the syntactic index. The correlations of syntactic rules (and index) with two sociological variables (age at time of immigration [A.T.I.] and duration of stay [D.S.]) also shown in Table 2 will be discussed on pages 18–21.

Figure 3 illustrates the correlation of the rules NC→Pro (8.2) and VC→VG (3.01) in the form of a scattergram.

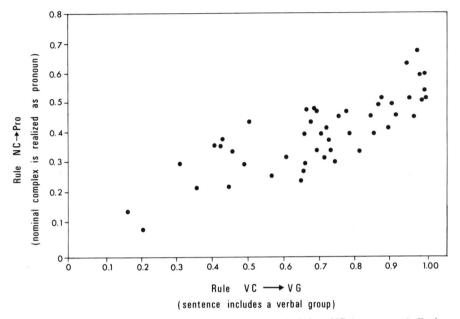

Figure 3. Correlation between rule NC → Pro and rule VC → VG (scattergram). Each point represents one informant, plotted according to frequency of the two rules.

OVERALL RESULTS AND CONCLUSIONS

Outline of Stages in the Acquisition of German Syntax

To obtain an accurate picture of syntactic development, the evolution of individual rules or rule clusters must be considered. We have made a detailed study of this kind, the results of which are summarized here in an informal and sketchy way. We concentrate here upon five principal areas of syntactic development: the structure of whole **propositions, verbal complexes** (VC), **nominal complexes** (NC), **adverbial complexes** (AC), and **subordinate clauses.** Although the terminology we use differs somewhat from standard nomenclature, there should be no difficulty in understanding it.

1. The proposition
   a. In the initial stage, propositions are formed without any finite element (verb or copula) and without a subject, e.g., /kɪnda traɪ/ '(I have) three children' or /aɪnə ta: aɪnə ma futɪ/, literally 'one day one mark fifty'.
   b. The most advanced learner never uses propositions without a finite element or a subject; this corresponds to the usage of native speakers.
2. The verbal complex
   a. The constituents of the verbal complex are learned in the following order: simple verb, copula, modal verb, auxiliaries. Combinations of modal verb, auxiliary + verb or copula are acquired very late.
   b. In the early stages, verbs are complementized by only one nominal complex (direct or indirect object) or one adverbial complex. There is a very regular and steady increase in the number of complexes depending on the verb.
3. The nominal complex
   a. Simple nouns (proper nouns, class nouns without an article or modifier, etc.) precede pronouns in order of acquisition.
   b. In the beginning, noun phrases do not have any modifier or determiner. There is a steady process of elaborating complex noun phrases.
   c. Within the class of determiners, there is a continuous shift from simple numbers (/svaɪ ma:/ 'two marks') and quantifiers (/fɪ: arbaɪ/, 'much work') to articles, i.e., numbers and quantifiers predominate at first; articles occur mainly in later stages.
   d. The first and most important adjectivals are adjectives. Prepositional phrases functioning adjectivally and relative clauses appear very late.
   e. Nominal clauses ('that . . .', 'whether . . .') first appear in the middle stages.
4. The adverbial complex
   a. The first adverbials are simple noun phrases without any preposition (/doisla/ 'in Germany, to Germany, for Germany'). This structure disappears rapidly. It is replaced by simple adverbs, prepositional phrases and adverbial clauses.
   b. Prepositional phrases with nouns are learned before prepositional phrases with pronouns (/baɪ maɪn kole:ga/ 'with my colleague' before /bai ɪ:m/ 'with him').
5. Subordinate clauses
   The acquisition of subordinate clauses shows a very clear and dis-

tinct order: Adverbial clauses are learned before nominal clauses, nominal clauses before relative clauses.

The whole process of the acquisition of syntax can then be described roughly as follows: The first utterances consist of simple or slightly expanded nominal complexes and/or adverbial complexes of a very simple kind. Then, the first finite verbs occur, sentences take on subjects, and the first pronouns are used. Verbal complexes and nominal complexes continuously increase in complexity during this process. Adverbial prepositional phrases and adverbs supplant simple noun phrases functioning as adverbials. Adverbial clauses, copulas, modal verbs, and adnominal prepositional phrases are learned. Only in the last stages is the expansion of verb or copula by auxiliaries and modal verbs learned. The same holds for the acquisition of nominal and relative clauses.

A Pattern of Overgeneralization: The Case of the Modal Verb *Müssen*

Overgeneralization of a specific form or rule of the target language during undirected second language learning process is a well-known fact. As an example, we will consider the acquisition of German modal verbs used as finite forms in connection with infinite verb forms. The co-occurrences of the finite modal and the infinite verb form are globally analyzed in our phrase structure grammar by rule 4.03 (see Figure 2, p. 10). For the application probability of this rule, we calculated the following values for the four groups of our sample[5]:

TABLE 3

Raw Scores and Application Probabilities for the Rule
VERBAL GROUP → MODAL VERB + VERB by Four Groups of Foreign Workers

Groups	Raw scores	Probabilities
I	4	.01
II	25	.03
III	94	.11
IV	72	.07

Table 3 shows a kind of **crossover** pattern for Group III. The rule is applied by this group with a rate substantially higher than not only Groups

[5]Each group includes 12 speakers. The sample was divided into groups on the base of the syntactic index. Consequently, Group IV covers IT-01 to IT-06, Group III IT-33 to IT-18, Group II SP-30 to SP-09, and Group I IT-13 to SP-35 (cf. Table 1). Group I shows the greatest and Group IV the smallest distance from the local Heidelberg vernacular.

I and II, but also Group IV, which corresponds most closely to the local vernacular and can be supposed to employ modal verbs in a wider and more differentiated range. In order to explain this crossover, it seems useful first of all to enumerate the lexical realizations of the modal verb rule. Altogether, we find the five modals *können, wollen, müssen, sollen,* and *mögen* appearing in a total of 195 sentences.

TABLE 4

Lexical Realization of Modal Verbs and Their Quantitative Proportions within the Rule MODAL VERB + VERB for Four Groups of Foreign Workers

Groups	Modal Verb					Total
	mögen	*sollen*	*müssen*	*wollen*	*können*	
I	-	-	-	3	1	4
II	-	-	13	9	3	25
III	-	1	75	12	6	94
IV	3	5	19	26	19	72
Total	3	6	107	50	29	195
Probabilities	.02	.03	.55	.26	.15	

Table 4 shows that (*a*) *müssen, wollen,* and *können* are the modals applied with greatest frequency; (*b*) *wollen* and *können* are applied at an earlier stage than *müssen;* (*c*) *mögen* und *sollen* are acquired very late; and (*d*) *müssen* contributes more than 50% to the applications of the rule. Most striking, however, is the fact that Group III applies *müssen* at a very high rate with 75 occurrences, 80% of their total modals. If we look at the values for Group IV, we note that *müssen, wollen,* and *können* are used in approximately the same proportion. The high value of *müssen* for Group III, which contrasts sharply with that of Group IV (cf. the crossover pattern of Figure 4), can then be supposed to be either a function of specific topics of discourse or of particular learner strategies. If the latter is the case, *müssen* acquires a broader meaning than standard German commonly allows.

A look at the interview passages of those learners in Group III who use the modal very often shows that particular verbal strategies rather than specific discourse topics seem to be responsible for the frequent application of *müssen*. We find that *muss* is apparently used as a substitute for morphological tense markers of the verb. It functions then as a feature of overgeneralization in the sense that it not only covers the meaning in standard German of *müssen* as an obligation to do something, but also the tense and aspect system of the verb.[6]

[6]The process of "overgeneralization" is discussed in Corder (1973, pp. 272–294).

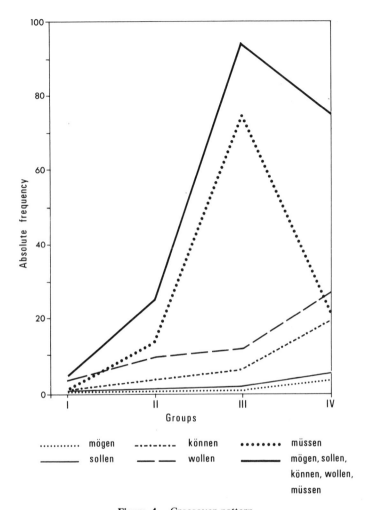

Figure 4. Crossover pattern.

The overgeneralized use of *müssen* can be explained in a preliminary way by **linguistic** and **sociological** arguments. Linguistically, *muss* functions as an **overgeneralized feature** and **covert error.** The application of *muss* here is overgeneralized because it covers a broader range of grammatical and semantic meaning than it does in German vernacular. The construction represents—in many cases—a covert error because the sentence is well formed on the surface, but erroneous in semantic deep structure (interpretation). The learner simply inserts *muss* in order to make the sentence acceptable, but the superficially correct formulation appears to be contextually and semantically inappropriate. The selection of *muss* as a suitable formal expression of the learning strategy may be explained by the fact that *muss* has the comfortable property of having the same form in first and third person singular.

From a sociological point of view, the overgeneralized use of *müssen* has three interesting aspects. First of all, it seems to be the modal that foreign migrant workers hear most frequently in everyday communication, particularly at work. Though its use in lieu of the verbal tense and aspect system seems to be socially motivated, its significance is mainly linguistic—since the specific meaning of *müssen* as an expression of an obligation is unconsciously extended to other meanings. Thus, the concept of *müssen* has been only partially recognized. Second, the insertion of *muss* before the verb form serves to avoid the use of the unmarked verb forms which represent a socially stigmatized feature of the use of German by foreign migrant workers. The use of *muss* has then the function of increasing their social acceptability by "improving" their speaking behavior.

Finally, the excessive use of the *muss* + Verb construction reflects characteristics of a particular group of learners who have acquired a level of German which may not be very good from a normative point of view, but which is sufficient for the resolution of everyday communication problems. These learners have lived in Germany for 4 to 6 years and are between 20 and 30 years old. Their contact with Germans, their style of living, and their jobs seem to indicate that these learners are involved in a process of social adaptation. These results, however, must be considered preliminary, awaiting further data collection and analysis as must our observation that the overgeneralized use of *müssen* is more apparent among women than among men.

Social Correlates of the Syntactic Acquisition Process

Finally, we outline the connection between the syntactic performance in German of the 48 Italian and Spanish workers and the social environment. In order to isolate factors which favor or hinder the process of second language learning, we have correlated the syntactic indices of the 48 informants with extralinguistic variables (cf. points 1–11 on p. 3). Correlations of the syntactic data with extralinguistic parameters show that the acquisition process is governed by the following six variables listed here in the order of their decreasing influence:

1. Contact with Germans during leisure time ($\eta = .64$)[7]

[7]"η" describes the correlation between an independent nominal variable and a dependent metrical variable: "In this case, 'η' is the most sensitive correlation coefficient [Benninghaus, 1974, p. 230]." This correlation coefficient turned out to be the most appropriate for the kind of data we are dealing with.

2. Age at time of immigration ($\eta = .57; r = .56$)
3. Contact with Germans at place of work ($\eta = .53$)
4. Professional training in the country of origin ($\eta = .42$)
5. Education (years of attendance at school) ($\eta = .35; r = .33$)
6. Duration of stay ($\eta = .28; r = .20$).

"Contact with Germans" and "age at time of immigration" seem then to be the most important factors governing the level of second language

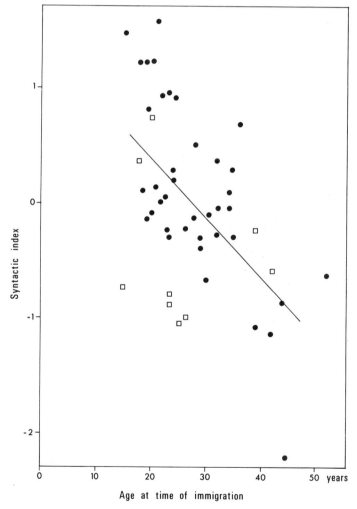

Figure 5. Scatter diagram: 48 foreign workers according to syntactic index and age at time of immigration. Informants with a duration of stay of less than 2.4 years are marked with open squares.

learning performance. At the beginning of our study, we hypothesized that "duration of stay" would play a major role in the process of acquisition of the second language. It turns out that this factor is only significant for the first 2 years of stay. After this, its effect is overridden by other social factors.

Figures 5 and 6 give some idea of these correlations and illustrate the differences between the correlation of the syntactic index with "age at the

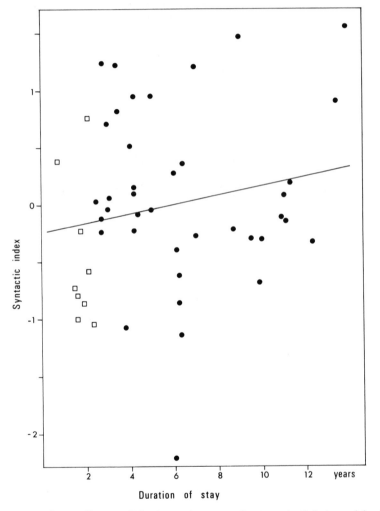

Figure 6.   Scatter diagram: 48 foreign workers according to syntactic index and duration of stay. Informants with a duration of stay of less than 2.4 years are marked with open squares.

time of immigration" and "duration of stay." Correlation coefficients between the syntactic index and subrules, on one hand, and "age at time of immigration" and "duration of stay," on the other, are found in Table 2.

REFERENCES

Becker, A., Dittmar, N., & Klein, W. Sprachliche und soziale Determinanten im kommunikativen Verhalten ausländischer Arbeiter. In U. Quasthoff (Ed.), *Sprachstruktur–Sozialstruktur. Zur linguistischen Theoriebildung.* Kronberg/Ts: Scriptor Verlag, 1977.

Benninghaus, H. *Deskriptive Statistik.* Struttgart: Teubner, 1974.

Clyne, M. Zum Pidgin-Deutsch der Gastarbeiter. *Zeitschrift für Mundartforschung,* 1968, *35,* 130–139.

Corder, P. *Introducing applied linguistics.* Harmondsworth: Penguin, 1973.

Dittmar, N. *Sociolinguistics. A critical survey of theory and application.* London: Arnold, 1976.

Dittmar, N., & Rieck, B.-O. Reihenfolgen im ungesteuerten Erwerb des Deutschen. Zur Erlernung grammatischer Strukturen durch ausländische Arbeiter. In R. Dietrich (Ed.), *Aspekte des Fremdsprachenerwerbs. Beiträge zum 2. Fortbildungskurs 'Deutsch als Fremdsprache', Heidelberg 1975.* Kronberg/Ts: Scriptor Verlag, 1976, 119–145.

Dittmar, N., & Rieck, B.-O. Datenerhebung und Datenauswertung im Heidelberger Forschungsprojekt 'Pidgin-Deutsch ausländischer Arbeiter'. In U. Bielefeld, E. W. B. Hess-Lüttich, & A. Lundt (Eds.), *Soziolinguistik und Empirie. Beiträge zum Berliner Symposium 'Corpusgewinnung und Corpusauswertung'.* Frankfurt: 1977, 59–96.

Grenander, U. Syntax-controlled probabilities. Technical report, Brown University, Division of Applied Mathematics. 1967.

Heidelberger Forschungsprojekt "Pidgin-Deutsch" (HPD). *Sprache und Kommunikation ausländischer Arbeiter. Analysen, Berichte, Materialien.* Kronberg/Ts: Scriptor Verlag, 1975. (a)

Heidelberger Forschungsprojekt "Pidgin-Deutsch" (HPD). Zur Sprache ausländischer Arbeiter: Syntaktische Analysen und Aspekte des kommunikativen Verhaltens. *Zeitschrift für Literaturwissenschaft und Linguistik,* 1975, 5 (18), 78–121. (b)

Heidelberger Forschungsprojekt "Pidgin-Deutsch" (HPD). *Untersuchungen zur Erlernung des Deutschen durch ausländische Arbeiter. Research report III.* Germanistisches Seminar, University of Heidelberg, 1976.

Heidelberger Forschungsprojekt "Pidgin-Deutsch" (HPD). Transitional grammars in the acquisition of German by Spanish and Italian workers. In Jürgen M. Meisel (Ed.), *Langues en contact—Pidgins—Creoles—Languages in contact.* Tübingen, 1977.

Klein, W. *Variation in der Sprache. Ein Verfahren zu ihrer Beschreibung.* Kronberg/Ts: Scriptor Verlag, 1974.

Klein, W., Ed. *Sprache ausländischer Arbeiter. Zeitschrift für Literaturwissenschaft und Linguistik,* 1975, 5 (18).

Labov, W., Cohen, P., Robins, C., & Lewis, J. *A study of the non-standard English of Negro and Puerto Rican speakers in New York City* (2 vols.). Final Report, Cooperative Research Project 3288. Washington, D. C.: U.S. Office of Health, Education, and Welfare, 1968.

Meisel, J. M. Ausländerdeutsch und Deutsch ausländischer Arbeiter. Zur möglichen Entstehung eines Pidgins in der BRD. *Zeitschrift für Literaturwissenschaft und Linguistik,* 1975, *5* (18), 9–53.

Salomaa, A. Probabilistic and weighted grammars. *Information and Control,* 1969, *15,* 529–544.

Suppes, P. Probabilistic grammars for natural languages. In D. Davidson & G. Harman (Eds.), *Semantics of natural language.* Dordrecht: Reidel, 1972, 741–762.

2

Semantic Field Variability

David Sankoff / Pierrette Thibault /
Hélène Bérubé

INTRODUCTION

In our study of socially conditioned variability in Montreal French, we
have been paying increasing attention to problems of lexical and semantic
variation. This chapter explores three aspects of such variation, illustrated
by quantitative data from our corpus of informal speech.

The first topic is the alternation among partial synonyms in a number of
syntactically well-defined contexts, the logical and semantic relations
between these forms, and the interaction between individual variability
and the socioeconomic differentiation of the speech community. This is
studied for the semantic domain spanned by the verbs which can mean 'to
dwell', where it seems reasonable to assure an underlying cognitive
organization common to all speakers.

By contrast, the second section deals with a situation where partial
synonymy among two or more lexical alternates is complicated by a
probable heterogeneity among members of the community at the semantic
or cognitive levels. The words of interest here are those which mean
'work', 'job', 'task', etc.

In studying the first two types of problem, we combine a basically
ethnosemantic methodology with distributional linguistic criteria. We

then raise the problem of a set of forms which are not tied to a highly
specific and concrete domain, such as is common in ethnosemantics and
related fields, but rather of a cluster of very general terms, meaning 'thing'
or 'something', which are almost pronominal in nature, whose function is
less referential than syntactic, for which the notion of semantic field is
hardly applicable, and for which we can no longer make use of a
methodology based on ethnosemantic intuition.

A SIMPLE MODEL FOR LEXICAL CHOICE

Insofar as we can extract words having a given meaning out of syntactic
context, using distributional criteria as well as ethnosemantic methodology, a simple formalism suffices to model the partial synonymy of generic
and specific terms, as well as the semantic field associated with a given
term. Details of this model have been published (Sankoff, 1971), so we
give only the necessary outlines here. In terms of linguistic adequacy, the
model is somewhat more general than the taxonomic treelike structures
used in ethnosemantics but is not of sufficient generality to account for all
the complex phenomena in a complete lexicon.

We shall use standard logical notation, where the symbol $\Rightarrow$ means
'implies', the symbol $\cap$ stands for 'and' (conjunction), and the symbol $\cup$
stands for 'and/or' (disjunction). Then the basic link between a word w
and its meanings is a logical implication of form, for example,

$$w \Rightarrow (a_1 \cap a_2) \cup (b_1 \cap b_2 \cap b_3 \cap b_4) \cup (c_1 \cap c_2 \cap c_3)$$

where the conjunction of features $a_1 \cap a_2$ is one of the "prime implicants," or most general meanings, of the word w. The other prime impli-
cants are $b_1 \cap b_2 \cap b_3 \cap b_4$ and $c_1 \cap c_2 \cap c_3$. The **semantic field** associated
with a word can then be defined to include any meaning, i.e., conjunction
of features, which implies one of its most general meanings. For the
example w, the semantic field consists of the three prime implicants plus
all other meanings of form $a_1 \cap a_2 \cap x$, $a_1 \cap a_2 \cap x \cap y$, $c_1 \cap c_2 \cap c_3$
$\cap z$, $\cdot \cdot \cdot$ as long as these conjunctions are not internally contradictory
or otherwise excluded, for example, on cognitive grounds.

This definition of the semantic field of a word is based on the rule of
thumb that **a word can be used to express any one of its most general
meanings**, e.g., $a_1 \cap a_2$, **as well as any more specific meanings**, e.g.,
$a_1 \cap a_2 \cap x$, where "more specific" indicates that additional features are
conjoined. A word may not be used for a meaning more general than one
of its prime implicants. Such phenomena as metaphor, for example,
would involve a violation of this restriction, and this characterization is

thus suggestive of a framework for the detection, classification, and analysis of these relatively rare usages.

The **lexical choice set** of a given meaning includes then any word, one of whose prime implicants is implied by the given meaning. For example, if

$$v \Rightarrow a_5 \cap a_6$$

then the lexical choice set of the meaning $a_1 \cap a_2 \cap a_5 \cap a_6$ would include both w and v, since both $a_5 \cap a_6$ and $a_1 \cap a_2$ are implied by $a_1 \cap a_2 \cap a_5 \cap a_6$.

Once the structure consisting of words and their semantic fields, or equivalently, meanings and their lexical choice sets, is established, a probabilistic model of lexical usage can be obtained by associating a nonnegative number to each pair consisting of one word and one meaning. This number must be zero if the word can never take on the meaning, and positive otherwise, and the sum of all the numbers must be one. For a given word, the sum of all the word-meaning probabilities expresses its overall frequency of occurrence. The probabilistic model we have constructed serves as a theoretical base for our statistical studies of word usage.

METHODOLOGICAL PROBLEMS

The basic ethnosemantic tool relevant to this study is a speaker's judgment of specific/generic relationships among terms referring to a class of entities or objects. From statements of the type *X is a special type of Y, but Y is not a special type of X,* or similar statements where "special type" is replaced by "subcategory," "part of," "aspect of," and so on, we may infer, in a logical way, a hierarchical structuring of the terms such as a taxonomic tree. Through componential analysis, this structure can then be described in an economical way by assigning to each term the conjunction of a small number of features. The logical relations between these formulas then reproduce the hierarchical structure. It should be noted that the features and their assignments are analytical constructions on the part of the researcher and while there are arguments in favor of various ways of devising and using feature sets, and for their connection with cognitive structure, these cannot be based solely on the restricted type of ethnosemantic evidence we have discussed.

In a more general investigation of the lexicon, we are not merely classifying terms referring to a restricted class of objects, but words that can have a variety of abstract usages, and that can involve specific/generic relationships of diverse and subtle types. Thus it becomes more and more difficult to have direct access to speakers' intuitions and impossible to elaborate a strictly ethnosemantic methodology. Fortunately, however, we can augment this to a considerable extent by observaticns of a distributional nature. Among a group of related words, there will be some syntactic contexts in which all may be used interchangeably. In other contexts, only a restricted subset may appear. In still others, only a different, perhaps partially overlapping, subset is possible. A little reflection suffices to identify "restricted usage" with "specific" and "general usage" with "generic." In practice, it is desirable that the distributional and ethnosemantic methodologies coincide as much as possible.

VERBS FOR 'TO DWELL'

Part of each interview making up our corpus is a discussion of the respondent's residential history. Thus there are many examples of verbs meaning 'to reside' or 'to dwell' (G. Sankoff & Thibault, 1977). These include *rester, vivre, demeurer,* and *habiter.* Of course these verbs take on a variety of other meanings. *Vivre* can mean 'to live' or 'to exist' more generally. *Rester* and *demeurer* can mean 'to stay' or 'remain'. *Rester* is somewhat more general in that it can always substitute for *demeurer* in any of the latter's usages while the opposite is not always true. Finally, all these verbs can be used in the more specific sense of 'live together'. We can ignore those semantic and syntactic features (e.g., +verbal, +stative, etc.) that all these verbs share, and concentrate on those that distinguish them.

We will denote by e (for exist) and u (for unchanging) the features distinguishing the most general senses of *vivre* and *rester*. The feature c (for continual) indicates the more specific thrust of *demeurer,* while h (human complement) will distinguish the more specific of the two meanings these four verbs all share. Thus the word-meaning formulas for the four verbs are:

$$
\begin{aligned}
rester &\Rightarrow u \\
demeurer &\Rightarrow u \cap c \\
vivre &\Rightarrow e \\
habiter &\Rightarrow u \cap c \cap e
\end{aligned}
$$

The lexical choice sets are:

$$
\begin{aligned}
u &: \{rester\} \\
u \cap c &: \{rester, demeurer\} \\
e &: \{vivre\} \\
u \cap c \cap e &: \{rester, demeurer, vivre, habiter\} \\
u \cap c \cap e \cap h &: \{rester, demeurer, vivre, habiter\}
\end{aligned}
$$

Note again that we could have conjoined to each of the above meanings other features which they all share, e.g., s (for stative). By the same token more generic verbs (e.g., *être*), which could take on these meanings and which could have been included in the lexical choice sets, have not been studied here. In neither case would the relation among lexical choice sets and semantic fields have changed.

Figure 1 shows how the lexical choice sets are ordered by set inclusion (indicated by the symbol ⊆), in a way opposite to how the meanings are ordered by logical implication.

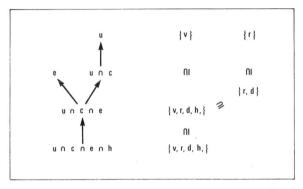

Figure 1.   Implications among meanings and inclusions among lexical choice sets.

The preceding outline is consistent with an analysis of 1222 occurrences of the four verbs, distributed among 60 interviews. The usages were identified with the aid of certain syntactic criteria. The most important was the restriction that to qualify as expressing the meaning $u \cap c \cap e$, a word had to take a locative complement referring to a residential situation, and that this had to be closer to the verb than any temporal complement which might also have been present. This was especially important for distinguishing among the meanings of the verb *vivre*. The usage of *rester* expressing the meaning u was generally identified through its presence in a surface form such as *il* (impersonal) *reste* ('there remains . . .') or *qui* [−human] *reste* ('which is left').

It should be noted the more general meaning of *vivre* which we denote by e is decomposable into a number of distinguishable meanings, but we will not go into the details in this analysis. The same is possibly true for the meaning $u \cap c$. Also we have documented, in some additional interviews, instances in which *demeurer* seems to have almost the same potential generality as *rester*,

> *Et puis, encore à date, c'est un des seuls qui*
> **demeure,** *pour combien de temps?* 76.92[1]
> [Speaking of a college] 'And still today, it's one of
> the few that are left, but for how long?'

and this can be seen as well in literary French,

> *Rien ne* **demeure** *plus des jours de grandes vacances.*
> [F. Jammes cited in *Le Petit Robert*, 1972, p. 437]
> 'Nothing remains from the days of the long vacation.'

Nevertheless, since this is restricted to one or two individuals and seems anomalous or archaic to informants, we have retained the generic/specific relationship between *rester* and *demeurer*.

There is also some question whether the meaning $u \cap c \cap e \cap h$ is necessary to the analysis. It could be argued that it is really the same as $u \cap c \cap e$ but that a slightly different connotation has been transferred to the word used by the presence of a [+human] complement. Nonetheless, for various reasons, such as that this usage seems to obviate the necessity or importance of a locative complement, and the existence of the specific verb *cohabiter* (which, however, is too rare to have occurred in our corpus), we prefer to distinguish this meaning.

Table 1 is a breakdown of the 1222 cases, according to lexical choice and meaning expressed, with examples and number of cases. These quantitative data enable us to construct a probabilistic model of word-meaning relationship in this domain as in Figure 2.

This model is, of course, an abstraction on the level of the speech community, and it is relevant as well to the receptive competence of individual speakers. Nevertheless on the productive level, individual speakers vary greatly from this scheme. Indeed, Figure 2 may be considered a composite of two major patterns. The majority of speakers use *rester* most of the time when expressing the meaning 'to dwell', and they never use *habiter*. A smaller number of speakers use *habiter* frequently for this meaning and use *rester* never or infrequently. Both groups also employ *demeurer* or *vivre*. Indeed, there is evidence that the use of *demeurer* is a stylistic resource available to all speakers, and most particularly as a "high-style" form for those who usually use *rester*. The use of *habiter*, however, would be characteristic of certain speakers and would not be apparent, even in careful style, in the speech of the majority.

Examining the social characteristics of the speakers who use *habiter*, we find that they are not evenly scattered among the population but are concentrated among the highly educated and professional class, with

---

[1]The identification number 76.92 refers to the ninety-second (92) line of interview number 76 in our corpus.

TABLE 1:
Verbs Meaning 'to Dwell' and Their Usages

Verb	Meaning	Example	Gloss	Cases
rester	*u*	Quand je suis arrivé il en **restait** quasiment plus. 36.166	'When I arrived there were hardly any left.'	26
	u ∩ c	Je la force pas à **rester** dans l'église avec moi. 9.894	'I don't force her to stay in the church with me.'	168
	u ∩ c ∩ e	On **restait** à Rosemont avant. 56.15	'We lived in Rosemount before.'	537
	u ∩ c ∩ e ∩ h	Lui, il **restait** avec son père puis sa tante. 18.305	'Him, he lived with his father and his aunt.'	26
demeurer	*u ∩ c*	Je pense que la signification **demeure** toujours pas mal la même chose. 25.548	'I think that the meaning still remains more or less the same.'	3
	u ∩ c ∩ e	Si on **demeure** en dehors de la ville... 30.583	'If you live outside the city...'	167
	u ∩ c ∩ e ∩ h	Ils **demeurent** encore ensemble... 120.94 [not in sample]	'They still live to-gether...'	0
habiter	*u ∩ c ∩ e*	A Montréal, on **habitait** au troisième étage. 39.143	'In Montreal, we used to live on the third floor.'	47
	u ∩ c ∩ e ∩ h	... peut avoir ses responsabilités aussi, tout en **habitant** avec la fille. 22.183	'... could assume his responsibilities as well, even while living with the girl.'	1
vivre	*e*	Je dis pas que je **vis** uniquement en fonction de l'avenir. 53.471	'I am not saying that I live only for the future.'	146
	u ∩ c ∩ e	Mon père a **vécu** à Sarnia. 9.964	'My father lived in Sarnia.'	85
	u ∩ c ∩ e ∩ h	On **vit** tous ensemble. 18.104	'We all live together.'	7
	frozen	Il y a du monde qui savent **vivre**. 2.881	'There are those who know how to behave.'	9

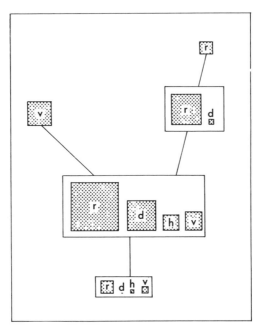

Figure 2. Probabilistic word-meaning model for verbs meaning 'to dwell'. Area covered by each letter proportional to its frequency of usage for the corresponding meaning.

perhaps a greater representation of female than male speakers. Indeed, the three speakers in our sample who use *habiter* more than 60% of the time for the meaning $u \cap c \cap e$ (the rest use it less than 25% of the time) are all women whom we have classified as belonging to the social groups consisting of professionals, owners, managers (and their families). All are very highly educated compared to others in their age groups. As for the speakers who use *rester* more than 50% of the time for this meaning, we see from Table 2 that they constitute a small minority of this same social

TABLE 2
Social Distribution of *Rester* Usage[a]

	Professionals, owner-managers	Office workers, small businessmen	Workers, unemployed
Over 50% *rester*	2	9	15
Under 50% *rester*	6	7	8

[a]Only the 47 speakers having at least 5 cases each of the meaning 'to dwell' are tabulated.

class. On the other hand, they constitute a clear majority of working class speakers.

In concluding this example, we remark that the social variation lies entirely in the lexical choice probabilities. Methodologically, it is rather straightforward to classify the tokens according to meanings with the help of syntactic criteria, and there is no question but that the meaning $u \cap c \cap e$, for example, has the same cognitive import for speakers of all classes.

WORK

Another interview topic was the work history of the respondent, and here, and in many other contexts, there is frequent use of words meaning 'job', 'position', 'task', or 'work'. These include *travail, ouvrage* (the two most important), *job, emploi, situation, position,* and *poste.* The structure of this semantic domain is more difficult to discern and the data is more difficult to analyze than with the preceding example.

The most abstract notion of 'work' or 'labor' is expressed almost exclusively by *travail,* which can also be used for the other meanings studied. The more specific meaning of a task, or a piece of work to be done, is frequently expressed by *ouvrage,* as well as *travail,* and occasionally, *job.* We include in this meaning the notion of the nature of work that one does, though hindsight suggests that this might have been more correctly classified separately. A clearly distinct meaning is that of 'paid employment' or 'job' which can be expressed by *emploi* as well as *travail, ouvrage,* and *job.* It is not clear, however, whether this should be considered a specification of the preceding meaning: 'task' or 'piece of work to be done', and we shall present reasons for and against. Words like *situation, poste,* or *position* would seem to have a more specific connotation, that of a particular, named position, such as 'chief X' or 'assistant Y', as distinguished from the idea of simply being hired to work. This specific meaning does not seem expressible by *ouvrage,* and this leads to the problem of whether or not it can be considered a specification of the preceding meaning. Finally, the words *travail, ouvrage,* and *job,* but not *emploi,* can be specialized in a locative sense to mean 'place of work'. Table 3 presents a breakdown of 752 occurrences of the various words, distributed among 120 interviews.

What sort of structure do these observations determine? First, we will use the notation w (for work) as the abstract meaning expressible only by the header term *travail.* Then $w \cap t$ will denote 'task'. The notion of 'paid employment' will be denoted by $w \cap t \cap r$ or simply $w \cap r$, depending on whether we consider it a specification of the previous meaning, or not.

TABLE 3:

Nouns Meaning 'Work' and Their Usages

Noun	Meaning	Example	Gloss	Cases
travail	'labor'	*L'amusement était dans le **travail**.* 3.121	'Enjoyment was in work.'	15
	'paid employment' and 'named position'	*Ils n'ont pas besoin d'aller en chercher des emplois, mais il y a des gens qui ont du **travail** depuis quarante ans.* 47.641	'They don't have to go looking for jobs, but there are people who have had work for forty years.'	68
	'task'	*Ils arrivaient dans un bureau puis il y avait un chef de bureau qui les entraînait à faire tel **travail**.* 73.93	'They would arrive in an office and there would be an office supervisor who would train them to do a certain type of work.'	68
	'location'	*Moi, de mon **travail**, ça me prend . . . ça me prend pas vingt minutes.* 30.601	'Me, from my work, it takes me . . . it doesn't take me twenty minutes.'	4
	frozen	*Ça m'intéresserait plus d'aller sur le marché du **travail**.* 50.56	'It would be more interesting for me to enter the labor force.'	44
	schoolwork	*Je sais pas moi, un certain nombre d'ateliers, un **travail** de session de 10 à 15 pages.* 53.208	'I'm not sure, me; a certain number of workshops, a term paper of 10–15 pages.'	25
ouvrage	'labor'	*Il y en a qui disent que l'**ouvrage** ne fait pas mourir.* 94.281	'There are those who say work won't kill you.'	1
	'paid employment' and 'named position'	*Je peux toujours me trouver un **ouvrage** dans mon métier.* 52.25	'I can always find a job in my line.'	57
	'task'	*D'abord que l'employé fait son **ouvrage**, il lui en demande pas plus.* 6.606	'As long as the employee does his job, he doesn't ask more.'	114
	'location'	*Il est venu me reconduire à l'**ouvrage**, puis il s'en allait chercher son patron.* 7.628	'He came to drive me to work, then he went to get his boss.'	6
	opus	*Lire un livre comme un **ouvrage** de Dagenais, ''Difficultés de la langue française''.* 115.706	'To read a book such as a work of Dagenais, *Difficultés de la langue française*.'	1

emploi	'paid employment' and 'named position'	*C'est parce que je vais avoir un autre emploi mais que je revienne.* 46.26	'It's because I will have another job when I come back.'	54
	'task'	*C'est pas assez créatif comme emploi: c'est trop . . . fais-ci, fais-ça, tape-ci, tape-ça.* 53.152	'It's not creative enough work. It's too much do this do that, type this type that.'	2
	frozen	*Ils n'ont pas de sécurité d'emploi, en somme.* 16.110	'They don't have job security, in effect.'	11
job	'paid employment' and 'named position'	*Alors, ils m'ont offert la job de chef de police.* 90.303	'So they offered me the job of chief of police.'	99
	'task'	*C'est moi qui avait la job de la poser cette maudite vitre-là.* 94.114	'It's me who had the job of installing that damned window.'	15
	'location'	*J'étais juste chauffeur pour s'en aller sur la job.* 32.171	'I was only driver for getting to work.'	1
position	'named position'	*Des gens qui vivaient au jour le jour, puis qui perdaient leur position, puis quand on dit il y avait plus rien nulle part.* 79.409	'People who lived from day to day, then lost their jobs, then, so to speak, there were no longer any anywhere.'	24
	others	*J'ai toujours eu des positions énormément supérieures à celles de mes amies.* 55.235	'I have always been enormously better placed than my friends.'	1
		Mais j'ai pas pris position vis-à-vis de ça. 13.632	'But I didn't take a position on that.'	7
situation	'named position'	*Mon père avait une bonne situation.* 79.338	'My father had a good position.'	5
	others	*Disons que c'était très tendu, la situation des jeunes là-bas.* 13.578	'Let's say that it was a very tense situation for the youth there.'	25
poste	'named position'	*C'était pour les administrateurs de conserver leur poste, voyez-vous?* 41.534	'It was for the administrators to keep their position, you see?'	8

TV - radio station, Post Office   97

Before we can decide this question, as summarized in Figure 3, let us examine the case of the 'named position' and locative meanings. Both of these would seem to be special cases or aspects of 'paid employment' as in Figure 4. But the locative meaning cannot be expressed by *emploi* while 'paid employment' can.

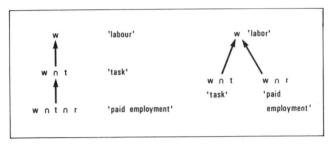

Figure 3.   Alternate configurations of meanings related to work.

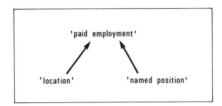

Figure 4.   Trial configuration of three meanings.

Similarly 'named position' cannot be expressed by *ouvrage* while 'paid employment' can. These facts would seem to necessitate either the counterintuitive classification of both 'location' and 'named position' as separate meanings not more specific than 'paid employment', or else the admission of counterexamples to our rule of thumb that a word which can express a generic meaning can also express a more specific one.

However, there is a third, more satisfactory analysis. We will present more detailed usage statistics than Table 3 suggesting a certain heterogeneity among speakers. The inconsistencies we have remarked can be shown to stem from the conflation of two different usage patterns. In one, *emploi* is rarely, if ever, used, for any meaning, so that there is no conflict in classifying 'location' as a more specific meaning than 'paid employment'. For this pattern, prevalent among working class speakers, the meaning 'named position' would not be directly relevant to the notion of 'task' or 'paid employment' and would either be classified out of the semantic domain in question or considered a specification of 'labor' only, thus avoiding the contradiction involving *ouvrage*.

The second pattern, characteristic of bourgeois or middle class speakers, does not make use of *ouvrage* for the notion of 'paid employment'. This leaves the way clear for us to consider 'named position' as a specification of 'paid employment' without contradiction. For speakers falling into this pattern, the 'location' of work would appear to be not so much an aspect of 'paid employment' as an aspect of the 'task' to be performed, and is thus considered as a specific aspect of the latter. The fact that in this second pattern, *ouvrage* is employed very frequently for 'task' is evidence for not classifying 'paid employment' and hence 'named position' as more specific than 'task'.

These considerations lead to the idealized structures in Figure 5 for the

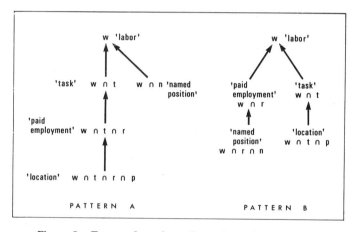

Figure 5. Two configurations of meanings related to work.

two types of meaning relationships. The word-meaning formulas for the two patterns are very similar:

Pattern A	Pattern B
travail $\Rightarrow w$	*travail* $\Rightarrow w$
ouvrage $\Rightarrow w \cap t$	*ouvrage* $\Rightarrow w \cap t$
job $\Rightarrow (w \cap t) \cup (w \cap n)$	*job* $\Rightarrow (w \cap t) \cup (w \cap r)$
emploi not used	*emploi* $\Rightarrow w \cap r$
poste *situation* $\Big\} \Rightarrow w \cap n$ *position*	*poste* *situation* $\Big\} \Rightarrow w \cap r \cap n$ *position*

The lexical choice sets are also similar:

Pattern A		Pattern B	
w	: {*travail*}	w	: {*travail*}
$w \cap t$	: {*travail, ouvrage, job*}	$w \cap t$	: {*travail, ouvrage, job*}
$w \cap t \cap r$	: {*travail, ouvrage, job*}	$w \cap r$	: {*travail, emploi, job*}
$w \cap t \cap r \cap p$	: {*travail, ouvrage, job*}	$w \cap t \cap p$	: {*travail, ouvrage, job*}
$w \cap n$	: {*travail, job, poste, situation, position*}	$w \cap r \cap n$	: {*travail, job, poste, emploi, situation, position*}

Based on the data summarized in Table 3, this analysis must be considered speculative at best. Of the six cases total per informant of the various words, almost two on the average fall outside the semantic domain being studied, and the rest are mostly *travail* and *ouvrage*. Thus we cannot seriously investigate the constraints and structures we have posited on an individual level. Nevertheless grouping the speakers on an occupational basis as in Table 4 confirms in large measure the crucial facts for our heterogeneity arguments.

TABLE 4

Social Distribution of Words Meaning 'work'

Meaning	Word	Professionals, owner-managers	Office workers, small business-men	Workers, unemployed
'paid employment'	*ouvrage*	17%	4%	30%
	travail	20%	43%	16%
	emploi	39%	22%	11%
	job	24%	30%	43%
	N	54	76	148
'task'	*ouvrage*	34%	48%	78%
	travail	59%	43%	13%
	emploi	3%	0%	0%
	job	3%	9%	9%
	N	58	54	87

First, there is the low rate of *emploi* (11%) for the meaning 'paid employment' among the working class speakers compared to a dominant 39% for the bourgeois speakers and 22% for the middle category. Second, there is the low rate of *ouvrage* among the latter two groups (17% and 4%, respectively) for the same meaning compared to 30% for the working class speakers.

The small number of examples is not the only difficulty in collecting and analyzing these data. An even more serious problem is that of classifying the examples according to meaning, and eventually, the definition of the various meanings themselves. In contrast to the previous example based on verbs meaning 'to dwell', there is a serious lack of distributional criteria here to distinguish, for example, among 'paid employment' and 'task', largely because we classed 'nature of one's work' together with 'task'. Had we created a separate category, however, this would have settled certain borderline cases, but would no doubt have created additional ambiguities between the new category and 'task', on the one hand, and 'paid employment', on the other. Thus the classification of many cases is based on an admittedly arbitrary but hopefully consistent process of judgment taking into account the larger context of the conversation. Of course, many distributional criteria were used; when the word in question is found in a locative complement, the meaning is clearly 'location'; when it is the direct object of verbs like *chercher* 'look for', *trouver* 'find', *perdre* 'lose', etc., the meaning expressed is generally 'paid employment' or possibly 'named position', but not 'labor', 'task', or 'location'.

The words *travail, ouvrage, job,* and *emploi* can be count or mass nouns. When *travail* is used to express 'labor' it must syntactically be a mass noun. In the rare cases when *emploi* is used for 'task' it is also a mass noun. Otherwise, as the meanings become more specific, both mass and count forms alternate without any clear-cut effect on meaning, until the most specific meanings, 'location' and 'named position', which strongly favor the count form (cf. Macnamara, this volume). This aspect of the distribution of forms is, however, of little help in classifying the occurrences, since it does not distinguish between 'paid employment' and 'task' and because it is very frequently not marked on the surface (e.g., *mon travail* 'my work').

THINGS

The study of semantic fields, and related areas such as ethnosemantics, usually focus on semantic domains whose meanings are relatively rich in semantic features. This is true of our previous two examples. In contrast to this, for our final example we set out to study a set of interrelated words which have very little or no referential content. These are words corresponding to 'thing' or 'something'. Montreal French is endowed with quite a number of these, including *chose, affaire,* the two most common, as well as the form *de quoi* and *histoire, patente, machin, truc,* and *bebelle.* We have examined the approximately 4000 occurrences of these words in the 120 interviews. To a large extent these words behave like partial synonyms, being intersubstitutable in many of their usages. On the other hand, their relationships cannot be easily represented in terms of a componential analysis based on semantic features, such as we used in the other examples. The reason for this is that with this class of ultrageneric words, the referential function is minimal. They serve instead a variety of syntactic and discourse functions.

In Table 5 we attempt to give a provisional classification of these functions. This is not an attempt at an exhaustive analysis, nor are the categories disjoint nor even completely comparable, of them being semantically based, others syntactic and others largely discourse related. The idea is rather to contrast the functional diversity of this group of words with the relatively homogeneous referentiality of the previous two examples.

In the table, we see that *chose* and *affaire* can be used for the very generic referent 'thing' but this represents a small fraction of their usage. (*Affaire, histoire,* and *truc* also occasionally have other more specific referents in other semantic fields.)

One of the major functions of *chose* and *affaire* is as dummy nouns. Verbs which require complements or adjectives which are required to modify a noun need sometimes be used without any substantive NP or noun being referentially necessary. *Chose* and *affaire* and the other words are readily available for this dummy function and this represents one of their major functions.

Another important usage of these words is to fulfill a certain discourse function. When in the course of an utterance a speaker fails to find an appropriate word to express a specific referent, or for various reasons having to do with the speech situation, does not wish to utter a certain word, he may use instead *chose* or *affaire,* either as a "stalling" device until he recovers the word he needs, or simply as a substitute.

Chose and *affaire* occur very frequently in a number of expressions meaning 'things like that', 'that sort of thing', etc., where they are largely interchangeable.[2] About half as frequently they appear in idiomatic expressions which are specific either to one or the other word.

Finally, there are the pronounlike usages of these words. To do justice to this phenomenon would warrant a lengthy description and analysis, but we present here only a brief discussion. We distinguish two major sub-

---

[2]The linguistic and social distributions of such tags has been studied in Australian English by Dines (1977).

classes based on the surface position of the tokens. In the first subclass, *chose* (or *affaire*) forms part of a preposed matrix sentence in which is embedded a lower sentence containing the coreferent of *chose*. The structure of these sentences may be summarized as:

1	2	3	4	5	6

$$\left(\left\{\begin{array}{l}\textit{Il y a}\\ \text{Impersonal}\\ \text{verb}\end{array}\right\}\right) \quad \left(\left\{\begin{array}{l}\text{Article (Adjective)}\\ \text{[-definite]}\\ \textit{quelque}\end{array}\right\}\right) \quad \textit{chose}(s) \quad \left(\left\{\begin{array}{l}\text{Adverb}\\ \text{PrepP}\end{array}\right\}\right) \quad \text{(S)} \quad (\textit{c'est})\ \text{S}$$

$$\left(\left\{\begin{array}{l}\text{'There is'}\\ \text{Impersonal}\\ \text{verb}\end{array}\right\}\right) \quad \left(\left\{\begin{array}{l}\text{Article (Adjective)}\\ \text{[-definite]}\\ \text{'some'}\end{array}\right\}\right) \quad \text{'thing}(s)\text{'} \quad \left(\left\{\begin{array}{l}\text{Adverb}\\ \text{PrepP}\end{array}\right\}\right) \quad \text{(S)} \quad (\text{'that is'})\ \text{S}$$

Obligatory elements of the construction are 3 and 6, the latter containing the coreferent. When an S is present as 5, elements 1, 2, and 3 can usually be substituted for by the demonstrative pronoun *ce*, with a consequent loss of emphasis, unless the optional adjective in 2 is present, as well as element 4.

In the second subclass, *chose* or its equivalent is found in the last half of an inverted equational sentence, where its coreferent has been preposed:

1	2	3	4	5	6

$$\left\{\begin{array}{l}(\textit{Ça})\\ \text{S}\end{array}\right\} \quad (\textit{c'est}) \quad \left(\left\{\begin{array}{l}\text{Article}\\ \text{[-definite]}\\ \textit{quelque}\end{array}\right\}\right) \quad \textit{chose}(s) \quad \left\{\begin{array}{l}\text{S}\\ \text{PrepP}\end{array}\right\} \quad (\textit{ça})\ \#$$

$$\left\{\begin{array}{l}(\text{'That'})\\ \text{S}\end{array}\right\} \quad (\text{'that's'}) \quad \left(\left\{\begin{array}{l}\text{Article}\\ \text{[-definite]}\\ \text{'some'}\end{array}\right\}\right) \quad \text{'thing}(s)\text{'} \quad \left\{\begin{array}{l}\text{S}\\ \text{PrepP}\end{array}\right\} \quad (\text{'that'})\ \#$$

The coreferent is in 1. Here we find that the elements 3 and 4 of the construction may often be replaced by the demonstrative pronoun *ça*, with a similar loss of emphasis to that of the first example.

Usually *affaire* may be substituted for *chose* in the above pronounlike usages. Indeed, the two types of constructions we have described serve more generally to allow the introduction of a topic of discourse or to permit a comment on some subject by the device of using a relatively generic word in the *chose* slot as a link to a coreferent in the body of the discourse.

The patterns of substitutability of *chose, affaire,* and related words, and their differential utility in different contexts (i.e., for different functions) is very reminiscent of the situation in the previous examples of verbs for 'to dwell' and nouns for 'work'. However the analysis must be based entirely

TABLE 5

Usage of *Chose* and *Affaire*[a]

Noun	Function	Example	Gloss	Cases
chose	Meaning 'entity'	*. . . de dire pour une **chose** son vrai nom.* 4.667	'. . . to call a thing by its real name.'	22
	Dummy noun supporting adjective	*Des rouets, des foyers, toutes des **choses** antiques.* 120.294	'Spinning wheels, fire places, all the antique things.'	5
	Dummy noun acting as verb complement	*Tu vas leur prêter quelque **chose** . . .* 24.485	'You lend them something . . .'	688
	Discourse device	*Un **chose** de médecin ou bien un papier des parents.* 80.222	'A thing from the doctor or else a note from the parents.'	222
	Expressions: Substitution possible	*Des morceaux de radar, d'aviation . . . des **choses** comme ça.* 7.267	'Bits of radar (machines), aviation (equipment) . . . things like that.'	797
	Expressions: Substitution not possible	*Je connaissais pas grand **chose**, j'avais 15 ans.* 46.182	'I didn't know much, I was 15 years old.'	300
	Coreference: Preposed	*Il y a une **chose** qui me fatigue, c'est qu'ils peuvent parler . . .* 54.430	'There is one thing that tires me; that's how they can talk.'	96
	Other coreference	*C'est des **choses** que je . . . qui ont un peu changé ma vie.* 6.284	'They are things which I . . . which have changed my life somewhat.	110
affaire	Meaning 'entity', 'Business (personal or commercial)'	*Les gens font leur **affaire**, puis moi, je fais la mienne.* 93.55	'People take care of their own business and I take care of mine.'	38
	Dummy noun supporting adjective	*. . . une **affaire** antique. On aime ça.* 2.67	'. . . an antique thing. We like that.'	41

40

Category	Example		Count
Dummy noun acting as verb complement	*On va dire des affaires des fois, on s'en rappelle même pas.* 2.1148	'We say things sometimes, we don't even remember.'	202
Discourse device	*Il y a beaucoup de français mal parlé: l'affaire, les sacres pour commencer.* 87.792	'There is much poorly spoken French; what-do-you-call-it, swear words for starters.'	192
Expressions: Substitution possible	*Sortir avec des petites filles, des affaires comme ça.* 24.61	'To go out with young girls and stuff like that.'	557
Expressions: Substitution not possible	*Ils ont fait l'affaire; on les a gardés.* 114.126	'They were suitable; we kept them on.'	283
Coreference: Preposed	*L'affaire, c'est que, quand je suis arrivé là-bas . . .* 54.168	'Thing is that when I arrived there . . .'	32
Other coreference	*Ça, c'est une affaire que j'aime pas.* 51.542	'That's a thing that I don't like.'	36

[a] All figures approximate. Tokens which fall in more than one category are only counted once.

on distributional criteria. Instead of an implicational pattern among meanings, we must be satisfied with inclusion relations among lexical choice sets. Again there are problems of individual variability among speakers and of a lack of data for the less common words, but we can discern the following general tendencies. There are some expressions where only *chose* is appropriate, and others where only *affaire* can be used, but the majority of the functions we have described can be fulfilled by the two. In many cases, such as the majority of referential usages as 'entity', or as a discourse device, none of the other words would be probable. The words *truc, machin, patente,* and *bebelle* are largely confined to the dummy noun function, and the contexts of possible usage are more and more restrained as we proceed from *truc* to *bebelle. De quoi* is sometimes usable in these contexts but only when certain syntactic conditions are met (e.g., nonplurality, mass noun). In some cases, such as in the complement of a verb such as *dire* 'say', *penser* 'think', etc., *histoire* can also be used.

A distinct class of functions, which involves most of the expressions where *chose* and *affaire* are interchangeable, as well as the coreferential functions, can also be fulfilled often by *de quoi,* sometimes by *histoire,* and sometimes either, but rarely if ever by the other words. These usage possibilities and restrictions may be summarized by relating the lexical choice sets as in Figure 6.

It should be clear that this diagram is only a general summary, and does not take into account a great number of syntactic and semantic factors

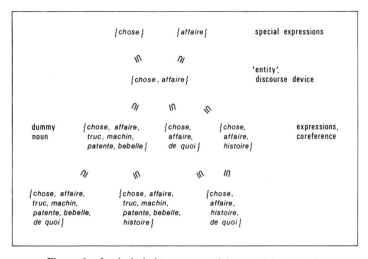

Figure 6.   Lexical choice sets containing word for 'thing'.

which may intervene to make a word appropriate or inappropriate in a given context. Only a complete analysis of the distribution of these forms within a general syntax and semantics of the noun phrase could hope to accomplish this. Nevertheless, as a general guide to the functions, uses, and relationships among these words, Figure 6 captures and depicts the situation in an economical and intuitively satisfying way.

As a final note, we cite one way in which the usage of these words varies from individual to individual. In expressions like *la même chose,* some people use *chose* exclusively, others prefer *choses* (plural), still others use *affaire* and/or *affaires.* A good proportion of speakers vary from one usage to another. The social aspects of this patterning remain to be investigated in detail, though a preliminary inspection shows bourgeois speakers to prefer *choses comme ça* while working class speakers use predominantly *ces affaires-là.*

REFERENCES

Dines, E. Variational analysis of a discourse pattern—"and stuff like that." Unpublished manuscript, University of Melbourne, 1977.

Sankoff, D. Dictionary structure and probability measures. *Information and Control,* 1971, *19,* 104–113.

Sankoff, G., & Thibault, P. L'alternance entre les auxiliaires *avoir* et *être* en français parlé à Montréal. *Langue Française,* 1977, *34,* 81–108.

3

Grammatical Ideology and Its Effect on Speech

Anthony Kroch / Cathy Small

INTRODUCTION

Modern linguistics entirely rejects prescriptivism in grammatical analysis. Rightly so, since prescriptivism is simply the ideology by which the guardians of the standard language impose their linguistic norms on people who have perfectly serviceable norms of their own. Unfortunately, rejection of prescriptivism as a basis for analysis is generally coupled with disregard for it as an object of study. The effect of prescriptivist ideology on language use and structure is rarely addressed. Indeed, linguists tend to believe that prescriptive norms have no significant effect on usage, at least in speech. The few instances where such norms are known to have influenced speech are termed isolated cases whose rarity and triviality make them exceptions that prove the rule. Recent sociolinguistic work on hypercorrection and the role of the upper middle class in the suppression of sound change, however, belies this view. Conscious prestige norms can have a powerful influence on speech, and the whole question of their role in language is worth another look.

PRESCRIPTIVISM AND GRAMMATICAL IDEOLOGY

This paper is a brief presentation of work currently in progress on the effect of prescriptive norms on the syntax of speech. The basis of the work is the hypothesis that one significant factor influencing speakers' choices among linguistic variants is the belief that the forms of the standard language are logically superior to those of nonstandard dialects. This supposed logical superiority of the standard language is asserted on a number of grounds, including accuracy in the use of inflections, precision of vocabulary, and richness of derivational morphology. In syntax, however, the claim to superiority is based on a grammatical ideology which (*a*) assumes that a syntactic alternant whose surface form more closely parallels the logical form of the proposition it expresses is more logical than one in which the parallel is less close and (*b*) claims that standard language constructions are consistently closer to logical form than nonstandard alternatives. Examples of this argumentation are easy to find. Thus, a double negation is said to be illogical because two negatives logically equal a positive, and the construction *the reason is because . . .* is similarly labeled on the ground that the clause following the verb *to be* is adverbial and adverbs cannot be predicate nominals. Interestingly, such reasoning is used not only against nonstandard forms but also to condemn certain pandialectal usages, as when grammar books insist that a sentence like (1) not be used with the meaning of (2):

(1)   *John only eats cabbage.*

(2)   *John eats only cabbage.*

The argument here is that the word *only* logically modifies the constituent to its immediate right; and therefore, sentence (1), while usable in a context like (3), is incorrect in the more usual context of (4):

(3)   *John only eats cabbage; he doesn't grow it.*

(4)   *John only eats cabbage; he eats nothing else.*

Similarly, the ubiquitous split infinitive is criticized for separating two parts of a single semantic unit.

Of course, the linguist can easily show that the superior logic claimed for the preferred constructions is spurious since the basic assumption—that there is a simple relation between surface syntactic form and logical form—is false. Thus multiple negation, while nonstandard in English, may be perfectly acceptable in other standard languages (for example, Spanish and Portuguese). Similarly, the placement of *only* in preverbal position when it modifies an object noun phrase is simply a particular case of the widespread syntactic process of quantifier movement. Even the stigmatization of *the reason is because* . . . loses its logical support when the linguist points out that adverbial phrases function quite often as semantic substantives.

We should note, of course, that prescriptivism, being ideological, does not use the argument from logic consistently. For example, according to the argument from formal logic, triple negation ought to be acceptable since three negatives are logically equivalent to simple negation (Burling, 1973); but, of course, sentence (6) is just as nonstandard as (5):

(5)   *John didn't sell no car.*

(6)   *John didn't sell nobody no car.*

Such inconsistencies are more the rule than the exception. Indeed, whenever a standard form appears to violate logic, as in the rule governing *shall* versus *will,* or when a stigmatized usage seems perfectly logical, as in the use of *-wise* as an adverb forming suffix, the appeal to logic is relinquished in favor of references to tradition and convention.

Inconsistent though it be, the grammatical ideology we have been discussing has a long history and a wide geographic distribution. It is perhaps universal in stratified societies with standard languages. As Chomsky (1966) has pointed out, the Cartesian linguists of the seventeenth century held that the form of speech reflected the form of thought; and some of them argued for the superiority of French over other languages on the grounds that its structure was more logical. Even the founder of modern linguistics, Saussure, had little to say about syntax, believing that sentence formation was less governed by linguistic rule than by the requirements of propositional thought. As far as geographic distribution is concerned, we refer to the Arab belief that classical Arabic is superior to other languages because of its logical structure (Ferguson, 1968) or to the Chinese attitudes concerning their standard language, Mandarin. The sociological importance in our society of the grammatical ideology of standard language syntax is clear. It provides the appearance of a reasoned basis for the stigmatization of nonstandard dialects by interpreting the syntactic conventions of these dialects as evidence of inferior reasoning. But of how much linguistic importance is this ideology? In particular, to what extent does it influence the syntax of actual speech? This question is a difficult one to answer, but we have some suggestive evidence that the influence is significant and that it goes beyond the obvious effect of promoting avoidance of nonstandard forms. What we have found is a tendency for people to make speech choices, even between standardly acceptable syntactic alternants, on the basis of the grammatical ideology.

TWO EXAMPLES

We have been studying two syntactic alternations, particle movement and complementizer *that* deletion after verbs: that is, the alternations responsible for the paired sentences of (7) and (8):

(7)   a. *John pointed out the mistake.*
                 b. *John pointed the mistake out.*

(8)   a. *Sally knows that Harry ate the salami.*
                 b. *Sally knows Harry ate the salami.*

Our sample, chosen both for availability and in the hope that it would include identifiably more and less standard speech, was several hours of talk-show conversation on Philadelphia's all-talk radio station WWDB-FM. In future studies, this sample should be supplemented with interviews, where the sampling of informants is more representative and controlled; but the taped broadcasts have proved an excellent source of pilot data, especially for studying the effect of standard norms. We defined two sociolinguistic groups of speakers in the shows, the callers and the show hosts with their studio guests. We assumed that for reasons both of social status and role in the radio talk-show interaction, the host/guest group generally speaks a more standard English than the caller group. This assumption seems justified based on our subjective impressions of the data, but could also be tested by a comparative frequency count of nonstandard linguistic features in the speech of the two groups.

The overall results of our analysis are given in Tables 1 and 2. These tables show that the caller group places the particle away from the verb and deletes complementizer *that* substantially more frequently than does the host/guest group. We have separated *think* from the other verbs in Table 2 because its frequency of occurrence and the frequency of complementizer deletion after it are both so high that including it with the other verbs would distort the results.

Our hypothesis is that the reason for the differences between the caller and host/guest groups exhibited in Tables 1 and 2 is a greater adherence by the latter to the grammatical ideology of the standard language that favors the most direct correspondence between propositional form and surface syntax. This greater adherence would follow from the group's generally greater loyalty to and concern for the norms of the standard. In

TABLE 1
Particle Placement, Overall Results (N = 305)[a]

	Speaker	
Particle position	Caller	Host/Guest
V NP Prt	$\frac{73}{138}$ (53%)	$\frac{62}{167}$ (37%)
V Prt NP	$\frac{65}{138}$ (47%)	$\frac{105}{167}$ (63%)

$p < .01$ (for the comparison)

[a]Chi square was used to check statistical significance. Chi square probabilities are reported for all comparisons for which there are at least ten tokens per cell.

TABLE 2
That Deletion, Overall Results (N = 506)

	Speaker				
	Caller		Host/Guest		
	$\emptyset$	*that*	$\emptyset$	*that*	
think	$\frac{112}{126}$ (89%)	$\frac{14}{126}$ (11%)	$\frac{122}{155}$ (79%)	$\frac{33}{155}$ (21%)	$p < .05$
Other verbs	$\frac{140}{233}$ (60%)	$\frac{93}{233}$ (40%)	$\frac{64}{173}$ (37%)	$\frac{109}{173}$ (63%)	$p < .001$

the case of the particle alternation the surface syntactic configuration V Prt NP would correspond to propositional form more directly than would V NP Prt because only the first reflects in its word order the semantic unity of the verb and particle (compare the split infinitive). In the case of *that* deletion the presence of the complementizer would correspond more directly to propositional form than its absence because the presence of the complementizer can be said to indicate more explicitly the logical relationship between the matrix verb and the complement clause.

LINGUISTIC CONDITIONING

In order to test our hypothesis and eliminate the possibility that the difference we had observed was actually due to the effects of linguistic conditioning factors, we analyzed the linguistic factors likely to influence each of the alternations. In the case of the particle alternation we analyzed the effects of the following factors: (a) length of object noun phrases (L), (b) degree of semantic dependence of particle on the verb (D), and (c) stress (S). The length of object noun phrase was given two values: L_1—the direct object is less than three words long; and L_2—the direct object is three or more words long. Sentences where the object noun phrase was a pronoun were excluded from analysis since, with normal intonation, the pronoun must be placed between the verb and the particle. The sentences of (9) and (10) illustrate the two values of L:

(9) L_1 a. *Bill pointed out John to the woman.*
           b. *Sally called Mary up on Saturday.*
           c. *The circus set the tent up.*
           d. *Carter played out his options.*

(10) L_2 a. *The FBI turned the incriminating documents over.*
            b. *We put up all three of my cousins.*
            c. *Harry mulled over the idea that his wife suggested.*

The semantic dependence factor was given three values, listed here in order of increasing semantic dependence of the particle on the verb: D_2—the particle functions as an adverb of direction; D_1—the particle can be interpreted metaphorically as an adverb of direction; and D_0—the particle has no semantic content except as part of the verb. Cases where the particle is an adverb and functions as such in nonparticle as well as particle constructions (e.g., *bring home the bacon*) were excluded from the analysis of this factor. The three values of D are illustrated in the following sentences:

(11) D_2 *The quarterback threw the ball away.*

(12) D_1 *Let me throw this idea out.*

(13) D_0 *He called the mayor up.*

The stress factor was given two values: S_1—heaviest stress falls on the constituent (particle or noun phrase) immediately following the verb; S_2—heaviest stress falls on the second constituent following the verb. Because of the complexities associated with contrastive stress, sentences containing it were excluded from the analysis of the stress factor. The values of S are illustrated in the following sentences:

(14) S_1 a. *I turned the lĭght ŏn.*
                       b. *I turned ón the lĭght.*

(15) S_2 a. *I turned the lĭght ón.*
                       b. *I turned ŏn the lĭght.*

The results of our analysis appear in Tables 3, 4, and 5, which show that the linguistic factors analyzed will not account for the difference between the host/guest and caller groups since when each factor is held constant the difference remains. Therefore, the difference between the two groups in particle placement choice is unlikely to be due to differences in the linguistic environments in which they customarily use the verb particle construction, although a multivariate analysis on a larger sample is still needed. The results in Table 4 are interesting for a further reason. They show that the degree of difference between the caller and host/guest groups (as measured by R = the ratio of the two groups' percentages of the V NP Prt alternant) decreases as the semantic independence of the

TABLE 3

Effect of Object NP Length on Particle Placement (N ≈ 305)

Length of object NP	Speaker				
	Caller		Host/Guest		
	V NP Prt	V Prt NP	V NP Prt	V Prt NP	
L_1	$\frac{58}{99}$ (59%)	$\frac{41}{99}$ (41%)	$\frac{48}{106}$ (45%)	$\frac{58}{106}$ (55%)	$p < .05$
L_2	$\frac{15}{36}$ (42%)	$\frac{21}{36}$ (58%)	$\frac{17}{64}$ (27%)	$\frac{47}{64}$ (73%)	$p > .05,$ NS

TABLE 4

Effect of Semantic Relationship between Particle and Verb on Particle Placement (N = 246)

Degree of semantic dependence	Speaker					
	Caller		Host/Guest			
	V NP Prt	V Prt NP	V NP Prt	V Prt NP	R^a	
D_0	$\frac{24}{63}$ (38%)	$\frac{39}{63}$ (62%)	$\frac{16}{90}$ (18%)	$\frac{74}{90}$ (82%)	2.11	$p < .01$
D_1	$\frac{11}{21}$ (52%)	$\frac{10}{21}$ (48%)	$\frac{12}{28}$ (43%)	$\frac{16}{28}$ (57%)	1.21	$p > .05$ NS
D_2	$\frac{15}{21}$ (71%)	$\frac{6}{21}$ (29%)	$\frac{16}{23}$ (70%)	$\frac{7}{23}$ (30%)	1.01	

a $R = \dfrac{\text{\% of V NP Prt alternant for Callers}}{\text{\% of V NP Prt alternant for Host/Guests}}$

TABLE 5

Effect of Stress Pattern on Particle Placement (N = 256)

| Stress pattern | Speaker | | | |
| | Caller | | Host/Guest | |
	V N Prt	V Prt NP	V NP Prt	V Prt NP	
S_1	$\frac{33}{35}$ (94%)	$\frac{2}{35}$ (6%)	$\frac{35}{42}$ (83%)	$\frac{7}{42}$ (17%)	
S_2	$\frac{28}{69}$ (41%)	$\frac{41}{69}$ (59%)	$\frac{20}{110}$ (18%)	$\frac{90}{110}$ (82%)	$p < .001$

particle increases. In other words, to the extent that the particle has an adverbial function the difference between the two groups tends to disappear; that is, the host/guest group uses the V Prt NP order more than the caller group only to the extent that this order reflects the closeness of the semantic relationship between verb and particle. This result, we would argue, confirms our hypothesis that grammatical ideology is the cause of the intergroup differences. After all, it is precisely and only when the particle is semantically independent of the verb that the grammatical ideology we have postulated would not favor its placement next to the verb.

Turning now to the *that* deletion alternation, we find similar results. Table 6 shows the deletion percentages for the five most common verbs. Together these verbs account for more than 90% of the tokens analyzed, and for each of them the difference between the caller and host/guest groups is clear. Another linguistic factor we analyzed was the effect of phrases intervening between the verb and the complement clause, on the assumption that the presence of such phrases would decrease the frequency of *that* deletion. The number of such cases was too small to allow any conclusions, but this factor certainly does not account for the variance between our two groups.

Tables 7 and 8 show the correlation of verb frequency and of Germanic versus Romance origin of the matrix verb with *that* deletion. Our findings on frequency agree with those of Cofer (1972). There is an effect but it is small. The effect of verb origin is much larger. Moreover, all of the verbs with 10 or more tokens are Germanic so that the relatively high deletion percentage for verbs with less than 10 tokens must be due to the infrequent Germanic verbs having a high enough deletion percentage to offset the low deletion percentage of the Romance verbs. These results

TABLE 6
That Deletion, Five Most Common Verbs (N = 621)

	Speaker				
	Caller		Host/Guest		
	ø	*that*	ø	*that*	
think	$\frac{112}{126}$ (89%)	$\frac{14}{126}$ (11%)	$\frac{122}{155}$ (79%)	$\frac{33}{155}$ (21%)	p < .05
say	$\frac{52}{85}$ (61%)	$\frac{33}{85}$ (39%)	$\frac{32}{73}$ (44%)	$\frac{41}{73}$ (56%)	p < .05
know	$\frac{25}{35}$ (71%)	$\frac{10}{35}$ (29%)	$\frac{16}{41}$ (39%)	$\frac{25}{41}$ (61%)	p < .01
tell	$\frac{18}{34}$ (53%)	$\frac{16}{34}$ (47%)	$\frac{9}{36}$ (25%)	$\frac{27}{36}$ (75%)	p < .05
believe	$\frac{6}{10}$ (60%)	$\frac{4}{10}$ (40%)	$\frac{11}{26}$ (42%)	$\frac{15}{26}$ (58%)	
Total	$\frac{212}{290}$ (73%)	$\frac{78}{290}$ (27%)	$\frac{189}{331}$ (57%)	$\frac{142}{331}$ (43%)	
Total (not including *think*)	$\frac{111}{174}$ (64%)	$\frac{63}{174}$ (36%)	$\frac{69}{176}$ (39%)	$\frac{107}{176}$ (61%)	

TABLE 7
Effect of Verb Frequency on *That* Deletion (N = 492)

	All speakers		
Verb frequency	ø	*that*	
Verbs with 10 or more tokens (not including *think*)	$\frac{134}{291}$ (46%)	$\frac{157}{291}$ (54%)	
			p > .05, NS
Verbs with less than 10 tokens	$\frac{76}{201}$ (38%)	$\frac{125}{201}$ (62%)	

indicate that lexical formality, which for English verbs correlates with Romance as opposed to Germanic etymology, is an important factor inhibiting *that* deletion. This is as we would expect. Speakers associate formality with the standard language so the grammatical ideology has more power when the context, here lexical, is more formal.

TABLE 8

Effect of Verb Origin on *That* Deletion (N = 502)

	All speakers		
Verb origin	∅	*that*	
Germanic (not including *think*)	$\frac{208}{442}$ (47%)	$\frac{234}{442}$ (53%)	$p < .001$
Romance	$\frac{10}{60}$ (17%)	$\frac{50}{60}$ (83%)	

CONCLUSION

Not surprisingly, people's prescriptive grammatical intuitions confirm our findings on the relationship between the alternants of particle movement and *that* deletion. As Table 9 shows, the sentence *John called up*

TABLE 9

Prescriptive Judgments on Particle Placement (N = 32 Temple University Undergraduates)

John called Mary up		*John called up Mary*	
Substantially more correct	Slightly more correct	Substantially more correct	Slightly more correct
2 (6%)	5 (16%)	14 (44%)	11 (34%)

Mary was judged to be substantially more correct than its alternant by 44% of a sample of Temple University undergraduates while only 22% favored the other alternant, whether marginally or strongly. Similarly, as Table 10 shows, 46% of a sample of Philadelphia speakers interviewed by Cofer (1972) thought deletion of *that* to be incorrect in both of the two cases presented to them. Only 31% thought deletion correct in both of the two cases. These figures illustrate how people do assign different prescriptive values to the alternants of particle movement and *that* deletion, thus providing further evidence for the existence of the grammatical ideology we have hypothesized and making more plausible our claim that this ideology is responsible for the pattern of the data in our speech sample.

TABLE 10

Prescriptive Judgments on *That* Deletion (N=26)[a]

Deletion correct:	
after *sure* only	2 (8%)
after *announce* only	4 (15%)
after both	8 (31%)
after neither	12 (46%)
Total	26

[a]Adapted from Cofer (1972).

REFERENCES

Burling, R. *English in black and white*. New York: Holt, Rinehart, and Winston, 1973.
Chomsky, N. *Cartesian linguistics: A chapter in the history of rationalist thought*. New York: Harper and Row, 1966.
Cofer, T. Linguistic variability in a Philadelphia speech community. Unpublished Ph.D. dissertation, University of Pennsylvania, 1972.
Ferguson, C. A. Myths about Arabic. In Fishman (Ed.), *Readings in the sociology of language*. The Hague: Mouton, 1968, 375–381.

4

Advances in Variable
Rule Methodology

Pascale Rousseau / David Sankoff

INTRODUCTION

The study of optional rule application from a probabilistic point of view
and using statistical methods was initiated by Cedergren and Sankoff
(1974). They enlarged on Labov's (1969) original concept, in discussing
the following three probabilistic models.

The Additive Model

In the environment or context consisting of features $i, j, \cdot \cdot \cdot, k$ the
probability that the rule will apply is p, where

$$(1) \qquad p = p_0 + p_i + p_j + \cdot \cdot \cdot + p_k,$$

where p_0 is a constant **input** parameter, and $p_i, p_j, \cdot \cdot \cdot, p_k$ are the effects
of the features $i, j, \cdot \cdot \cdot, k$, respectively. The feature i may be a particular
phonological or syntactic condition; it may represent the tendencies of a
particular speaker, or social group, or social variable.

The Multiplicative Nonapplication Probabilities Model

$$(2) \qquad (1 - p) = (1 - p_0) \times (1 - p_i) \times \cdot \cdot \cdot \times (1 - p_k),$$

where we require that $p_0, p_i, \cdots, p_k$ all be probabilities, that is each is constrained to the interval between 0 and 1, inclusive.

The Multiplicative Application Probabilities Model

(3) $p = p_0 \times p_i \times p_j \times \cdots \times p_k,$

where, again, we require that $p_0, p_i, \cdots, p_k$ all be probabilities.

The Data

The models above were proposed to account for a specific type of data set. These data are in frequency form; we observe the total number T of occurrences of a given environment where a particular grammatical rule may or may not apply, and count the number A of times the rule actually applies. Each data element requires a fraction of form

(4) $\dfrac{A}{T} = \dfrac{\text{rule applications}}{\text{eligible environments}}$

as well as a series of symbols representing the features making up the environment.

The Goal of a Variable Rule Analysis

The different models all represent ways to describe the combined effect of all the features in the environment on the application probability of a rule. Each feature is considered to have a specific effect, and from these the model generates rule probabilities for all possible environments, which are generally far more numerous than features. If the observed frequencies for the environments correspond well, in a statistical sense, to the probabilities generated, we consider that the model accounts well for the data.

We illustrate with the following (somewhat simplified) example from Labov (1972):

Rule: Copula contraction
Model: $(1 - p) = (1 - p_0) \times (1 - p_i) \times (1 - p_j)$
i: Represents the preceding phonological environment (consonant or vowel)
j: Represents the following syntactic environment (verb, predicate adjective, etc.)

Data:

(5)

A/T	Predicative adjective	Verb
Consonant	8/32	9/14
Vowel	16/23	12/14

Results of an estimating procedure:

(6)

$$p_0 = .25 \qquad p_{\text{pred adj}} = 0$$
$$p_{\text{cons}} = 0 \qquad p_{\text{verb}} = .49$$
$$p_{\text{vowel}} = .65$$

Predicted frequencies generated by model and values in (6):

(7)

8/32	8.7/14
17/23	12.1/14

Judgment: (Comparing (5) and (7), model accounts well for the data (e.g., as indicated by a χ^2 test).

As in this example, the set of features which may be present in environments should, for linguistic and statistical reasons, be broken down into a number of mutually exclusive, and exhaustive **factor groups**. Exactly one feature from each factor group is present in each environment.

PROBLEMS AND METHODS

Statistical and Computational Problems

In statistical terms, variable rule analysis can be thought of as a multidimensional problem on binomial data, where each dimension represents one feature. For our purposes, however, we will consider each factor group as constituting a single dimension.

The statistical problems associated with the models are:

1. To estimate $p_0, p_i, p_j, \cdots , p_k$, the parameters of the proposed model, on the basis of frequency data.
2. To evaluate the accuracy and other qualities of the estimating procedure.

3. To decide how well the model accounts for the data, in particular whether the data may be broken down into two or more subsets (corresponding, e.g., to different groups of speakers) each obeying somewhat different models of the same general type.

4. To test whether there are significant differences between the effects of the various features in a given factor group, and hence to see whether the factor group contributes significantly to explaining the data, or whether it may be eliminated from consideration, thus reducing the dimensionality of the problem.

There are also the usual types of computational problems.

5. We must have a program that does not require too much computer time.
6. It must not require too much computer memory storage.
7. It should be easily usable.

The Analysis of Variance

Let

(8) $r = \log(1 - p), \qquad q = \log p.$

Then the two multiplicative models become:

(9) $r = r_0 + r_i + \cdots + r_k, \qquad q = q_0 + q_i + \cdots + q_k.$

Additive models, such as (1) and (9), are usually analyzed by statisticians using the method called analysis of variance (ANOVA). Because of the inappropriateness, for linguistic variation data, of some of the assumptions underlying this method, however, it was rejected. (See Cox, 1970, for the difficulties in applying ANOVA to binomial data in general.) The main problem is the great variability in T, the total number of observations per environment, especially the many environments where $T = 0$ because they consist of linguistically impossible or improbable configurations of features. This leads to a breakdown of ANOVA with respect to accuracy and interpretability.

Maximum Likelihood

For this reason we have recourse to methods based on the well-known maximum likelihood principle. Let us recall briefly what such methods are like. For a given model and a given set of data, the likelihood is a measure of how likely these data are to have been generated by the model. For the frequency data which interest us, this likelihood is essentially the product of terms of form

$$(10) \qquad p^A (1 - p)^{T - A},$$

where the product contains one such term for each environment for which we have data. But because of (1), (2), or (3), this likelihood depends on the value we choose for the model parameters $p_0, p_i, \cdots, p_k$. The values of the parameters which together with the given data result in the highest value of the likelihood are by definition the most "likely." These are the maximum likelihood estimates and they have many desirable properties known as consistency, efficiency, and asymptotic normality. The question remains—how to find these most likely values?

The Estimation Procedure

Despite the apparently simple form of (10), when the entire product making up the likelihood is considered, and the p's are replaced by the model parameters, the likelihood function becomes rather complicated. No algebraic method, such as solving some simple equations containing the data, can exist for finding the values of the parameters which maximize the likelihood. These estimates have to be found iteratively: That is, at each step of a process of successive approximations we are driven closer and closer to the exact solution. Though we never attain it exactly, we can approximate it as close as we want (e.g., five decimal places).

In 1971 the VARBRUL program was written and implemented for carrying out such an iterative solution for models (1), (2), and (3). This was done in conjunction with Cedergren's (1973) work on Panamanian Spanish. For other applications, see Guy (1975).

Problems with Tests and Models

A χ^2 test was included in VARBRUL to give an idea of how well the various models fitted the data. This was based on calculating

$$(11) \qquad \frac{(\text{observed cases} - \text{expected cases})^2}{\text{expected cases}}$$

both for rule applications and nonapplications in all environments and summing up all these terms. Unfortunately the resulting sum is well approximated by a χ^2 distribution (if the model fits) only when the expected

number of rule applications and the expected number of rule nonapplications are both at least 5 in all environments, which is seldom the case with
linguistic data. Thus the use of (11), while indicative, is not really a
rigorous statistical test. This gave rise to the following complication: How
can we decide, for a given data set, which of the models should be chosen
since the test based on (11) is not reliable enough to do it automatically?
This problem turned out to be one of the greatest drawbacks associated
with the use of VARBRUL.

RECENT WORK

The Logistic Model

Rather than patch up the various deficiencies of VARBRUL, such as its
ad hoc programming, the problems with the test of fit and the choice of
models, a reexamination was undertaken of the whole question of which
model should be used. On the basis of this reexamination, and for several
reasons to which we can only allude here, a single new model was
proposed to replace the previous three:

$$(12) \quad \left(\frac{p}{1-p}\right) = \left(\frac{p_0}{1-p_0}\right) \times \left(\frac{p_i}{1-p_i}\right) \times \left(\frac{p_j}{1-p_j}\right) \times \cdots \times \left(\frac{p_k}{1-p_k}\right).$$

This model is perhaps the most generally used for the analysis of binary
data (Cox, 1970; Jones, 1975; Lindsey, 1975). It is symmetric[1] with respect to application probabilities and nonapplication probabilities, unlike
(2) and (3). As in these other two multiplicative models, the p_i in (12) are
probabilities, which lead to interpretations impossible in the additive
model (1). Model (12) is susceptible to a knockout analysis (see the section on knockout analysis, p. 66) for features which deterministically either
prohibit or require rule application, while models (2) and (3) permit each
only one type of knockout.

Note that when the p_i are all close to 1, model (12) reduces to model (2).
When the p_i are all close to 0, it reduces to model (3). It is also possible to
show that (12) behaves like the additive model when all the p_i have
intermediate values, i.e., around $\frac{1}{2}$.

---

[1]Let $B = T - A$. With (12), carrying out the variable rule analysis on the fractions B/T
instead of A/T will directly give the same estimates for nonapplication probabilities as first
analyzing A/T to find p and then subtracting $1 - p$. Model (2) does not have this property and
neither does (3).

Uniqueness Problem

Mathematically speaking, data sets such as we have been discussing do not uniquely determine the estimated values of the parameters in the models (1), (2), (3), and (12). They determine only certain relationships among the parameters within the same factor group. For example, consider the data on copula contraction in (5). The optimal parameter values in (6) predict the frequencies in (7). But the very different set of values in (13) are also optimal in that they also predict (7), and we could construct any number of such optimal parameter value sets for these data.

(13)
$$p_0 = 0 \qquad p_{\text{pred adj}} = .06$$
$$p_{\text{cons}} = .2 \qquad p_{\text{verb}} = .52$$
$$p_{\text{vowel}} = .72$$

In order for these types of models to be uniquely determined by the data and by the estimating procedure, it is necessary to add one mathematical constraint to each factor group. In ANOVA this constraint is that the sum of the parameters in each factor group be 0. In model (1), we may do the same though it may be preferable (for the sake of comparability with the other models) to require that the average value within each group be $\frac{1}{2}$.

The appropriate constraint for model (2) is that the minimum parameter within each factor group be equal to 0, and for model (3), that the maximum parameter within each group be equal to 1.

For model (12) we may adopt either the same constraint as for the additive model, or else require that the average of $\log(p_i/1 - p_i)$ within a group be 0.

Probabilistic Interpretations

Let us consider the application or not of an optional rule as being the outcome of a number of independent binomial "experiments," one for each feature in the environment. The experiment corresponding to a feature i has probability p_i of being a "success." Then if we say that the rule applies whenever at least one feature in the environment is associated with a successful experiment, then we are in effect defining model (2). If the rule applies only when all the features simultaneously involve successful experiments, we define model (3). These interpretations of formulas (2) and (3) are clear from the definition of statistical independence.

The interpretation of formula (12) is less apparent. However it is an easy matter to derive (14) and (15) from (12).

(14)
$$\frac{p_0 p_i \cdots p_k}{(1 - p_0)(1 - p_i) \cdots (1 - p_k) + p_0 p_i \cdots p_k}$$

(15) $$(1 - p) = \frac{(1 - p_0)(1 - p_i) \cdots (1 - p_k)}{(1 - p_0)(1 - p_i) \cdots (1 - p_k) + p_0 p_i \cdots p_k}.$$

These formulas have the following interpretation: As in the other models, the experiments associated with the various features in the environment are presumed to act independently, except that the outcome is conditioned on the event either that all the experiments are successes or that none are. If they all are, the rule applies. If none are, it does not.

It should be pointed out that despite the attractiveness, for explanatory purposes, of these probabilistic interpretations, and despite the fact that they are natural extensions (cf. Cedergren & Sankoff, 1974) of conjunctive and disjunctive ordering of linguistic constraints, these interpretations have not yet proved to be of any great use in practice.

The VARBRUL 2 Program

Sankoff (1975) wrote a program to implement an algorithm for estimating the parameters of the logistic model. The algorithm converges quickly and the program is easy to use. It has the feature that the factor groups do not need to be given by the user as input, the features are automatically grouped together in such a way that no two factors in the same groups occur together in any environment. The first part of the program is devoted to finding this grouping of the factors, while the other part performs the algorithm. The factors to be studied must be nominal as in the above example, and cannot be ordinal or interval. This program, which is well documented, is now in general use (Labov & Labov, 1977; G. Sankoff & Thibault, 1977; Naro & Lemle, 1976, 1977; Lefebvre, 1975).

FURTHER STEPS

Despite the improvements incorporated in VARBRUL 2, many of the problems of the original remain. Recently we have been working on the statistical and computational level with the aim of solving all of these. We have succeeded to a larger extent and have tested all the solutions on S. Laberge's various data sets mentioned elsewhere in this volume. Currently we are assembling the various algorithms and tests into a flexible and easy-to-use package to be called VARBRUL 3. We shall now discuss some of these aspects.

Continuous Factors

Features such as age, education, economic indices, etc., are most naturally considered as continuous dimensions, and the grouping to achieve nominal factors necessary in the previous programs tends to introduce too many meaningless parameters into the estimation process. If z is a continuous factor, we can generalize (12) as follows:

(16) $$\left(\frac{p}{1-p}\right) = \left(\frac{p_0}{1-p_0}\right) \times \cdots \times \left(\frac{p_k}{1-p_k}\right) \times \left(\frac{p_z}{1-p_z}\right),$$

where

(17) $$\log\left(\frac{p_z}{1-p_z}\right) = c(z - \bar{z}).$$

The mean value of z in the data is $\bar{z}$ and there is just one parameter, c, to be estimated for this factor (group).

Tests of Significance

We have looked in some detail into the logistic model to answer the statistical problems noted earlier. The first to be studied was: Are the values of the parameters from contrasting features, as estimated from the data, significantly different? When we accumulate data we tend to record a great number of factors, not knowing in advance if every factor studied has a significant effect on the applicability of the rule. We can explain this concept in terms of an example.

Suppose the model we are studying includes 25 factors; in this case, there are 25 parameters to be estimated in maximizing the likelihood of the data. Suppose further, as in (18),

(18)

	Analysis 1	Analysis 2
Factor group 1	A,B,C,D,E,F (6 factors)	$A = B = C = D = E,F$ (2 factors)
Factor group 2	L,M,N,O,P,Q,R,S (8 factors)	$L,M = N = O = P = Q = R = S$ (2 factors)
Factor group 3	$X,Y,Z,$	X,Y,Z
	etc.	etc.
	25 factors total	15 factors total

that we suspect that 5 of the factors in group 1 really have no different effect from each other and 7 in group 2 are also homogeneous. Then we collapse the 5 into one single factor and the 7 into another, which leaves us with $25 - 4 - 6 = 15$ factors, which we estimate by maximizing the likelihood of the reduced model. If the two likelihoods are about the same, then we can say that the 10 disregarded distinctions gave no higher precision. There is a way to test accurately the difference in likelihood based on the fact that the difference between the logs of the two likelihoods should approximate a $\frac{1}{2}\chi^2_{10}$ distribution if there is no effect.

Reduction of the Dimensionality of the Model

Using the same test, entire factor groups can be tested for significance, and the model rebuilt to contain only dimensions which add significantly to the explanation of the variability in the data. We have developed systematic procedures for doing this exactly analogous to the forward and backward selection procedures for doing multiple regression (Draper & Smith, 1966).

Knockout Analysis

Among linguistic variation data, we frequently find some features which are present only in environments in which the rule is always applied, i.e., in which $A = T$. Similarly, for other features $A = 0$, that is, their presence in environment categorically prevents a rule from applying. There is no need to use a statistical estimating procedure to analyze the effect of such **knockout** factors. In equation (12) a knockout feature i is equivalent to either $p_i = 1$ or $p_i = 0$. Further, data collected on environments containing knockout features is useless for estimating the effect of other features present, because the nature of knockouts overwhelms any other effects, as can easily be proved.

It is thus necessary to identify knockouts and to remove data pertaining to them from the data set, prior to further statistical analysis. With small data sets it is possible to carry out this "data purification" manually, but such a procedure becomes too time consuming with large data sets. In our program, an automatic search is made by counting for each feature, ΣA, the total rule applications over all environments containing it, and ΣT, the total occurrences of such environments. If $\Sigma A = 0$ or if $\Sigma A = \Sigma T$, the factor is a knockout, and data on all environments containing it are automatically eliminated from further processing.

This being done does not necessarily mean that we can perform a variable rule analysis straight away on the remaining features. It sometimes happens that in eliminating one knockout feature, we inadvertently create others. This is illustrated by the data in (19).

(19)

Environment	A	T
KC	10	10
KD	5	5
BC	1	5
BD	0	4
ED	0	2

As we can see K is a knockout feature and the first two environments must be removed. This leaves the reduced data set in (20), in which D has

(20)

Environment	A	T
BC	1	5
BD	0	4
ED	0	2

now become a knockout feature.

Indeed, there may be a whole hierarchy of successively weaker knockout features, in the sense that those features which are recognized as knockout at a certain step in the analysis, did not have this knockout effect in the presence of at least one of those which had been recognized at an earlier step.

This may seem an unduly complicated structure to attribute to a data set; nonetheless it is completely and uniquely well defined for each data set, and it is the only structure compatible with a probabilistic model such as (12).

Computational Considerations

VARBRUL 3 continues the computational improvements of VAR-BRUL 2 and takes them several steps further.

Whereas the earlier program was limited as to the amount of data it could handle and, more seriously, the number of features allowed, we can now handle a thousand or so environments without difficulty, and well over a hundred factors. This latter property is very important if we wish to consider each speaker as a separate feature in the analysis, rather than use an a priori extralinguistic characterization (in terms of age, sex, etc.). Thus we can now analyze the Montreal French corpus, with 120 speakers, without grouping data from different speakers.

With increased capacity in terms of the size of problem which can be handled by the program, it became necessary to have more efficient programming from the computer time viewpoint. To achieve this efficiency, we abandoned the factor-by-factor approximation method of VARBRUL 2 in favor of a Newton–Raphson type algorithm which improves the estimates of all parameters at once. In addition, the actual programming has been carried out with much greater attention to algorithmic efficiency, with respect both to time and memory.

Detection of Subpopulations Obeying Different Models of the Same Type

A converse problem to the reduction of the dimensionality of the model is adding dimensions: For example, if the description of the whole population where all individuals have the same estimate for all the factors is inadequate statistically, it is perhaps because some subset of this population follows a different model. For example suppose that one group in the population has a tendency to apply the rule more frequently in the presence of feature X than when feature Y is present, while another group applies it more for Y than for X in corresponding contexts. This means perhaps that two parameters X and X' and two parameters Y and Y' should be included in the model, two for the one group (X,Y), the other two for the second group (X',Y').

A program is now operating which examines the population to see whether it may be divided into two, three, etc., groups, each of which is homogeneous, but among which there may be very different values for one or more parameters or even different significant factor groups. The log likelihood test in conjunction with simulation studies shows whether the grouping obtained explains the data significantly better than a single-group model.

The procedure is again based on the maximum likelihood method. Some examples are given in Rousseau and Sankoff (this volume). This method was developed in collaboration with E. Diday.

REFERENCES

Cedergren, H. J. Interplay of social and linguistic factors in Panama. Unpublished Ph.D dissertation, Cornell University, 1973.

Cedergren, H. J., & Sankoff, D. Variable rules: Performance as a statistical reflection of competence. *Language*, 1974, *50*, 333–355.

Cox, D. R. *The analysis of binary data*. London: Methuen, 1970.

Draper, N. R., & Smith, H. *Applied regression analysis*. New York: Wiley, 1966.

Guy, G. The Cedergren–Sankoff variable rule program. In R. W. Fasold & R. W. Shuy (Eds.), *Analyzing variation in language*. Washington, D.C.: Georgetown University Press, 1975, 59–69.

Jones, R. H. Probability estimation using a multinomial logistic function. *Journal of Statistical Computation and Simulation*, 1975, *3*, 315–329.

Labov, W. Contraction, deletion, and inherent variability of the English copula. *Language*, 1969, *45*, 715–762.

Labov, W. *Language in the inner city.* Philadelphia: University of Pennsylvania Press, 1972.

Labov, W., & Labov, T. L'apprentissage de la syntaxe des interrogations. *Langue Française*, 1977, *34*, 52–80.

Lefebvre, C. Plural agreement in Cuzco Quechua: Some aspects of variation. Unpublished Ph.D. dissertation, University of California, Berkeley, 1975.

Lindsey, J. K. Likelihood analyses and tests for binary data. *Applied Statistics*, 1975, *24*, 1–16.

Naro, A., & Lemle, M. Syntactic diffusion. In S. Steever, C. Walker, & S. Mufwene (Eds.), *Papers from the parasession on diachronic syntax.* Chicago: Chicago Linguistics Society, 1976, 221–247.

Naro, A., & Lemle, M. Syntactic diffusion. *Cienca e cultura*, 1977, *29*, 259–268.

Sankoff, D. VARBRUL version 2. Unpublished manuscript, 1975.

Sankoff, G., & Thibault, P. L'alternance entre les auxiliaires *avoir* et *être* en français parlé à Montréal. *Langue Française*, 1977, *34*, 81–108.

5

Variable Rules, Community Grammar, and Linguistic Change[1]

Paul Kay

INTRODUCTION

This chapter will show that if a variable rule is a rule of community grammar, then the mathematical assumptions inherent in published variable rule analyses are incompatible with a pattern of language change which has in fact frequently been observed. An assumption in each of the variable rule models so far proposed is that linguistic constraints and social constraints operate independently, that is, that there is no interaction between linguistic and social constraints. In fact, a very common pattern of observed language change, probably the characteristic pattern, involves precisely such interaction.

An attractive aspect of variable rule theory is the manner in which the linguistic constraints in the model represent propensities shared throughout a speech community while the social constraints and/or the input probabilities are what distinguish among social groups or individual speakers. On this interpretation, the effect of each linguistic environment on the probability of rule application is constant across speakers. The

[1]Don Forman, Chad McDaniel, and especially David Sankoff have given me a lot of help with this paper, and I would like to blame all the errors it contains on them if only I could get away with it.

differences in application frequencies in a given linguistic environment observed in different speakers are attributed to social constraints and to the effect of speaker-linked input probabilities.

The variable-rule-as-community-grammar assumption has been propounded not so much in clear theoretical statements as in the large number of empirical studies that tacitly adopt it. In most variable rule studies (e.g., those reported in Cedergren & D. Sankoff, 1974; G. Sankoff, 1974; Wolfram, 1974; Cedergren, 1973; Fasold, 1972), one simply applies one or several variable rule models to a data table representing the breakdown by linguistic and social environment of the application frequencies observed in the entire sample under study. In these studies no attempt is usually made to investigate whether or not linguistic constraints are shared; the method of analysis tacitly assumes they are.[2] It is implied by this method that linguistic constraints are in fact shared throughout the speech community. The notion that linguistic constraints are shared communitywide and that speakers differ only with respect to their input probabilities is a plausible and attractive notion because it is the theoretical pillar of the doctrine that a variable rule expresses at once what is shared (the linguistic constraints) and what is not shared (the group or speaker constraints) in a community grammar.

Unfortunately, this notion of community grammar is shown in many of Labov's data to be contradicted by observed synchronic facts. We will demonstrate below that it is also contradicted by a pattern of language change commonly observed in real communities. Labov has often remarked that linguistic constraints are not in fact always uniform throughout a speech community (e.g., 1972b, p. 81 and passim). In the next section, the following relationship between the uniform constraints assumption and language change is demonstrated: If a single variable rule

---

[2]There have been two exceptions of which I am aware. Cedergren and D. Sankoff (1974, p. 347) in their study of r spirantization in 79 speakers of Panamanian Spanish, checked for uniformity of linguistic constraints using the following procedure. Applying linguistic constraint parameters and social-class-linked input probabilities derived from the variable rule analysis of the full sample of 79 speakers, they calculated for each speaker separately the expected frequencies for each environment. Using a chi-square test of goodness of fit, which they characterize as too stringent, they found a discrepancy between those predicted and the observed frequencies significant at the 5% level for about 20% of the informants.

Guy's recent study (1975) is a stronger exception in that Guy takes as a central issue the investigation of the degree to which linguistic constraints are shared across speakers. His conclusion is that for the variable studied, deletion of final -d and -t in Philadelphia English, the relative strengths of linguistic constraints within a family are widely shared among speakers. (He does not attempt to assess the relative importance of different constraint families across speakers.) It is worth noting that the feature studied by Guy is not one that appears to be the focus of a change in progress.

applies to an entire speech community at time t_0, and if at a later time t_1 it is found that the community obeys an equally uniform but numerically distinct set of linguistic constraints on the application of the rule, then, if change has occurred according to the empirically most characteristic pattern, the community must have passed through a phase in which there was no uniform set of linguistic constraints characteristic of it, that is, in which the relevant part of its grammar was not specifiable by a single variable rule. Thus, observed language change frequently, if not invariably, involves interaction of linguistic and social constraints while the variable-rule-as-community-grammar model prohibits this interaction. Perhaps this fact has received less than complete recognition because it was the same person, Labov, who (*a*) invented variable rules (1969), (*b*) proposed the variable-rule-as-community-grammar model (1972a), (*c*) pointed out that variable constraints are not always shared throughout the community (1972a), and (*d*) documented in the finest detail that pattern of interaction between linguistic and social constraints that vitiates the variable-rule-as-community-grammar model (1972a, 1972b, 1972c, and elsewhere).

In the third section, I will briefly discuss several of the classic cases of change studied by Labov and others and show that these cases are not consonant with the postulate that linguistic constraints are shared throughout the speech community (hereinafter the **uniform constraints assumption**).

THEORETICAL INDEPENDENCE OF CONSTRAINTS

There have been four distinct models to date for variable rules proposed: additive, multiplicative applications, multiplicative nonapplications, and logistic. The respective defining equations are given in (1)–(4):

(1) $\qquad p = p_o + p_a + \cdots + p_n$

(2) $\qquad p = p_o \times p_a \times \cdots \times p_n$

(3) $\qquad p = 1 - (1 - p_o) \times (1 - p_a) \times \cdots \times (1 - p_n)$

(4) $\qquad p = \dfrac{p_o \times \cdots \times p_n}{[p_o \times \cdots \times p_n] + [(1 - p_o) \times \cdots \times (1 - p_n)]}$,

where p designates the probability of application, p_o designates the input probability (which may vary by social group, including groups of one), p_a designates the constraint selected from the first linguistic constraint family, $\cdots$, and p_n designates the constraint selected from the nth linguistic constraint family. As has been pointed out by J. B. Kruskal (personal communication) as well as by D. Sankoff (personal communication), under the apparent diversity of these models lies an interesting mathematical uniformity, namely that in each model we can assign weights $k_o, \cdots, k_n$ to the linguistic constraints which correspond to the probabilities $p_o, \cdots,$ p_n in such a way that the application probability p is a monotone function of the sum of the weights. That is for each model (1–4) there exists a function f such that

(5) $$p = f(k_o + \cdots + k_n).$$

Consider first the additive model. Here we just take the weights k_i as identical to the probabilities p_i.

In the applications model (2) we let $k_i = \log p_i$. By taking the log of equation (2) we get

(6) $$\begin{aligned} \log p &= \log(p_o \times \cdots \times p_n) \\ &= \log p_o + \cdots + \log p_n \\ &= k_o + \cdots + k_n. \end{aligned}$$

Hence

(7) $$p = \log^{-1}(k_o + \cdots + k_n).$$

In the nonapplications model we set $k_i = \log(1 - p_i)$ and by reasoning analogous to the above we obtain

(8) $$p = 1 - \log^{-1}(k_o + \cdots + k_n).$$

Similarly, in the logistic model, if we take the weight k_i to be $\log\left(\dfrac{p_i}{1 - p_i}\right)$, we can derive

(9) $$p = 1 - \frac{1}{1 + \log^{-1}(k_o + \cdots + k_n)}.$$

Thus we see that the four particular variable rule models so far proposed belong to a general class of models defined by equation (5) in which the application probability is always a monotone function of the sum of the weights assigned to relevant linguistic and social constraints.

The significance of equation (5) for the present discussion is that it allows us to see that the independence of constraints property is the same in all four models. Since all models are transformations of the additive model, all have the independence of constraints property as defined in the additive model. Because of this property, any such transformed-additive model is incapable of accounting for a very common situation of linguistic change. In the next section we will see that change often begins with an increase or decrease in frequency of rule application in a single context, that is, under a single combination of constraints, while the frequencies in other contexts remain stable. Consider the case of two constraint families each containing two constraints: (k_{o_1}, k_{o_2}) the speakers, say, and (k_{a_1}, k_{a_2}) the linguistic constraints. Is it possible for the rule probability p to change in only one context? For example can $k_{o_1} + k_{a_1}$ change over time while the sums of weights for the other three contexts $(k_{o_2} + k_{a_1}, k_{o_1} + k_{a_2}, k_{o_2} + k_{a_2})$ remain constant? The answer is no, since if $k_{o_1} + k_{a_1}$ changes then either k_{o_1} or k_{a_1} (or both) must change, and the change in one cannot be merely equal and of opposite sign to the change in the other. If, meanwhile, $k_{o_2} + k_{a_1}$ and $k_{o_1} + k_{a_2}$ are each to remain unchanged, then k_{o_2} must change to compensate for any change in k_{a_1} and k_{a_2} must change to compensate for any change in k_{o_1}. But then $k_{o_2} + k_{a_2}$ must change by an amount equal and of opposite sign to the change in $k_{o_1} + k_{a_1}$. This shows that we cannot have a change in one context only.

This effect is independent of the variable rule model chosen and of course of the procedure used to estimate the constraint values from the data. As long as the number of different contexts is large enough in comparison with the number of constraints—and no model is of any interest otherwise—a change in rule probability in one context implies a change in at least one other context. According to the mathematics of all the variable rule models, an increase or decrease in application probability in a single context, to the exclusion of all others, is an impossibility. We will see in the coming section that this theoretical impossibility is a frequent concomitant of observed linguistic change.

A second, and more obvious, consequence of the independence of constraints property is that if constraints become reordered for any speaker, they must be similarly reordered for all speakers. This theoretical constraint is also violated by some of the data discussed in the next section.

EMPIRICAL DEPENDENCE OF CONSTRAINTS

We have shown that none of the proposed variable rule models accounts for interaction of speaker and linguistic constraints. In particular, we saw that:

a. The theory cannot model the shift of a single group's usage in a single linguistic environment while other groups and environments remain stable.

b. The models imply that if the relative strengths of two linguistic constraints become reordered over time for one group of speakers, they must be similarly reordered for all groups of speakers in the community to which the variable rule applies.

We will first consider a few examples from Labov's work on variation and change in progress that violate one or both of these theoretical propositions and then some examples from the work of the wave theorists.

Perhaps the first of the modern studies of variation and change in progress that employed actual counts of linguistic tokens to get frequencies of rule application was Labov's study of the centralization of the vocalic nucleus [a] of the diphthongs [aw] (*bout*) and [ay] (*bite*) in Martha's Vineyard. Here it was found that the centralization of [a] experienced an initial jump in frequency in the environment [__y] among the fishermen of the old Yankee town of Chilmark. Thus proposition (a) is violated by the data. From here the change spread to the linguistic environment [__w] and to other speaker groups in the community, the Portuguese and Indian inhabitants, but not independently in the two dimensions: "In these two ethnic groups [Portuguese and Indian], centralization of (aw) overtook and surpassed centralization of (ay) [Labov 1972b, p. 525]." Thus proposition (b) is also violated by these data.

If the raising of front and back peripheral tense vowels in New York is considered as a uniform linguistic process with [+front] and [+back] functioning as differential linguistic environments in a single variable rule, then there is interaction between these conditioning linguistic environments and the ethnic differentiation, Jewish versus Italian, with the former favoring the front and the latter the back vowels (Labov, 1966, p. 11 and passim). Labov has more recently reported (1972d, p. 58 and passim) that with respect to deletion of postvocalic [r], younger upper middle class New Yorkers are dramatically adopting the nondeleted pronunciation in relaxed style without any significant comparable shift in other social classes. The former example constitutes a violation of proposition (b) and the latter of proposition (a).

Labov (1972c) discussed the reported merger and split of Early Modern English long [a:] (*mate*) and long [ε:] (*meat*), which had the apparent effect of first merging these two classes so that *meat* and *mate* became homophonous and then splitting the resultant class mysteriously along the lines of the original separate classes to produce the current circumstance in which *meat* and *meet* are homophonous. Here Labov states clearly the generality of the empirical principle that linguistic and social constraints characteristically interact in the process of language change: "When a set of associated sound changes spreads from one group to another, different elements are advanced more rapidly by different groups [Labov, 1972c, p.

834]." He then discusses by way of illustration the Martha's Vineyard (ay/aw) change, making it clear that by "different elements" he means to include also the case of a single element in contrasting environments. If we frame our linguistic rules so as to make the process of peripheral vowel raising a uniform phenomenon, then the information specifying the precise height of the vowel before the upward shift is part of the conditioning environment of the rule. Labov's discussion makes clear that the strength of this constraint varied across vowel heights in a way that interacted with social class. Thus:

> There is reason to think that the sixteenth century movements of long ā and ēa [ɛ:] followed a pattern similar to the current sound changes we have been studying. In London, the long ā and ēa variables were most advanced among speakers from the merchant class, not the highest social class. Hart, who was one of the landed gentry and a court herald, had low ā and lower-mid ēa. Those who testified to the merger of ēa and long ā were tradesmen's sons, like Bullokar and Laneham. We can see the general outlines of a middle-class pattern opposed to an upper-class pattern. If our present understanding of sociolinguistic patterns is at all applicable, we would not expect to find sharp divisions between the two which would establish them as separate dialects. The predominance of the merchant class in the raising was a matter of more-or-less [Labov, 1972c, p. 834].

That is, there was an interaction between the social class of the speaker and the environmental feature consisting of the initial height of the vowel to be raised in the variable rule that specifies that long tense front vowels are raised. This analysis depends again on the presumption that we would want to express the tendency to raise the vowels sharing these features in a single rule. This presumption seems appropriate in terms of general considerations of economy in grammar and especially so in terms of the data Labov has introduced that show such "chain shifts" or parallel shifts to have very much the character of a single unified process.[3] If we arbitrarily assign the heights of the relevant four front vowels as follows $H(a:) = 1$; $H(\varepsilon:) = 2$; $H(e:) = 3$; $H(i:) = 4$ and allow x to be an integer variable with the values $\{1,2\}$, the main outlines of the variable rule in question can be represented[4]

[3]It is common in such processes for the sounds in question to move in parallel so that while the lower vowel ends up in the position the higher vowel vacated, the higher vowel has itself moved so that roughly the same distance between the two is maintained at all times. For example, "In the south of England (ay) is often backed and raised to the original position of (oy) [ɔɪ] but at the same time (oy) moves upward in a chain shift to high-position [uɪ] [Labov, 1972c, p. 834]."

[4]The analysis is complicated by the fact that not only is the frequency of application of the rule a quantitative variable but also the output of the rule is itself a variable. That is, not only is the frequency of raising a variable conditioned by various linguistic and nonlinguistic constraints but also the degree of raising is a variable. Lacking detailed phonetic data for the

(10)

$$
\begin{bmatrix}
\rule{2cm}{0.4pt} \\
[+ \text{ Vowel}] \\
[+ \text{ Front}] \\
[+ \text{ Tense}]
\end{bmatrix}
$$

$$
H \rightarrow H + x \ / \ \left\langle \begin{matrix} [H = 1] \\ [H = 2] \\ [H = 3] \end{matrix} \right\rangle
$$

$$
\left\langle \begin{matrix} [\text{Nobility}] \\ [\text{Merchant class}] \\ [\text{Lower than merchant class}] \end{matrix} \right\rangle
$$

Rule (10) says that tense front vowels are raised variably depending on the initial height of the vowel and the social class of the speaker. There is interaction between these two variable constraint families in that the merchant class has, according to Labov's report, a much greater tendency than the other class groups to apply the rule in the "$H = 1$" linguistic environment, that is, to raise [a:] to [e:], creating the *mate/meat* merger.

We turn now to another class of empirical examples, those that have been discovered by scholars working in the wave theory/implicational scale paradigm. Fasold has attempted to resolve the differences between variable rule and implicational scale theorists. He says, "As I tried to argue in [Fasold, 1975], variable rules generate 'multivalued' implicational scales and are quite compatible with scale analysis [personal communication]." This statement is correct.[5] By simply arranging the constraint values in each constraint family in ascending or descending order, we may produce a multivalued implicational scale of the sort to which Fasold makes reference. An example is given in Table 1, where for convenience the multiplicative application probabilities model is assumed. In Table 1, it is further assumed that there are three speaker

---

historical period in question, Labov treats degree of raising tacitly as discrete valued, but we may be assured from results obtained in parallel instrumental studies in the present and reported in the same paper (and elsewhere, e.g., Labov, Yaeger, & Steiner, 1974) that in fact this phonetic variable was continuous. The variable "degree of raising" is ignored in the present treatment as it is not germane to the point of this paper, although it would appear that the demonstrated existence of phonetically continuous output variables cries for an extension of the variable rule formalism. What would be needed, it appears, are rule schemata that yield not a single probability, interpreted as an application frequency, but rather a probability distribution over some continuous interval of a linguistic scale, say, vowel height.

[5]We assume that Fasold has in mind cases in which there are no more than two constraint families since implicational scales, as used by wave theorists, are usually no more than two dimensional (cf. Bailey, 1973, p. 86ff.) and we restrict our attention here to such cases.

groups o_1, o_2, o_3 and one linguistic constraint family with three constraint values a_1, a_2, a_3.

However, although Fasold's statement is correct, its converse does not hold. It is true in general that frequencies predicted by a variable rule model will satisfy a multivalued implicational scale model, but it is not true in general that data satisfying an implicational scale model will be well fit by a variable rule model. Moreover, and more to the point, those empirical bodies of data that have been offered as the paradigmatic exemplifications of the implicational scale model of the wave theory do not satisfy any variable rule model precisely because they entail the interaction of linguistic and speaker constraints. An example is Bickerton's corpus on the alternation of the complementizers *tu/fu* in the Guyanese creole continuum (Bickerton, 1971). The more basilectal form is *fu* and the more acrolectal *tu*. The relevant linguistic environments are a_1 following inceptive verbs such as *start*, a_2 following desiderative verbs such as *want*, and a_3 following other verbs. Of Bickerton's 28 speakers, data were gathered for all three linguistic environments on 8 speakers. Those data are presented in Table 2 and may be generated by a variable rule of the form

(11)
$$fu \rightarrow tu \ / \ \left\langle \begin{array}{l} [+V, +\text{Inceptive}] = a_1 \\ [+V, +\text{Desiderative}] = a_2 \\ [+V, -\text{Inceptive}, \\ \quad -\text{Desiderative}] = a_3 \end{array} \right\rangle \left[\underline{\hspace{3cm}} \atop +\text{Complementizer} \right] \left\langle \begin{array}{l} \text{speaker group} = o_1 \\ \cdot \\ \cdot \\ \cdot \\ \text{speaker group} = o_n \end{array} \right\rangle$$

To solve for the arithmetical values of the constraint parameters we would of course have to know the observed numbers of application and nonapplications. For purposes of the following argument, we may without loss of generality assume that *tu* corresponds to 0, *fu* to 1, and *tu/fu* to ½. The resulting assumed observed application frequencies are given in Table 3. Let us now consider fitting a variable rule to the numerical data presented in Table 3. Again for convenience we use the multiplicative applications model, but analogous arguments apply to any variable rule model. The data in Table 3 will not fit the variable rule model because of strong interaction between linguistic and speaker constraints. Since the first row of the table consists of all 1's, $p_{a_1} = p_{a_2} = p_{a_3} = 1$. (If the product of two probabilities is unity both of them must be unity.) But by the inde-

TABLE 1

Table of Predicted Frequencies Assuming Multiplicative Applications models[a]

Variable rule parameters			Linguistic constraints		
Speaker constraints	Linguistic constraints	Speaker constraints	$p_{a_1} = 1.0$	$p_{a_2} = .4$	$p_{a_3} = .1$
$p_{o_1} = .8$	$p_{a_1} = 1.0 \implies$	$p_{o_1} = .8$	.80	.32	.08
$p_{o_2} = .6$	$p_{a_2} = .4$	$p_{o_2} = .6$	.60	.24	.06
$p_{o_3} = .3$	$p_{a_3} = .1$	$p_{o_3} = .3$	.30	.12	.03

[a]Illustration with hypothetical underlying constraints that a variable rule generates a multivalued implicational scale. The predicted frequency in each cell is greater than that in all cells to its right and in all cells below it.

TABLE 2

Implicational Scale Data on Guyanese Complementizer Usage in Three Linguistic Environments by Speaker Group[a,b]

	Linguistic environment		
Speaker group	a_1	a_2	a_3
o_1	*tu*	*tu*	*tu*
o_{14}	*tu*	*tu*	*tu/fu*
o_8	*tu*	*tu*	*fu*
$o_{11,25}$	*tu*	*tu/fu*	*fu*
o_{26}	*tu*	*fu*	*fu*
o_{27}	*tu/fu*	*fu*	*fu*[c]
o_9	*fu*	*fu*	*fu*

[a]Adapted from Bickerton (1971, Table VI).

[b]The fourth speaker group contains two members, the rest one each.

[c]In fact this entry was *tu/fu* but I have changed it for illustrative purposes, as with this single change the data scale perfectly, except for some of the speakers with missing data, who also have scaling errors.

TABLE 3

Bickerton's Guyanese Creole Complementizer Data
Converted to Numerical Observations (See Text)

Speaker group	Linguistic environment		
	a_1	a_2	a_3
o_1	1	1	1
o_{14}	1	1	.5
o_8	1	1	0
$o_{11,25}$	1	.5	0
o_{26}	1	0	0
o_{27}	.5	0	0^a
o_9	0	0	0

aSee footnote b Table 2.

pendence of constraints assumption, if one row of the table has all entries equal, every row of the table has all entries equal. For example, since p_{a_1} $= p_{a_2} = p_{a_3} = 1$, every entry in the fourth row of the table must be equal to the input constraint $o_{11,25}$. Note further that the difficulty cannot be removed by simply eliminating the top and bottom rows, which represent speaker groups for which the rule is categorically present and absent respectively. (The logistic model could accommodate such data.) If in fact we consider only the five internal rows of the table (dropping the top and bottom rows from consideration), 9 of the 10 pairwise comparisons among these rows involve a logical inconsistency. In general, the sort of data presented by wave theorists, in which for each speaker group there is categorical behavior in many or all linguistic environments and variable behavior in few or no environments, offers objection in principle to the variable rule theory because they show strong evidence of interaction between social and linguistic constraints.[6]

[6]It was pointed out by J. B. Kruskal (personal communication) and by D. Sankoff (personal communication) that these data of Bickerton's can be fitted fairly well by the logistic model and in effect as closely as desired by creating a special model for this purpose within the family of variable rule models defined by equation (5). But the point should not be lost that the lack of fit of a variable rule model to observed data is supposed to be due to sampling error. The reason that variable rules fit this particular implicational scale data set fairly well is that the number of rows and columns is small. If, as wave theorists maintain, change situations characteristically produce data which form implicational scales with large numbers of rows and columns where variability is confined to a narrow band along the diagonal, then the data of these change situations is inimical to variable rule analysis.

CONCLUSIONS

I have attempted to show in this chapter that (*a*) the variable-rule-as-community-grammar postulate requires that there be no interaction between speaker and linguistic constraints—that is, that linguistic constraints be shared throughout the community; (*b*) that synchronic studies have shown that this is often not the case; and (*c*) that empirical studies of change in progress have shown that interaction between social and linguistic constraints is a common and probably the characteristic pattern of relation between linguistic and social constraints. Indeed, it would appear that Labov's notion of the mechanism of linguistic change depends in part on the interaction of linguistic and social constraints. It follows that the variable-rule-as-community-grammar postulate must be rejected if community grammars are going to be applicable in situations of ongoing change.

The question then arises, if variable rules are not rules of a community grammar, what are they? Because of the independence of constraints assumption, variable rules are, as we have seen, applicable only to communities or subcommunities that are homogeneous with respect to linguistic constraints. Hence the **theoretical** utility of variable rules in modeling the normal heterogeneity of speech communities would appear limited, since the heterogeneity frequently entails interaction of linguistic and social constraints. Variable rules will no doubt remain a valuable statistical tool for the analysis of the differential strengths of linguistic and social variables in determining linguistic behavior in subsections of speech communities that are **homogeneous** and **stable** with respect to the relevant linguistic constraints on rule application. We have seen that variable rules do not furnish an adequate model of speech communities in which the linguistic heterogeneity present is part of an ongoing linguistic change.

REFERENCES

Bailey, C.-J. N. *Variation and linguistic theory.* Arlington, Va.: Center for Applied Linguistics, 1973.
Bickerton, D. Inherent variability and variable rules. *Foundations of Language,* 1971, 7, 457–492.
Cedergren, H. J. On the nature of variable constraints. In C.-J. Bailey & R. Shuy (Eds.), *New ways of analyzing variation in English.* Washington, D.C.: Georgetown University Press, 1973, 13–22.
Cedergren, H. J. & Sankoff, D. Variable rules: Performance as a statistical reflection of competence. *Language,* 1974, 50, 333–355.
Fasold, R. W. *Tense marking in Black English: A linguistic and social analysis.* Arlington, Va.: Center for Applied Linguistics, 1972.

Fasold, R. W. The Bailey wave model: A dynamic quantitative paradigm. In R. W. Fasold & R. W. Shuy (Eds.), *Analyzing variation in language.* Georgetown University Press, 1975, 27–58.

Guy, G. Variation in the group and the individual: The case of final stop deletion. *Pennsylvania Working Papers on Linguistic Change and Variation,* 1975, Vol. I, No. 4.

Labov, W. *The social stratification of English in New York City.* Washington, D.C.: Center for Applied Linguistics, 1966.

Labov, W. Contraction, deletion, and inherent variability of the English copula. *Language,* 1969, *45,* 715–762.

Labov, W. Where do grammars stop? In R. Shuy (Ed.), *Proceedings of the 23rd Annual Round Table on Languages and Linguistics.* Washington, D.C.: Georgetown University Press, 1972, 43–88. (a)

Labov, W. On the mechanism of linguistic change. In J. Gumperz & D. Hymes (Eds.) *Directions in sociolinguistics.* New York: Holt, Rinehart and Winston, 1972, 512–537. (b)

Labov, W. On the use of the present to explain the past. In L. Heilmann (Ed.), *Proceedings of the Eleventh International Congress of Linguists.* Bologna: Società Editrice il Mulino Bologna, 1972, 825–851. (c)

Labov, W. The social stratification of (r) in New York City department stores. In W. Labov *Sociolinguistic patterns.* Philadelphia: University of Pennsylvania Press, 1972, 43–69. (d)

Labov, W., Yaeger, M., & Steiner, R. *A quantitative study of sound change in progress.* Report on NSF Contract GS-3287. Philadelphia: U.S. Regional Survey, 1972.

Sankoff, G. A quantitative paradigm for the study of communicative competence. In R. Bauman & J. Sherzer (Eds.), *Explorations in the ethnography of speaking.* Cambridge, England: Cambridge University Press, 1974, 18–49.

Wolfram, W. *Sociolinguistic aspects of assimilation: Puerto Rican English in New York City.* Arlington, Va.: Center for Applied Linguistics, 1974.

6

Language Variation and Linguistic Competence

Ralph W. Fasold

HYPOTHESES ABOUT COMPETENCE

The use of variable rule methodology has proven a successful heuristic procedure for determining the linguistic and other influences on a substantial number of variable linguistic processes. Even as only a heuristic tool, variable rule research would be well worthwhile, but it seems likely that a concept that allows the insightful analysis of a wide range of language data would also be part of a theory of human linguistic competence. Most proponents of variable rules in linguistics have not made detailed attempts to integrate variable rules into linguistic theory, beyond adapting the notational conventions of generative phonology and answering those critics who claim that variable rules are unlearnable.

The fact of patterned variation in language leads to several possible hypotheses about what speakers know, which enables them to produce the patterns of variation. The strongest of these is that speakers somehow "know" the precise frequency percentage they should have as the output of a variable rule in some environment. The well-known rule for the deletion of word-final alveolar stops in English, for example, is known to be sensitive to the nature of the initial segment of the following word. Suppose that a given group of speakers, say, black adolescents in Harlem, are observed to delete final alveolar stops 80% of the time when the next word begins with a consonant. If speakers have knowledge of precise frequency percentages, this would mean that this group of speakers constantly and unconsciously monitors their own speech so that their deletion rate would be precisely 80% when averaged together with the deletion rate for other speakers of the same group. Although some of Labov's early work (e.g., Labov, 1969) has been interpreted as implying that this is what speakers "know" and has been severely criticized by Bickerton (1971), no linguist who has worked on variation in language has actually proposed that speakers aim at precise percentages of application of variable rules.

Currently used variable rule models, following Cedergren and Sankoff (1974), make use of probability numbers assigned to variable constraints. In our example, some probability value, say .75, would be assigned to the presence of a following consonant in the rule for deleting final alveolar stops. This value, taken together with the values for the other constraints on the rule in a given environment, can be used to compute the probability that an alveolar stop will be deleted in that particular environment. This second value gives the **probability** that the rule will be applied in that particular environment, but the frequency is not expected to match the probability value in every data set even from the same group of speakers. A possible hypothesis, then, is that the probability values (like .75) are part of a speaker's linguistic competence.

A third hypothesis can be derived from Labov's pioneering work on variable rules (Labov, 1969). Labov's classical model incorporated the implicit hypothesis that a speaker knows the factors that favor a variable rule and also a hierarchical order of strength or weight among them. In the case of the rule for deleting final alveolar stops, a following consonant favors application more than a following vowel so that utterances like *morning mist hovers over the river* are more likely to be pronounced with the *t* of *mist* deleted than utterances like *morning mist is over the river.* Another constraint has to do with the morphemic status of the deletable stop. Thus, the *t* of *missed,* which represents the *-ed* morpheme, is less likely to be deleted than in the phonetically identical *mist,* in which *t* does not represent a separate morpheme. Moreover, the constraint about the following consonant is stronger or heavier than the one about the morphemic status of *t* for most speakers. This means that where the two conflict, as in *missed my bus* versus *mist on the river,* deletion is more frequent in the former type of utterance than the latter. According to this hypothesis, the speaker "knows" that following consonants and the morphemic status of the stop both affect the deletability of the stop and that the following segment has more effect than morphemic status, but probability values associated with each are not directly part of his linguistic competence, let alone the exact frequency with which final stops are to be deleted in the various environments. The heirarchy of constraints is to be interpreted as Labov proposed (Labov, 1969), namely, "each constraint in the hierarchy outweighs the effects of all constraints below it [p. 741]." That is, in a variable rule with three constraints, when the highest weighted constraint is present and the lower two are absent, the rule applies more often than when the two lower weighted constraints are present, but the highest is absent.

A fourth hypothesis, somewhat weaker than the third, would be that linguistic competence should include (a) knowledge of what environmental factors contribute to application of the rule, and (b) knowledge of the relative weight of each. The relative weight might be indicated simply by interpreting the constraint with the highest probability value as the heaviest constraint, the one with the second highest probability as the second heaviest, and so on. The actual numbers, though, are not taken as part of the speaker's competence. This hypothesis is similar to the one I have just attributed to Labov's early proposal, except that it is apparently not necessarily the case that each constraint in the hierarchy outweighs all others below it. The heaviest weighted constraint may contribute more to the application of the rule than either of the next two taken separately, but the hypothesis as described would not predict that the heaviest one inevitably produces more output in the absence of the next two than the second and third constraints would produce in the absence of the first.

A fifth and still weaker hypothesis would be that speakers know what features in the environment of a variable rule favor application of the rule, but their competence does not include knowledge of which ones favor application more than others. As far as I know, no one has argued strongly for this hypothesis, although in one of his articles, Labov (1971) writes variable rules which conform to it, saying that such a rule format "describes conditions which hold for English generally and for many Creole continua" although "it is sometimes useful to show relative strengths of these constraints [p. 467]."

A sixth and the weakest hypothesis is the one implicit in all generative theories which do not include variable rules, with equivalents in all other linguistic theories I know about. This is the competence associated with optional rules. Optional rules, in effect, mean that the speaker knows that there is variation at certain points of syntax and phonology, but that environmental factors influencing frequency of application of an optional rule are not subject matter for linguistic theory.[1]

---

[1]Kay and McDaniel (1977) point out that hypotheses such as the first through fifth are not simply stronger versions of optional rules but are qualitatively different. The goal of theories with optional rules is to account for just what utterances are possible in a language, not to predict the likelihood of occurrence of various options.

EVIDENCE FROM GROUP AND INDIVIDUAL DATA

In what follows, I will argue that most of the evidence so far indicates that the third hypothesis is the correct one, with the fourth as a possible "fall-back" position. An example of the evidence that leads me to this conclusion is Wolfram's three-constraint rule for d deletion in the speech of New York Puerto Rican male adolescents (Wolfram, 1973).[2] His data appear as Figure 1.

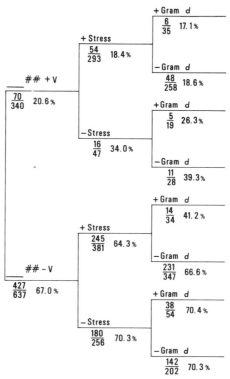

Figure 1. Final d deletion for N. Y. Puerto Rican adolescents. [From Wolfram, 1973, p. 122.] [Errors corrected.]

If the third hypothesis were perfectly supported by these data, the percentages would become progressively larger as we move down the chart. The percentages do in fact increase in value from top to bottom, aside

[2]Wolfram (1973) actually presents data for a rule with four constraints, but many of the cells showing the fourth-order constraint are very sparsely populated and the fourth-order constraint appears weakly ordered in any event and may not be an actual factor influencing application of the rule.

from a negligible statistical fluctuation at the bottom of the chart. The literature on linguistic variation contains numerous empirical studies like Wolfram's and the data I have seen conform to the principle about as well as Wolfram's do.

It might be objected that data such as those in Figure 1 are group data and that the patterns would not work for individual speakers. Since linguistic competence is related to individual competence, if the relationships in data displays like Figure 1 are the result only of averaging the data for groups of speakers, they would say nothing about individual linguistic competence. However, there are a number of studies in which it has been shown that the patterns hold for individuals as well as for groups. This has been shown for final stop deletion in the speech of black peer groups in Harlem (Labov, Cohen, Robins, & Lewis, 1968, p. 76), for the same rule in Philadelphia (Guy, 1977), in Detroit (Wolfram, 1973, p. 6), and in Appalachian English (Wolfram & Christian, 1976, p. 36), for postvocalic *r* deletion in Appalachian English (Wolfram & Christian, 1976, p. 47), and for *que* deletion in Montreal French (Sankoff, 1974, p. 37, but for an objection, see Bickerton, 1973, pp. 28–29). It is reasonably clear that the group patterns hold as well for individuals when enough data are collected from each speaker.

CONNECTIONS WITH THE WAVE MODEL

The hypothesis that linguistic competence involves knowledge of constraints on variable rules and also a hierarchy of constraints fits well into the Bailey wave model of linguistic change (Bailey, 1973). According to Bailey, a variable rule for a linguistic change in progress begins in the heaviest environment (the one in which the constraints favoring application are all present) then spreads to successively lighter environments until it reaches the lightest environment (the one in which no favoring constraints are present). While the rule remains variable, output is more frequent in heavier environments than in lighter ones. If the rule is destined to become categorical, it becomes categorical first in the heaviest environment, then in successively lighter environments. When the rule becomes categorical in the lightest environment, the rule as a whole ceases to be variable and takes its place among the obligatory rules of the language. For Bailey's model to work, it is necessary to be able to calculate the rule environments in order from heaviest to lightest. This can readily be done, given the third hypothesis. For example, a rule with three constraints would have its environments ranked by weight as follows: (1) first-order, second-order, and third-order constraints all present;

(2) first-order and second-order constraints present; (3) first-order and third-order constraints present; (4) first-order constraint only present; (5) second-order and third-order constraints present; (6) second-order constraint present; (7) third-order constraint present; (8) no favoring constraints present. The existence of such simple ranking rules, and hence perfect compatibility with the wave model, is a mathematical consequence only of the third competence hypothesis.

The description of the Bailey wave model just given has to be modified somewhat to allow for *reordering*. Occasionally, during the development of a variable rule through time, a lower-order constraint takes a higher position in the hierarchy. In these cases, the rule moves toward categoricality according to the old hierarchy up to the point of reordering, after which it proceeds according to the new hierarchy (Fasold, 1973).

The Bailey model has shown considerable promise when applied to data on language variation. An example is the application of the model by Fasold (1975) to the data in Sankoff (1974).

SOME METHODOLOGICAL PROBLEMS

The determination of constraint hierarchies was originally done heuristically by cross-product analysis. Figure 1, presenting Wolfram's data, is an example. Rule environments were determined by selecting from a set of factors arranged in pairs, each pair consisting of the presence and absence of a favoring constraint. Each combination arrived at by selecting one member from each pair (provided that such a combination is a possible one) determines an environment. If all combinations are possible, the number of environments is 2^n, where n is the number of pairs of constraints. The environments are then listed in order by frequency of output in that environment. The result will be an arrangement like Figure 1.

In spite of the fact that many rules could be written employing the cross-product technique, the method was plagued by two chronic problems. One was the problem of missing cross-products. Because of certain characteristics of language in general or of the particular language being investigated, some combinations of factors are inherently impossible. In my research on the final stop deletion rule in Washington, D.C. vernacular Black English (Fasold, 1972), this problem was encountered. Deletion of a final stop is favored if the final stop appears in an unaccented syllable and also, in the case of verbs, if the final stop is preceded by a formative boundary rather than a word boundary. If a verb form has a formative boundary rather than a word boundary, there is a difference in vowel quality as well as the addition of a suffix in the past tense. This rule in

English yields contrasts such as *toll−toll#ed* versus *tell−tol+d* and *step−steppe#ed* versus *sweep−swep+t*. The *-ed* of *tolled* and the *d* of *told,* of course, are identical, as are the *-ed* of *stepped* and the *-t* of *swept.* But it became impossible to determine the correct ranking between the absence of the accent constraint and the formative boundary constraint, because of a particular fact about English: All English verbs that take the formative boundary in the past tense are monosyllables and are therefore all accented. The combination of unaccented syllable and presence of the formative boundary, then, is inherently impossible and there is no way to determine which constraint is the stronger.

The other problem is somewhat less serious, as it turns out, but has still been troublesome. There are situations in which a two-way division of factors is not the most natural one. A problem of this type arose in my work on the final stop deletion rule. It turns out that the least deletion occurs, in the case of final consonant clusters, if the penultimate consonant is a stop, more if it is a fricative, and most if it is a sonorant. If pairs of constraints are to be insisted upon, it is not quite clear if fricatives and sonorants are to be grouped together first as against stops (by some feature based on continuing airstream), or if the correct initial grouping is stops and fricatives (both [+obstruent]) against sonorants. Neither answer is entirely satisfactory, and both necessarily leave one combination of constraints empty. But the problem is to some extent an artifact of the cross-product approach, and the most obvious solution would be to allow a set of three factors appear at that point in the hierarchy instead of two (see Figure 2).[3]

As in Figure 1, there are few deviations in the ordering, the only serious one from a statistical point of view resulting from skewing by a particular lexical item, *kept,* which was by far the most frequent item in these sets and almost always appears without the final stop.

USE OF THE VARIABLE RULE PROGRAMS

The Cedergren–Sankoff variable rule programs can be used in the solution of both difficulties. The coding of factors and factor groups must be done with an eye to the production of a display like Figure 1 or Figure 2. Each set of branchings in the horizontal tree represents a factor group. Most often, it will probably be the case that a factor group consists of two factors, a constraint and its absence, but sometimes a three- or four-way branching, yielding a three- or four-member factor group, may be more

---

[3]It is also a consequence of binary features in generative phonology.

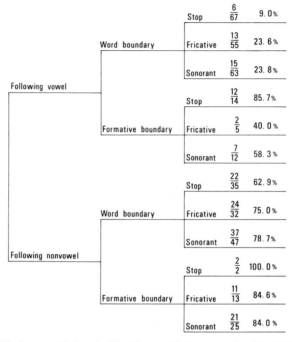

Figure 2. Final stop deletion in Washington, D.C. vernacular Black English. [From Fasold, 1972, p. 26.] [Errors corrected.]

appropriate. In the case of inherently impossible cross-products, no data would be entered for that environment. The program then assigns probabilities to each factor, using the inherently possible subset of the logically possible environments. The constraint hierarchy is then determined from the numerical values of the probabilities. The nonapplications model of the original variable rule program was particularly easy to use in this way. Since the least favorable factor in each factor group would be set at 0, it was a simple matter to rank the constraints by simple observation of the numerical order of their probabilities. For example, the nonapplications model gave the following results, based on the data in Figure 2.

Following vowel : 0
Following nonvowel : .655

Word boundary : 0
Formative boundary : .525

Stop : 0
Fricative : .148
Sonorant : .150

A reading off in numerical order of the probabilities would show that a following nonvowel is the first-order constraint, a formative boundary is the second-order constraint, and that sonorants and fricatives, as against stops, make up the third-order constraint, with a negligible difference between them. In this case the probability values do not provide any information toward establishment of the constraint hierarchy not given by Figure 2. Had there been impossible environments due to impossible combinations of constraints, however, the probabilities could have told us which constraint outranks the other anyway, while the horizontal tree diagram would not.

The use of a variable rule computer program to obtain the correct constraint hierarchy is only valid if the program achieves a sufficiently snug fit between the observed and predicted rule applications in each environment. The variable rule nonapplications model results for the stop deletion data reported above gave a total chi-square value of 10.336; with an input probability of .096. While this is not an excellent fit, given the two deviations in Figure 2 due to *kept,* it is not too bad either. In fact, the worst fit by far is for the deviant following vowel, formative boundary, stop environment whose contribution to the chi-square value was 4.68. In any event, the fit in this example seems good enough to give what appears to be the correct hierarchy.

The variable rule 2 program (see Rousseau & Sankoff, this volume) for the same data gives equally good results, although interpreting them is not quite as transparent. The results for the latter program were the following.

Following vowel : .250
Following nonvowel : .750

Word boundary : .301
Formative boundary : .699

Stop : .433
Fricative : .523
Sonorant : .545

In the newer program, values above .500 favor the rule, values of less than .500 disfavor the rule and a value of .500 means a constraint has no effect. Given this interpretation, it is clear that, as before, a following nonvowel is the first-order constraint, the formative boundary is the second-order constraint, and the third-order constraint is to be found in the group stop, fricative, and sonorant. Again it is apparent that the difference between the effect of sonorant and the effect of fricative is negligible, and the presence of a prefinal stop disfavors the rule. But it appears from these results that a prefinal sonorant or fricative has almost no effect and the rule should perhaps be written so that a prefinal stop disfavors the rule rather than stating that some feature common to sonorant and fricative favors it.[4] The total chi-square value for this version was 16.876, with an input probability of .639; which is comparable to the fit achieved by the older program. The worst fit is in the same environment as before, where the contribution of the chi-square value is 6.718. In order for the Cedergren–Sankoff programs to be used to determine constraint hierarchies in conformity with the third hypothesis, it is important that the data be coded in the manner I have described.

CONCLUSION

My major conclusion is that the original proposal about the nature of constraint hierarchies on variable rules made by Labov in 1969 should be maintained as a competence principle. The Cedergren–Sankoff computer programs can be used in overcoming two problems that might be insoluble by simple inspection of the data, if the factors are coded in the appropriate manner. When certain combinations of constraints yield an impossible environment, constraints can still be assigned the appropriate relevant weighting on the basis of probability estimation using the possible environments. Second, the Cedergren–Sankoff procedures have shown us that constraints do not always have to be placed in pairs; this insight can be applied to construction of horizontal tree displays as well as to coding of data for computer analysis. No competence claims are made for the procedures involved in the computer program itself. The precise probability values are not important, and any estimation procedure available now or in the future would be equally valuable, provided that the estimates achieve a reasonably good fit with the observed data. Linguists interested in variation but disinclined to learn the details of mathematical reasoning and computer technology can take courage from the fact that a great many variable rules can have constraint hierarchies correctly assigned on the basis of horizontal tree displays alone. Where computer assistance is necessary, the interpretation of the results is straightforward and not nearly as mystical as it may seem.

---

[4]If, as seems likely, the feature used to designate the absence of a prefinal stop is the converse of the one used to designate what is common to fricatives and sonorants, the matter becomes purely academic.

REFERENCES

Bailey, C.-J. N. *Variation and linguistic theory*. Arlington, Va.: Center for Applied Linguistics, 1973.

Bickerton, D. Inherent variability and variable rules. *Foundations of Language*, 1971, 7, 457–492.

Bickerton, D. Quantitative versus dynamic paradigms: The case of Montreal *que*. In C.-J. N. Bailey & R. W. Shuy (Eds.), *New ways of analyzing variation in English*. Washington, D.C.: Georgetown University Press, 1973, 23–43.

Cedergren, H. J., & Sankoff, D. Variable rules: Performance as a statistical reflection of competence. *Language, 1974, 50,* 333–355.

Fasold, R. W. *Tense marking in Black English: A linguistic and social analysis*. Arlington, Va.: Center for Applied Linguistics, 1972.

Fasold, R. W. The concept of 'earlier–later': More or less correct. In C.-J. N. Bailey & R. W. Shuy (Eds.), *New ways of analyzing variation in English*. Washington, D.C.: Georgetown University Press, 1973, 183–197.

Fasold, R. W. The Bailey wave model: A dynamic quantitative paradigm. In R. W. Fasold & R. W. Shuy (Eds.), *Analyzing variation in language*. Washington, D.C.: Georgetown University Press, 1975, 27–58.

Guy, G. A new look at *-t, -d* deletion. In R. W. Shuy & R. W. Fasold (Eds.), *Studies in language variation*. Washington, D.C.: Georgetown University Press, 1977, 1–11.

Kay, P. & McDaniel, C. On the logic of variable rules. Unpublished manuscript, University of California, Berkeley, 1977.

Labov, W. Contraction, deletion and inherent variability of the English copula. *Language, 1969, 45,* 715–762.

Labov, W. The notion of 'system' in creole languages. In D. Hymes (Ed.), *Pidginization and creolization of languages,* London: Cambridge University Press, 1971, 447–472.

Labov, W., Cohen, P., Robins, C., & Lewis, J. A study of the non-standard English of Negro and Puerto Rican speakers in New York City (Vol. 1). Final Report, Cooperative Research Project 3288, U.S. Office of Education (ERIC ED 028 423), 1968.

Sankoff, G. A quantitative paradigm for studying communicative competence. In R. Bauman & J. Sherzer (Eds.), *The ethnography of speaking*. London: Cambridge University Press, 1974, 18–49.

Wolfram, W. *Sociolinguistic aspects of assimilation: Puerto Rican English in East Harlem*. Arlington, Va.: Center for Applied Linguistics, 1973.

Wolfram, W., & Christian, D. *Appalachian speech*. Arlington, Va.: Center for Applied Linguistics, 1976.

7

A Solution to the Problem
of Grouping Speakers

Pascale Rousseau / David Sankoff

INDIVIDUAL VERSUS GROUP ANALYSES

Which of two or more variants of a linguistic variable is realized in a given utterance can depend on many factors, including aspects of the specific linguistic and pragmatic context in which the variable is situated as well as individual speakers' characteristics which tend to affect their choice of variant in a consistent way in all contexts.

Given a collection of data on a linguistic variable collected from a number of speakers, we can identify two polar approaches toward the evaluation of contextual and noncontextual influences. One favors a separate analysis first of each context (more precisely, context type) for each individual, resulting in a list of **categorical** contexts where that individual uses only one or only the other variant, as well as another, preferably much smaller, list of **variable** contexts. The motivation behind this approach is the hope that as a second step, some generalizations can be found to distinguish an individual's categorical contexts where one of the variants occurs exclusively from those where the other occurs, with the variable contexts constituting a small transitional class. A third step would attempt to relate one individual's pattern to those of the other speakers. The drawback of this procedure is that there is no guarantee that the categorical and variable contexts will indeed pattern in any obvious or interesting way, especially since the categorical appearance of some of the contexts may well be an artifact of scanty data. (If in a given type of context, an individual produces but a single token, this context will necessarily appear categorical since $0/1 = 0\%$ and $1/1 = 100\%$. Even if there are two tokens, the odds are that the context will still appear categorical, and so on.) In its fear of losing possible categorical distinctions through grouping data, this approach deliberately ignores the fact that linguistic constraint effects tend to be shared, if not by an entire community, then at least by sizable groups of speakers. In addition, these procedures risk producing artificial categorical analyses which will break down when more speakers and more data per speaker are added to the data set, and they forgo the possibility of discovering interesting quantitative generalizations.

The opposite approach would group data from different speakers together for each type of context in order to improve the statistical significance of the analysis. To account for the existence of obvious differences among speakers, it might only combine data within each of a (small) number of sociologically defined groups. An alternative procedure is simply to add sociological characterizations of speakers as if these were part of the context, prior to statistical processing. At the same time, this approach attempts to assure a simple and economical analysis by modeling the set of all possible contexts for the variable in terms of combinations of a relatively small number of parameters. These procedures have the advantage of immediately allowing statistically valid generalizations, and the clear evaluation of both contextual, linguistic constraints as well as sociological effects. Their disadvantages are that they necessarily assume a high degree of sharedness among speakers with respect to parameter values; they risk imposing irrelevant sociological distinctions on the linguistic data; and they are not specifically equipped for the discovery of categorical contexts where these do exist.

As is clear in the work of Labov and others, there is a continual tension between these two approaches in the course of a variational analysis. The theoretical goals and substantive questions of classical linguistics push the analysis toward the search for categoricality, while the validity criteria of statistical inference, and the modeling procedures of empirical science encourage grouping and a minimization of the number of parameters to be estimated. In the next section, we introduce a method which steers a middle course between the two extremes. It does involve grouping speakers and restricting the number of parameters according to statistical criteria. Nevertheless, this grouping is done not on a sociological, a priori basis, but solely in terms of similarity in linguistic performance as evaluated during the execution of the procedure. In addition, the method automatically searches out classes of categorical contexts. We have written a computer program which efficiently performs the method. In the third, fourth, and fifth sections of this chapter, we present results of analyzing three data sets on Montreal French variation.

THE ALGORITHM

The goal of the analysis is a **partition** of the speakers into a number of groups, with a statistical analysis within each group, independent of the others, estimating the effects of linguistic context factors as well as individual speaker tendencies. Each group should be as homogeneous as possible and the number of groups should reflect the number of significantly different performance patterns which can be discerned within the community.

Parameter Estimation

The central part of the algorithm is the statistical analysis within each group. We illustrate with a hypothetical example. Suppose there are 20 different linguistic contexts possible for a given variable, each context determined by one of four possible phonological factors W, X, Y, and Z and one of five possible syntactic factors A, B, C, D, and E and suppose there are 10 speakers, labeled from 1 to 10, in the group. Then, there are at most 200 data items, each classified by one factor from the phonological factor set, one from the syntactic set, and one number identifying the speaker, and specifying the number of times each of the two variants has occurred in this speaker's speech sample. The statistical problem is to fit a **variable rule** model to this data, that is to estimate values for the 20 parameters,

$$p_0, p_A, p_B, p_C, p_D, p_E, p_W, p_X, p_Y, p_Z, p_1, p_2, \cdots, p_{10},$$

(where p_0 is called the **input** parameter) corresponding to the effects of the various factors on the tendency to use the first variant rather than the second. The three parameters corresponding to the three factors associated with each data item, e.g., p_B, p_Y, and p_4, are assumed to combine their effects according to the formula

(1)
$$\frac{p_{BY4}}{1 - p_{BY4}} = \frac{p_0}{1 - p_0} \times \frac{p_B}{1 - p_B} \times \frac{p_Y}{1 - p_Y} \times \frac{p_4}{1 - p_4},$$

where p_{BY4} is the theoretical probability that Speaker 4 will use the first variant rather than the second in the context BY. (Note that for this model to be well defined, all parameters must be between 0 and 1. In addition,

$$\log \frac{p_W}{1 - p_W} + \log \frac{p_X}{1 - p_X} + \log \frac{p_Y}{1 - p_Y} + \log \frac{p_Z}{1 - p_Z} = 0,$$

so that there are in effect only three independent parameters in this set and analogously only four in the syntactic set and nine in the speaker set.)

If f_{BY4} is the actual proportion of times that Speaker 4 used the first variant in context BY, then it is desirable that p_0, p_A, p_B, etc.,be estimated in such a way that (1) predicts values of p_{BY4} equal to or close to f_{BY4}, and likewise for all the other contexts simultaneously. Of course, since we can independently choose values for only 17 parameters, we cannot assure that the proportions in all 200 speaker contexts be well approximated by the model probabilities. The best we can do is choose the most **likely** value of the parameters. This is done by finding those values which maximize the **likelihood,** as in Rousseau and Sankoff (this volume), or equivalently the **log likelihood:**

(2) $$\sum nf \log p + n(1 - f) \log(1 - p),$$

where n is the number of occurrences of a specific speaker context, f is the actual proportion of the first variant, and p is the first variant probability such as on the left hand side of formula (1). The Σ indicates that two terms such as those displayed are added in from each speaker in each context to form a grand sum. (Actually, the true log likelihood differs from (2) by a constant, which does not concern us here.) The precise values of p_0, p_A, etc., which maximize (2) are found by methods of mathematical programming (Rousseau & Sankoff, this volume).

The Grouping Procedure

Once we have a procedure for the statistical analysis within groups it remains to elaborate criteria to decide what constitutes a meaningful partition of the set of speakers into groups, and a method for finding groups which satisfies these criteria. Fortunately, the same likelihood principle used to estimate parameter values also provides an approach to evaluate partitions. Suppose we wish to partition the speakers into two groups. Instead of just finding one set of values of the parameters which maximize the formula (2), we want to divide the set of speakers into two groups, within each of which a separate model of type (1) can be estimated as before, but such that the total value of (2) is maximized. Thus all the parameters are to be estimated twice, once for the speakers in one group and once for the other. The same generalization can be extended to three or more groups. Unfortunately, it is easier to define this criterion than to satisfy it. Indeed, it is not possible to set up an efficient algorithm which will always guarantee the optimal grouping.

Nevertheless we can define an algorithm of a type well known in the statistical theory of classification, which is **locally optimal,** and which when used with good judgment generally provides the best grouping or close to it. Now, suppose we wish a partition into three groups. As a starting point we divide the speakers randomly into three groups. An estimation of the variable rule parameters is carried out within each of these groups independent of the others. This produces three different parameter sets. Then, the data set for each individual speaker is compared in turn with the three parameter sets to see which fits best, the group he or she presently belongs to or one of the others. The way this fit is calculated is simply to see which of the three sets of parameters yields the highest value for formula (2) when only the given individual's contexts, ns and fs are included in the sum, and when the speaker's own parameter is allowed to take on whatever value maximizes the fit. In this way three new groups are formed, each containing all the individuals who correspond best to one of the parameter value sets.

A new cycle is then initiated by recalculating the parameter values within each group. All individuals are tested against the three new sets of estimates and reassigned to new groups if necessary. The procedure continues until at some cycle, all individuals stay in their previous group, at which point we say that the algorithm has **converged.** (It can be proved that it always converges—that it is impossible for individuals to keep switching groups indefinitely under the criteria set out above.)

We can then hope we have the optimal or a nearly optimal grouping.

Some Problems with the Method

The first step of the algorithm involves an arbitrary partition of the speakers into groups. Unfortunately, different initial random groupings generally result in different final groupings when convergence has been attained. Nevertheless, as we shall see in the examples in the next sections, these final groupings generally are quite similar. They have approximately the same level of likelihood and differ largely because a number of speakers fit equally well into two or more groups. Furthermore, examining 10 such locally optimal groupings to find membership patterns in common enables us to run the algorithm one last time, with a nonarbitrary initial partition, namely, the one based on this common grouping pattern. The algorithm then tends to converge after only one or two cycles, the final result always proving to be more likely than any of the initial runs.

Another problem associated with the procedure involves the number of groups to be constructed. There is no feasible, strictly mathematical way now available for judging, for example, whether the increase in likelihood obtained by allowing four groups instead of three is significant enough to warrant considering the extra distinction meaningful. The same is true even for evaluating the difference between a single unified analysis of all the speakers and an optimal partition into two groups, that is, for deciding whether any subgrouping at all is justified.

There are, however, at least five types of criteria which, when applied with judgment, can help decide how many groups are meaningful. The first uses the log-likelihood function (2) directly. If for example the likelihood of the optimal two-way partition is 10% better than a unified analysis, but a three-way partition adds only another 1%, we would certainly hesitate before adopting the three-way group analysis. If on the other hand the three groups added another 10%, but a four-way analysis added only 1%, then we would be justified in settling on the former. These considerations can be put on a more solid quantitative basis with the help of **simulation** studies as will be illustrated below.

The second criterion has to do with similarities among the different locally optimal solutions obtained from successive runs of the program. If in all or almost all the two-group analyses, the same two groups, plus or minus a few individuals in each case, are discernible, this is reason for confidence in the meaningfulness of these groups. If for the three groups, however, the program converges at very dissimilar groupings each time, we would tend to doubt the existence of a significant three-way partition. This criterion can be made more rigorous through the use of certain **analyses of affinity** as illustrated below.

The third criterion is a check on whether one of the groups appears spurious. This can take several forms. The group may contain a very small number of speakers who do not really differ much from one of the other groups. Many of the speakers in a group may have little data and many contexts with no data. Many of the speakers may be categorical, or almost so, in their preference for one variant. These types of results do not disqualify a grouping per se, but since such speakers can easily be fitted into almost any group by appropriate adjustment of their individual parameters, attention must be paid to the possibility that such groups are artifacts of the method.

A fourth criterion compares the groups obtained at one level with those at the next. If in the passage from a two-group analysis to a three-group analysis, one of the two original groups remains almost unchanged while the other divides neatly into two internally more homogeneous groups, this seems reasonable as a result of the grouping algorithm. A similar case occurs if two of the three final groups represent "core" members of two of the original groups, while the third regroups the "peripheral" members of both. But if all three of the final groups are made up of more or less equal proportions of the two original groups, this inconsistency sheds doubt on at least one of the analyses, most likely the three-group one.

The fifth criterion is based on an examination of the input parameters for each group. If these are very different, say .1, .5, and .9 for three groups, it is quite possible that there is really no grouping inherent in the data, that all individuals are consistent with the same parameters for model (1) and that what the program is doing is simply classifying speakers according to their overall tendencies to use one variant or the other. Were model (1) perfectly appropriate for all linguistic variables and were there plenty of data for each speaker in each context, such artificial divisions of the spectrum of input parameters would not occur. But given the gaps and uneven distribution of data and the fact that (1) is an analytic convention which may be more or less appropriate for different variation phenomena, it is important to be aware of this possibility.

The existence of the five criteria we have enumerated, none of them hard and fast, highlights the common-sense judgment element which must enter into the evaluation of the results of the two-group, three-group, and higher analyses. And, of course, any additional linguistic evidence which may be pertinent should also be integrated into the final choice.

There is still another class of difficulties associated with the method, and these have to do with so-called **knockout** constraints. In an ordinary variable rule analysis, a given contextual factor or an individual may not be compatible with one of the variants. This individual or factor is always assigned a parameter value of 0 or 1, depending on which variant is excluded, so that the probability predicted by (1) is 0 or 1 for any context containing this factor, irrespective of the other factors which may be present. This is fine when there is no subgrouping problem, but as soon as we apply our grouping method, two types of difficulty emerge. First, suppose at one point during the execution of the algorithm, a knockout factor is found for one group but not the others. Then it would seem impossible to modify this fact in later cycles of the algorithm because no individuals can enter such a group unless their data are consistent with the knockout. This can be seen in formula (2): If $p = 0$ for a speaker context, then it is infinitely unlikely, i.e., impossible, that f be other than 0 since $\log 0 = -\infty$. Conversely if $p = 1$, then f must be equal to 1, since $\log(1 - p)$ will be $-\infty$. Thus the analysis can accumulate knockouts but cannot get rid of them. This is an undesirable property, in light of the possibility that knockouts may occur in nonoptimal groups, especially ones with few speakers or missing data.

A second type of difficulty is that in the criterion (2) a context which is both empirically categorical in that $f = 0$ or $f = 1$ and theoretically categorical, i.e., contains a knockout factor so that $p = 0$ or $p = 1$, always has a higher likelihood than if p is somewhere between 0 and 1. Thus the program has a tendency to search for groupings which contain as many knockouts as possible even though this may require juxtaposing rather different individuals to take advantage of corresponding gaps in their data. What is worse, when the total number of empirically noncategorical contexts within a group does not sufficiently exceed the number of parameters to be estimated, a certain pathological behavior is exhibited by the variable rule subprogram itself. We will not enter into the details here, the main problem being that the program, by assigning unrealistic large or small values to parameters which can compensate for each other in the variable contexts in which they co-occur, in effect creates **technical knockout** factors, producing many high-likelihood contexts while these factors are still compatible with a certain amount of variability (Rousseau & Sankoff, 1977).

All of the aforementioned problems associated with knockout factors have been effectively resolved with the aid of a single adjustment to the algorithm. Instead of allowing parameters to take on all values between 0 and 1 inclusively, they are restricted to the range between ϵ and $1 - \epsilon$ where ϵ is a very small fraction, which becomes progressively smaller with each iteration of the algorithm. At first this adjustment introduces its own distortion into the analysis, but as the algorithm proceeds, these gradually disappear, while still preventing the difficulties associated with unwarranted knockout tendencies. And true knockout behavior is still detected by the algorithm and reflected in the final organization of the groups.

LABERGE'S *ON/TU–VOUS* DATA

The first variable to be analyzed is drawn from Laberge (forthcoming). The indefinite subject pronoun in Montreal French can be either *on*, as is normatively prescribed, or one of the second-person forms *tu* (singular or familiar) or *vous* (plural or formal). One factor set whose effects are analyzed is the syntactic set, which distinguishes whether the variable is found in an implicative type of structure, in a sentence embedded in a presentative matrix, or simply co-occurrent with a lexical marker of indefiniteness. The other factor set distinguishes between two discourse effects, one which may be called situational insertion and the other, formulation of a moral. The 4356 tokens of this variable documented by Laberge are distributed among 120 speakers. Twenty-six of these use only *on* or only *tu–vous*, involving 495 tokens, and hence are not susceptible to further statistical analysis.

A variable rule analysis, without any grouping of the 94 remaining speakers, results in the contextual parameter values in Table 1 plus the 94

TABLE 1

Single-Group Analysis of *on* / *tu-vous* Data[a]

Number of speakers	Syntactic			Discourse		Input	Log likelihood
	I	*L*	*P*	*S*	*M*		
94	.31	.50	.70	.35	.65	.70	-1550

[a] *I* = implicative; *L* = lexical marker; *P* = presentative; *S* = situational insertion; *M* = formulation of a moral. Parameters indicate tendency to use *on*.

individual speaker parameters. Note that presentatives favor *on* while implicatives favor *tu*, with lexical markers in between, a configuration which accords well with semantic and syntactic considerations. The formulation of a moral tends to favor *on* more than situational insertion, and this is also easily interpretable.

Ten runs of a two-group analysis produced the figures in Table 2. The results for Speaker Group 1 in all of the runs resemble the total population figures of Table 1 with respect to the implicative/presentative contrast, while in 7 out of 10 cases, the other group shows little or no difference among the syntactic parameters. In all cases, the discursive effect remains relatively unchanged. The log likelihood increases by 4% for the two-group analysis in comparison with the unified analysis of Table 1.

In themselves, the lists of speakers in each group are not very revealing and would require too much space to reproduce here. It suffices to note that there is a core of 39 speakers in all 10 of the Group 1s, and a core of 31 speakers in all of the Group 2s. We define the **affinity** between two speakers to be the number of runs (between 0 and 10) in which they end up in the same group. Then we find that we can define three groups containing 49, 37, and 8 speakers, respectively, where within each group every pair of speakers has an affinity of at least 6. Speakers in the first and last groups also have for the most part a large affinity, so we group them together, yielding one group of 57 speakers and one of 37. Using these two groups as the starting point for a further run of the grouping program gives immediate convergence, no speakers changing from one group to the

TABLE 2

Two-Group Analysis of *on* / *tu-vous* Data

Run	Speaker group	Number of speakers	Syntactic			Discourse		Input	Log likelihood
			I	*L*	*P*	*S*	*M*		
1	1	57	.18	.59	.76	.38	.61	.72	−1485
	2	37	.52	.48	.50	.33	.67	.71	
2	1	54	.20	.71	.63	.35	.65	.71	−1482
	2	40	.43	.39	.67	.37	.63	.71	
3	1	57	.17	.59	.76	.39	.61	.72	−1485
	2	37	.52	.48	.50	.33	.67	.71	
4	1	49	.15	.61	.78	.41	.59	.69	−1484
	2	45	.47	.50	.53	.32	.68	.73	
5	1	55	.20	.71	.62	.35	.65	.70	−1482
	2	39	.43	.39	.68	.37	.63	.73	
6	1	54	.20	.71	.63	.35	.65	.71	−1482
	2	40	.43	.39	.67	.37	.63	.71	
7	1	55	.17	.66	.71	.37	.63	.69	−1485
	2	39	.47	.43	.60	.36	.64	.74	
8	1	57	.18	.59	.76	.39	.61	.72	−1485
	2	37	.52	.48	.50	.33	.67	.71	
9	1	49	.15	.61	.78	.41	.59	.69	−1484
	2	45	.47	.50	.53	.32	.68	.73	
10	1	57	.18	.59	.76	.39	.61	.72	−1485
	2	37	.52	.48	.50	.33	.67	.71	
Final	1	57	.18	.59	.76	.39	.61	.72	−1485
	2	37	.52	.48	.50	.33	.67	.71	

other after the initial variable rule analysis within each group displayed on the last line of Table 1.

Table 3 presents an analogous set of results for a three-group analysis. Here the general pattern is for two of the three groups to resemble the single-group results of Table 1, except that in one group the lexical marker parameter is close to the implicative parameter and in the other it is close to the presentative parameter. For the third group a new pattern emerges where the syntactic effect is the complete opposite of what we have previously seen. Again, for all three groups the discursive effects are to a greater or lesser extent what we obtained in the two-group and single-

TABLE 3

Three-Group Analysis of *on* / *tu-vous* Data

Run	Speaker group	Number of speakers	Syntactic			Discourse		Input	Log likelihood
			I	L	P	S	M		
1	1	43	.17	.71	.66	.37	.63	.69	-1448
	2	34	.30	.39	.79	.38	.62	.74	
	3	17	.71	.52	.28	.25	.75	.76	
2	1	42	.16	.71	.67	.38	.62	.70	-1448
	2	36	.31	.41	.77	.38	.62	.71	
	3	16	.70	.50	.30	.24	.76	.77	
3	1	40	.15	.72	.69	.38	.62	.71	-1458
	2	31	.41	.32	.76	.42	.58	.75	
	3	23	.42	.62	.46	.25	.75	.67	
4	1	47	.17	.70	.68	.37	.63	.70	-1452
	2	32	.29	.28	.86	.36	.64	.86	
	3	15	.55	.57	.38	.36	.64	.47	
5	1	41	.17	.77	.61	.36	.64	.69	-1449
	2	36	.29	.43	.76	.38	.62	.66	
	3	17	.70	.41	.38	.26	.74	.85	
6	1	35	.19	.79	.52	.40	.60	.63	-1456
	2	31	.22	.47	.80	.33	.67	.70	
	3	28	.57	.43	.50	.37	.63	.75	
7	1	29	.18	.77	.57	.46	.54	.50	-1457
	2	35	.20	.49	.80	.32	.68	.77	
	3	30	.56	.46	.49	.36	.64	.75	
8	1	41	.13	.83	.59	.41	.59	.77	-1460
	2	24	.38	.78	.32	.17	.83	.95	
	3	29	.45	.43	.62	.39	.61	.42	
9	1	43	.17	.71	.66	.37	.63	.69	-1448
	2	34	.30	.39	.79	.38	.62	.74	
	3	17	.71	.52	.28	.25	.75	.76	
10	1	39	.13	.61	.81	.44	.56	.68	-1462
	2	26	.30	.58	.63	.25	.75	.74	
	3	29	.57	.44	.49	.38	.62	.73	
Final	1	43	.17	.72	.65	.38	.62	.68	-1448
	2	35	.30	.40	.78	.38	.62	.74	
	3	16	.70	.50	.30	.24	.76	.77	

group analyses. The three-group analyses are 2.5% more likely than the two-group ones.

An affinity analysis of the number of runs in which each pair of speakers was classified in the same group yields one group of 30 speakers with affinities of at least 6 and seven smaller groups. Collapsing together those groups which had relatively higher number affinities reduced the number to three. When these three groups are used as the starting point of a further run of the algorithm, convergence is achieved in the second cycle, after only four speakers change groups. The results are listed as the final line of Table 3.

We have also gone one step further, to a four-group analysis. This increases the log likelihood only about 1.3%. No clear pattern emerges from the 10 locally optimal solutions and the affinity analysis could only be carried out approximately by arbitrarily grouping together speakers with generally high affinities. As we shall see, these results do not warrant tabular presentation and analysis.

Thus we have obtained maximum likelihood (or close to it) analyses of the unified sample of speakers, of the sample partitioned into two groups, into three groups, and into four groups. In what ways do these four analyses agree and in what ways do they differ? Where they contradict one another, which one best reflects empirical reality? As a first approach to this question, we carried out the following simulation study.

Given the parameters of the unified sample analysis in Table 1, we generated five random data sets with the same characteristics as the real data. That is, corresponding to each speaker in each context we generated n random numbers between 0 and 1, where n is as before the total number of occurrences of both variants for that context in that speaker's speech sample. For each random number, if it was less than p as calculated for the context by formula (1), it was considered to indicate an occurrence of the first variant, otherwise it was counted as an instance of the second variant. Each complete data set so generated constitutes a typical sample under the single group hypothesis.

We then carried out, on each artificial data set, a single-group analysis and a two-group analysis. We reasoned that if a single-group analysis were all that was warranted for the real data, then the increase in likelihood with a two-group analysis should be about the same as the increase for the random data sets. This follows from the knowledge that for a random set there is no meaningful partition into two groups since the entire sample was generated as one group. Table 4 compares the increase in likelihood in the real data and in the simulated data and shows that the two-group analysis seems significantly more likely than a single group.

To test whether a three-group analysis is better than a two-group

TABLE 4

Likelihood Analysis of Simulated *on / tu-vous* Data Sets under Single-Group Hypothesis, under Two-Group Hypothesis, and under Three-Group Hypothesis

Run under single-group model	Log likelihood Single-group	Two-group	Increase
1	-1489	-1451	38
2	-1520	-1490	30
3	-1537	-1513	24
4	-1510	-1488	22
5	-1537	-1513	24
Real Data	-1550	-1485	65

Run under two-group model	Log likelihood Two-group	Three-group	Increase
1	-1434	-1415	19
2	-1407	-1388	19
3	-1416	-1403	13
4	-1399	-1385	14
5	-1402	-1374	28
Real Data	-1485	-1448	37

Run under three-group model	Log likelihood Three-group	four-group	Increase
1	-1363	-1350	13
2	-1360	-1332	28
3	-1380	-1369	11
4	-1327	-1307	20
5	-1379	-1365	14
Real Data	-1448	-1429	19

configuration, we carried out the same procedure, except that the artificial data were generated using two formulas of type (1), where the parameters were taken from the most likely two-way grouping at the bottom of Table 2. We see again in Table 4 that the increase in likelihood with three groups is greater in the real data than in the simulated data. Despite this result, we find this three-way grouping to be of little interest, for reasons to be explained below.

Proceeding with a test of significance for four groups, Table 4 shows that this is clearly not significant.

From the simulations, the statistical evidence seems to point toward accepting at least two groups and possibly three. The same is true for the second criterion mentioned in the section "Some Problems with the Method" (p. 102), since the 10 different local optimal results are very similar to each other in the two-group case and the 10 three-group analyses also resemble each other. Neither do the third, fourth, and fifth criteria help us distinguish the two-group and the three-group analyses. What are the differences between the two? First, we note that all agree that in each group there is a marked discursive effect, with moral formulations favoring *on*. All agree that for a large proportion of the speakers, the presentatives most favor *on*, while the implicatives favor *tu*. In Group 1 of the two-group analysis, however, the effect of lexical markers is situated halfway between presentatives and implicatives, while in the three-group results it is either equal to the presentative effect (Group 1) or equal to the implicative effect (Group 2). A more striking difference is that in the two-group analysis there is one group, namely Group 2, with negligible syntactic effect, but in the three-group case there is a group (Group 3) where the syntactic effect is completely reversed. Group 3 is unexpected, and there is no evident syntactic reason why some speakers might favor *on* more with implicatives than with presentatives. One clue that this group may be a statistical artifact is that it contains only 16 speakers, 10 of whom have no data or categorically *on* data for moral formulation contexts. This explains why the discursive effect, which is quite stable elsewhere, seems exaggerated, and this poor distribution of the data can be shown to be at least partially responsible for the reversed syntactic effect, as follows. By modifying our program to include the condition that the discursive effect must be identical in all three groups, we still obtain a group with syntactic effects reversed, but only to the extent of a .6:.4 comparison between implicatives and presentatives, rather than .7:.3.

We conclude from this study that the discursive effect is common to all variable speakers and the contrast between implicative and presentative effects is shared by most. There is a minority of speakers, however, who do not make this contrast and may even reverse it. No generalization can be made about lexical marking other than that its effect seems quite variable among speakers. Possibly this reflects the fact that the lexical category in effect contains many different types of markers which may have different effects and which may be differently distributed among speakers.

KEMP'S *CE QUE/QU'EST-CE QUE* DATA

Montreal French has four frequently occurring types of complement structures in which the initial term varies between *ce que* and *qu'est-ce que* (G. Sankoff, Kemp, & Cedergren, forthcoming; Kemp, 1978). There are indirect questions, which are headed by verbs belonging to a certain class; dislocated (extraposed) complements; headless relative clauses, and equational sentences. These four types serve as the single-factor set for our analysis, and there are 66 variable speakers who produced a total of 822 tokens. (Fifty categorical speakers produced an additional 413 tokens.)

Tables 5, 6, and 7 summarize the results of single-group, two-group, and three-group analyses. With only one group, indirect questions clearly favor *qu'est-ce que* more than the other complement constructions. With two groups, a subset of the speakers emerges where dislocated structures favor *qu'est-ce que* more than indirect questions. As indicated by the input probabilities, these tend to be speakers with a higher overall rate of *qu'est-ce que* usage. With three groups, a third pattern emerges, where some of the speakers who favor *qu'est-ce que* in indirect questions also favor it in headless relatives.

With this variable, simulation studies summarized in Table 8 clearly indicate that two groups are better than one, but that the third group is not statistically significant. It should be recalled that in addition to the two

TABLE 5
Single-Group Analysis of *ce que* / *qu'est-ce que* Data[a]

Number of speakers	Q	D	R	E	Input	Log likelihood
66	.83	.51	.42	.21	.28	-342

[a]Parameters indicate tendency to use *qu'est-ce que*. Q = indirect questions: D = dislocated; R = headless relatives; E = equational.

TABLE 6

Two-Group Analysis of *ce que* / *qu'est-ce que* Data

Run	Speaker group	Number of speakers	Q	D	R	E	Input	Log likelihood
1	1	22	.37	.77	.32	.52	.56	-290
	2	44	.96	.26	.41	.16	.14	
2	1	24	.47	.81	.46	.24	.50	-290
	2	42	.96	.24	.36	.19	.13	
3	1	27	.49	.69	.41	.40	.58	-291
	2	39	.96	.14	.23	.00	.12	
4	1	23	.37	.77	.32	.52	.57	-290
	2	43	.96	.26	.41	.16	.14	
5	1	21	.33	.85	.25	.52	.55	-291
	2	45	.93	.30	.45	.18	.19	
6	1	24	.47	.81	.46	.24	.50	-291
	2	42	.94	.26	.37	.21	.15	
7	1	21	.33	.85	.25	.52	.55	-291
	2	45	.93	.30	.45	.18	.19	
8	1	24	.47	.81	.46	.24	.50	-291
	2	42	.94	.26	.37	.21	.15	
9	1	22	.41	.86	.34	.31	.52	-296
	2	44	.89	.32	.44	.26	.23	
10	1	25	.48	.67	.42	.42	.62	-296
	2	41	.91	.19	.28	.19	.17	
Final	1	24	.47	.81	.46	.24	.50	-291
	2	42	.96	.24	.36	.19	.13	

groups there are categorical *ce que* speakers and categorical *qu'est-ce que* speakers.

The predominance of the indirect question construction for speakers who use very little *qu'est-ce que* represents a natural extension of the interrogative function of this marker from the direct to indirect contexts. That the heavy *qu'est-ce que* users prefer it so much in dislocated structures may reflect the susceptibility of the postverbal contexts (indirect questions, headless relatives) to variation under normative pressure in favor of *ce que*.

TABLE 7

Three-Group Analysis of *ce que* / *qu'est-ce que* Data

Run	Speaker group	Number of speakers	Q	D	R	E	Input	Log likelihood
1	1	18	.42	.80	.22	.55	.55	-277
	2	13	.71	.39	.76	.17	.60	
	3	35	.96	.15	.18	.00	.09	
2	1	16	.26	.85	.22	.64	.59	-271
	2	12	.71	.31	.55	.43	.60	
	3	38	.97	.16	.14	.00	.08	
3	1	15	.31	.78	.28	.62	.65	-286
	2	15	.79	.51	.80	.06	.38	
	3	36	.91	.34	.30	.31	.16	
4	1	17	.30	.83	.21	.64	.61	-276
	2	14	.75	.34	.79	.15	.65	
	3	35	.97	.33	.17	.22	.05	
5	1	18	.42	.78	.24	.55	.51	-283
	2	14	.77	.32	.79	.15	.63	
	3	34	.90	.28	.23	.02	.16	
6	1	19	.37	.72	.50	.39	.56	-289
	2	9	.78	.62	.19	.43	.63	
	3	38	.88	.22	.33	.02	.22	
7	1	17	.27	.86	.20	.65	.58	-276
	2	12	.80	.47	.82	.06	.51	
	3	37	.97	.28	.20	.24	.08	
8	1	18	.38	.90	.34	.26	.51	-275
	2	12	.75	.34	.48	.41	.55	
	3	36	.98	.10	.15	.00	.08	
9	1	16	.27	.86	.20	.65	.58	-276
	2	15	.75	.34	.79	.15	.61	
	3	35	.97	.34	.16	.22	.05	
10	1	18	.43	.79	.22	.55	.52	-277
	2	15	.77	.32	.79	.15	.61	
	3	33	.97	.20	.10	.01	.05	
Final	1	19	.29	.83	.23	.64	.57	-275
	2	14	.84	.29	.75	.13	.63	
	3	33	.98	.41	.07	.26	.04	

TABLE 8

Likelihood Analysis of Simulated *ce que* / *qu'est-ce que* Data Sets under Single-Group Hypothesis and under Two-Group Hypothesis

Run under	Log likelihood		
single-group model	Single-group	Two-group	Increase
1	-276	-261	15
2	-299	-276	23
3	-317	-292	25
4	-277	-262	15
Real data	-342	-291	51

Run under	Log likelihood		
two-group model	Two-group	Three-group	Increase
1	-259	-236	23
2	-273	-250	23
3	-268	-234	34
4	-265	-243	22
5	-239	-227	12
6	-272	-264	8
Real data	-291	-275	16

THE AUXILIARY DATA OF G. SANKOFF AND THIBAULT

The final set of data to be discussed here concerns the alternation between the auxiliaries *avoir* and *être* in the compound tenses of 16 verbs (G. Sankoff & Thibault, 1977). These verbs constitute the linguistic factor set and there are 104 variable speakers producing 2163 tokens. Fifteen categorical speakers produce an additional 126 tokens.

Table 9 presents the single-group, two-group, and three-group analyses. This illustrates well the tendency of the program to search for categoricality. Whereas the single-group analysis shows a somewhat gradual increase in *avoir* usage from left to right in the list of verbs, two-group analysis indicates the tendency for each group to have as many verbs as possible with parameters at, or close to, 0 and 1 and few transitional verbs. This trend continues in the three-group analysis.

Studying the input parameters of the various groups leads us to suspect that grouping is not warranted with this example, according to the fifth criterion elaborated on page 103. Aside from the differences in inputs,

TABLE 9

Single-Group, Two-Group and Three-Group Analysis of Auxiliary Data[a]

Speaker group	Number of group speakers	aller	revenir	venir	arriver	partir	retourner	monter	sortir	rentrer	descendre	tomber	rester	déménager	passer	changer	demeurer	Input	Log likelihood
	104	.00	.00	.01	.04	.38	.57	.72	.77	.81	.68	.85	.85	.85	.94	.98	.97	.54	-501
1	55	.00	.00	.01	.00	.00	.03	.72	.99	.75	.00	.99	.86	.93	.99	1.0	1.0	.35	-425
2	49	.00	.01	.00	.08	.76	.74	.80	.58	.92	.81	.75	.91	.89	.87	.94	.95	.65	
1	49	.01	.00	.00	.03	.01	.03	.02	.99	.88	.00	.99	.96	.98	1.0	1.0	1.0	.18	-386
2	23	.00	.00	.01	.11	.60	.46	.92	.46	.94	.71	.32	.97	.99	.79	.38	.93	.73	
3	32	.00	.01	.00	.01	.78	.88	.72	.86	.84	1.0	.97	.85	.51	.90	1.0	1.0	.63	

[a] Parameters indicate tendency to use *avoir*.

115

there are no dramatic, systematic reversals differentiating the groups. The second criterion also sheds doubt on the validity of the groups. An affinity analysis of 10 runs for the three-group analysis (not presented here) produces only a large number of very small groups, showing no consistent grouping. Further evidence is provided by the simulation experiments in Table 10. The three-way analysis does not show a significant improve-

TABLE 10

Likelihood Analysis of Simulated Auxiliary Data Sets under Single-Group Hypothesis and Under Two-Group Hypothesis

Run under	Log likelihood		
single-group model	Single-group	Two-group	Increase
	-436	-410	26
2	-432	-400	32
3	-460	-429	31
4	-432	-421	11
5	-445	-424	21
Real data	-501	-425	76

Run under	Log likelihood		
two-group model	Two-group	Three-group	Increase
1	-383	-377	6
2	-396	-364	32
3	-428	-391	37
4	-412	-380	32
5	-402	-344	58
Real data	-425	-386	39

ment over the two-way. The two-way does seem more likely than the single-group, but given the other criteria, a better analysis would consider the verbs as constituting a continuum in their tendency to use *avoir,* with perhaps a greater discontinuity between *arriver* and *partir* than elsewhere.

REFERENCES

Kemp, W. Description linguistique et sociale de la variation entre *ce que* et *qu'est-ce que* dans le français de Montréal. Unpublished M.A. thesis, Université du Québec à Montréal, 1978.

Laberge, S. The changing distribution of indeterminate pronouns in discourse. In R. W. Shuy & A. Schnukal (Eds.), *Language use and the uses of language*. Washington, D.C.: Georgetown University Press, forthcoming.

Rousseau, P., & Sankoff, D. Singularities in the analysis of binary data. Unpublished manuscript, 1977.

Sankoff, G., Kemp, W., & Cedergren, H. J. The syntax of *ce quelqu'est-ce que* variation and its social correlates. In R. W. Shuy & J. Firsching (Eds.), *Dimensions of variability and competence*. Washington, D.C.: Georgetown University Press, forthcoming.

Sankoff, G., & Thibault, P. L'alternance entre les auxiliaires *avoir* et *être* en français parlé à Montréal. *Langue Française*, 1977, *34*, 81–108.

8

Statistical Dependence among Successive Occurrences of a Variable in Discourse

David Sankoff / Suzanne Laberge

INTRODUCTION

Labov's (1970) demonstration of the inadequacy of a code-switching analysis of a short passage containing a bewildering alternation of standard and vernacular forms was a key argument in establishing the variationist paradigm. It has since become accepted practice to treat successive occurrences of a variable, even in the same utterance, as independent binomial trials. Those who use such a model realize, of course, that various types of co-occurrence relationships may hold between neighboring tokens of a variable (cf. Berdan, 1975). We generally proceed under this assumption (independence), however, not only because it simplifies the analysis, but also because in terms of their relative infrequency in the data, co-occurrence relationships should not seriously affect the results of statistical procedures for estimating the effects of other linguistic and sociolinguistic constraints. It is in this spirit that we will discuss the interactions of neighboring tokens as an interesting phenomenon in its own right.

More specifically, the aim of this chapter is to characterize the effect of syntagmatic proximity of two occurrences of a variable on the two tokens realized. We will discuss three variables drawn from a study of the evolution of the Montreal French pronominal system (Laberge, 1977), namely *on/tu–vous* (see also Laberge, forthcoming), *on/ils* (see also San-koff & Laberge, this volume) and *nous/on*. The first of these subject clitic variables pertains to a general indefinite (human) referent, the second to an indefinite referent exclusive of speaker and hearer, and the third to the first person plural. The data base consists of all tokens of these variables in the 120 interviews making up our corpus, as well as the order in which they appear in the discourse. This includes some 4500 tokens of the first variable, 1800 of the second, and 12,000 of the third.

TYPES OF CONSTRAINTS

For each variable, we define four types of syntagmatic proximity be-tween two tokens, focusing on the relation the second bears to the first.

The case of **embedding-constrained** tokens occurs when a single referent is the subject of two (or more) sentences, one of which is embedded in the other. We always work in terms of the surface order of the tokens, independent of whether the matrix sentence is positioned before or after the embedded one(s). Examples (1) and (2) involve the *on/ils* and *on/tu– vous* variables respectively.

(1)   *Qu'est-ce qu'on ressent quand on fume du pot?* (114:20)[1]
        'What do they feel when they smoke pot?'

(2)   *Ah bien c'est entendu qu'on est mieux, mieux en campagne quand on est jeune.* (116:26)
        'Well for sure you're (one is) better off in the country when you're young.'

The case of **sequence-constrained** tokens occurs when a single referent is the subset in a sequence of two or more independent sentences which are conjoined or simply juxtaposed. Examples (3) and (4) again involve the *on/ils* and *on/tu–vous* variables:

(3)   *On m'a dit chez nous que je parlais mal; aujourd'hui on m'en parle plus.* (117:44)
        'At home they used to tell me that I spoke badly; now they don't talk to me about it any more.'

(4)   *L'influence de la finance, c'est ça, vous payez tout en l'utilisant, vous en êtes pas privé.* (41:18)
        'The point about borrowing money is that you pay for it while you're using it, so you don't have to go without.'

---

[1]Figures in parentheses represent speaker and page number in the corpus from which the example is drawn.

The weakest relationship is that between **unconstrained** successive tokens, which involves simply two successive occurrences of a same variable which are too distant to qualify for either of the above categories. The working hypothesis underlying these first three categories states that the weaker the syntagmatic relationship between the two tokens, the greater the chance of a **switch** of variant when the second token is uttered. Examples (5) and (6), however, demonstrate that a switch can occur even in the most constrained environment, that of embedding-constrained tokens.

(5)   *On a été avisé que nous étions dans une zone*
        commerciale. (61:23)
        'We were advised that we were in a commercial zone.'

(6)   *Ah bien avec la vie chère comme elle l'est là, quand*
        ils en ont trois on arrête. (5:11)
        'Oh well with the cost of living as high as it is, when
        they have three (children), they stop.'

There is one additional type of constraint, involving the repetition of a subject variable and its verb after a **hesitation**. This is not to be confused with repetition for emphasis or similar discourse function. Hesitation repetitions cannot really be ranked among the other types of relationships for the purposes of testing our hypothesis, since they include deliberate switches of variant to serve disambiguating functions or as stylistic corrections, as well as simple lapses or hesitations in the flow of the discourse.

(7)   *Et puis je sais que ils passaient, on passait toujours les*
        mêmes films. (75:25)
        'And I know that they used to show, they always used to
        show the same films.'

(8)   *Je suis pas pour ça non plus parce que nous sommes pas,*
        nous sommes de descendance française. (61:28)
        'I don't believe in that either because we're not, we're
        of French descent.'

THE DATA

For each speaker, and for each variable, we have the total number of each variant. We have as well the number of switches involving embedding-constrained, sequence-constrained, and hesitation repetitions, as well as the number of cases involving no switch. We have the number of switches for unconstrained successive tokens, and the number of nonswitches, for a small number of speakers only, but we shall use these figures to show why it is not worthwhile to collect this latter type of data for the whole corpus.

RESULTS

The most interesting comparisons are those between the switching rates for sequence-constrained variables and overall proportions of the two variants. Were there no dependence between two tokens in sequence (the null hypothesis), the rate of switches from one variant to another should be equal to the proportion of the second type of variant. The scattergram in Figure 1 compares each speaker's switch rate from *on* to *tu–vous* with his or her overall proportion of *tu–vous*. The fact that the overwhelming majority of speakers lie below the diagonal rejects the null hypothesis and shows that variables in sequence are highly constrained not to switch. We can depict an average trend by plotting the proportion of switches in each decile. This suggests that speakers switch only about one-third of the number of times they might if there were no dependence. Figure 2 shows that an almost identical pattern holds true for switches in the opposite direction, from *tu* (or *vous*) to *on*.

Despite the dozens of tokens of the *on/tu–vous* variable produced by the average speaker, there are usually less than 10, and often only 2 or 3 sequence-constrained contexts where a given type of switch might take place. This accounts for much of the statistical fluctuation in the switching rate in the figures as well as for the concentration of speakers at exactly 0%, i.e., those who demonstrate no switches. About 40% of our speakers do not have even a minimum of 2 tokens of both variants in their recordings, and these have not been included in the analysis.

In the case of embedding-constrained and hesitation-repeated variables, the data are even thinner and no comparable graphical analysis is possible. It is clear, however, that embedding constrains switching much more strongly than do sequences, and embedding-constrained switches such as those occurring in (5) and (6) are very rare. Hesitation repetitions, being a rather mixed category, involve switching at about the same rate as sequences.

Is sequence constraint a form of text coherence, albeit quantitative, operating on coreferential variables in adjacent syntactic units, or does it simply reflect stylistic homogeneity within relatively short passages of conversation?

The first option is at least partly valid, as we can see by comparing

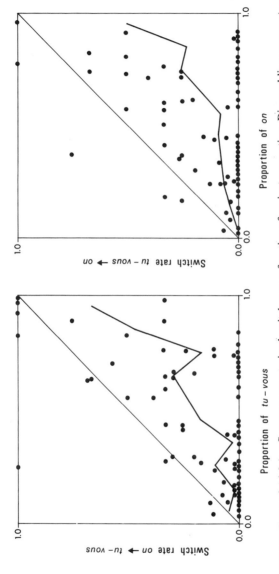

Figure 1 (left) and Figure 2 (right). Sequence-constrained switches as a function of variant proportion. Diagonal line represents null hypothesis that switch rate is independent of sequence constraints. Heavy line connects total rate of switch in each decile.

123

TABLE 1

Comparison of Variant Proportions with Switch Rates for Two Types of Neighboring Variable Pairs[a]

Speaker number	Proportion of *on*	*tu-vous → on* switch rate for unconstrained pairs	*tu-vous → on* switch rate for sequence-constrained pairs	Proportion of *tu-vous*	*on → tu-vous* switch rate for unconstrained pairs	*on → tu-vous* switch rate for sequence-constrained pairs
5	.45	.50	.12	.55	.25	.37
6	.24	.33	.12	.76	.60	.33
13	.24	.17	.06	.76	.63	.24
44	.30	.33	.19	.70	.67	.57
115	.39	.50	.20	.61	.73	.05

[a]In almost all cases, variant proportion approximates switch rate for unconstrained pairs, while sequence-constrained switch rates are much lower.

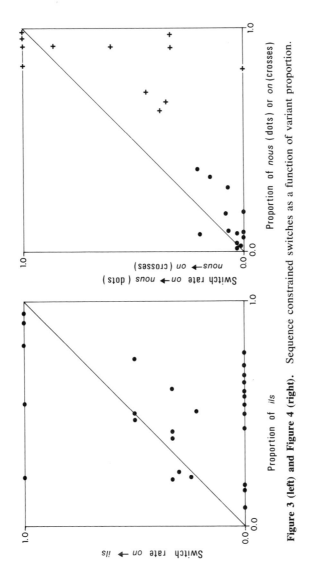

Figure 3 (left) and Figure 4 (right). Sequence constrained switches as a function of variant proportion.

switching rates in sequences and in unconstrained successive pairs for a number of speakers. For this analysis, we deliberately chose speakers who showed at least a minimal degree of switching behavior in their sequence data. Nevertheless, as Table 1 shows, the sequencing context is much more restrictive than just simple proximity between variables. Indeed, the switching rates for unconstrained pairs are not clearly different from the overall proportion of the variants, indicating little or no effect of stylistic homogeneity. This also explains why an exhaustive examination of switching in unconstrained pairs for all speakers is of little interest.

Turning to the other variables, we again encounter a data problem. There are too few sequence-constrained contexts for switching from *ils* to *on* in our corpus to permit analysis. However, almost 30 speakers do show both enough variation in this variable and enough sequence-constrained pairs for *on* to *ils* switches to warrant the graphical representation in Figure 3. Although less dramatic than the previous two, the tendency is for the same effect to be present, restricting switching in the sequence environment.

The case of *on/nous* is somewhat more clear-cut. The data problem here is that there are less than 200 tokens of *nous* as a subject clitic in our corpus. These are, however, concentrated among a small number of conservative speakers and we can portray their switching behavior as in Figure 4. Once again the sequencing constraint is unequivocally present, though it cuts out perhaps only half of prospective switches rather than the two-thirds suggested in the case of *on/tu–vous*.

REFERENCES

Berdan, R. The necessity of variable rules. In R. W. Fasold & R. W. Shuy (Eds.), *Analyzing variation in language*. Washington, D.C.: Georgetown University Press, 1975, 11–26.
Laberge, S. The changing distribution of indeterminate pronouns in discourse. In R. W. Shuy & A. Schnukal (Eds.), *Language use and the uses of language*. Washington, D.C.: Georgetown University Press, forthcoming.
Laberge, S. Etude de la variation des pronoms sujets définis et indéfinis dans le français parlé à Montréal. Unpublished Ph.D. dissertation, Université de Montréal, 1977.
Labov, W. The study of language in its social context. *Studium Generale 23*, 1970, 30–87. Reprinted in W. Labov, *Sociolinguistic patterns*. Philadelphia: University of Pennsylvania Press, 1972, 183–259.

9

Modeling of Duration Patterns in Reiterant Speech

Mark Liberman

INTRODUCTION

This chapter reports on some preliminary attempts at quantitative modeling of duration patterns in English. The intent is to demonstrate the feasibility and interest of such modeling, rather than to present a particular model as a finished product. I will begin by suggesting why duration data is an especially appealing candidate for quantitative modeling, and will describe then the particular body of data that was used, the modeling method, and some of the results.

Why Speech Timing Is Interesting

Patterns of duration in speech are quite reproducible. If the same speaker repeats the same utterance a number of times, without changing the stress pattern or the intonation, the durations of comparable segments or syllables (for those aspects of the speech signal which have conveniently measurable durations) typically have quite small variances: Standard deviations of 10 and 15 msec are fairly typical. This remains true, in my experience at least, even when there are fairly long periods of time between repetitions. Large variations in overall rate increase the variance somewhat, and variations across speakers also blur the sharpness of the patterns, but there remains substantial agreement.

An understanding of such duration patterns, and of the processes which generate them, is of great interest both practically and theoretically. Practical applications include speech synthesis by rule and speech recognition, for which any source of information describing reliable connections between language and sound is useful. The theoretical interest of this area of study has several aspects, of which I will mention three. First, linguistic constructs such as stress pattern, syllabic structure, surface constituent structure, and so on, affect timing, and an understanding of these relationships provides evidence which can help to choose among alternative linguistic theories. The relative stability of duration patterns, previously mentioned, means that in principle a substantial amount of information is available for such efforts. Second, there is reason to suppose that much of the information present in patterns of timing is used by the perceptual system. This raises, in a very pointed way, the perceptual problem posed by the dynamic aspects of speech, the problem of how our perceptions orient themselves amid the incoming stream of acoustic information, not only "normalizing" the variable dynamics of acoustic cues, but actually using this variation to provide information of value to the decoding process. Third, speech rhythms (exemplified for present purposes in patterns of duration) can be studied in relation to the problem of rhythmic organization in other human activities, notably music.

Some Problems

Although the study of speech timing is interesting and important for the reasons just mentioned, it faces a number of very substantial difficulties. Two classes of these difficulties are especially worthy of note: the number and nature of factors influencing duration, and the arbitrariness of duration measurements.

There are a large number of factors known to influence duration in speech. A nonexhaustive list includes the nature of the segment in question, the local segmental environment, syllabification, stress pattern, constituent structure, and intonation contour. Each of these variables has a large number of possible values. It is clearly not feasible to vary all of them orthogonally—life is too short. Indeed, many of them are nonorthogonal by nature. The usual practice is to pick some feature (e.g., position in the word) and vary it systematically, while trying to obtain some reasonable sampling of values for other variables. A lot has been learned by such techniques; however, in averaging across categories, much of the precision of temporal control is thrown away.

It has long been known that linguistic phonetic elements do not correspond to discrete portions of the acoustic signal, but rather produce a complex pattern of overlapping acoustic effects. Thus it is in some very real sense meaningless to talk about the **duration** of phonetic elements in speech. When phoneticians use this somewhat loose way of talking, they refer to the fact that in many cases there are local discontinuities in the acoustic signal which can be taken to specify the boundaries of **something**; generally these are points of closure and release, points of voicing onset or offset, the beginning and end of turbulence, and so on. Such points can often be measured with an accuracy of 5 msec or better; it is by reference to such points that we discuss **segment durations** or **syllable durations**. But sometimes there are several such measurable points in close succession—in the case of aspirated stops, for example, the interval of aspiration could be assigned to the stop, to the vowel, or to neither (with three different results for the body of data a theory of speech timing is asked to describe). Furthermore, we cannot even be sure that it is by reference to these apparent discontinuities in the acoustic signal that human beings reckon duration. In fact, there is good reason to suppose that this may not be the case—segments such as [y] or [r] do not create any such discontinuities, but duration cues do not seem to be obscured in utterances that happen to contain such segments. So from a theoretical point of view there is a very serious amount of arbitrariness in any decision about how to interpret duration measurements, even for those cases where measurements are possible.

A Solution

In order to get around such difficulties, phoneticians have traditionally resorted to nonsense. The advantages of nonsense syllable strings over (more or less) natural speech are obvious—segmental variables can be eliminated from the model, to whatever extent is desired, and the necessary arbitrariness of measurement criteria can be minimized by reducing the number of boundary types to one or two. Of course, the usual sort of nonsense **words** will not do for the study of phrase-level prosodic effects, so Lynn Streeter and I developed[1] the idea of mimicking a natural utterance while substituting some nonsense syllable, such as *ma*, for each syllable of the original.

This technique, for which Nakatani and Schaffer (1976) have suggested

---

[1]Actually, we redeveloped this idea, which was previously used by various Swedish researchers and reported in (apparently) unpublished manuscripts referred to in Lindblom and Rapp (1973).

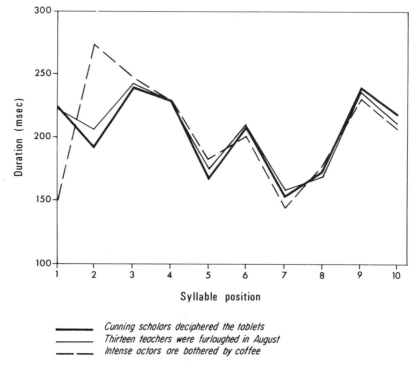

Syllable position

———— Cunning scholars deciphered the tablets
———— Thirteen teachers were furloughed in August
— — Intense actors are bothered by coffee

Figure 1. Syllable duration in reiterant speech imitations of three sentences.

the term **reiterant speech (RS)**, is described and justified in some detail in Liberman and Streeter (1976). The relevant findings of that study can be summarized as follows: (*a*) The reproducibility of durations in reiterant speech is comparable to what is found in natural speech; and (*b*) utterances with the same stress pattern and constituent structure produce nearly indistinguishable reiterant speech durational patterns, even when the durations of the originals are very dissimilar due to segmental effects.

Figure 1, taken from Liberman and Streeter (1976), presents syllable[2] durations in *mama* imitations of three target sentences:

(1)   *Cunning scholars deciphered the tablets.*

(2)   *Thirteen teachers were furloughed in August.*

(3)   *Intense actors are bothered by coffee.*

[2]For simplicity of exposition, we will use syllable (rather than segment) durations throughout this paper. In some ways segment durations are more interesting, but the issues involved are not relevant to this paper.

Note that the first two cases, in which stress and constituent structure are nearly the same, have very similar duration patterns, while the third case, in which the first word has a different location of main word stress, differs greatly in the first two positions, but remains quite similar to the previous cases in positions 2 through 10.

MATERIALS AND METHODS

It appears that different utterances with the same prosodic structure (stress and constituent structure) have the same reiterant speech timing pattern. It follows that we should, in principle, be able to predict such RS timing patterns as a function of the prosodic structure of the target utterance. In order to attempt such a prediction, we need three things: (a) RS duration data for some set of utterances; (b) a precise definition of the notion **prosodic structure** for those utterances; and (c) some assumption about the function which maps prosodic structure, as defined in (b), into durations, as measured in (a).

Data

The modeling described in this chapter is based on a body of data collected by Lynn Streeter and myself for other purposes. It consists of 20 utterances (and their RS imitations) spoken at least 10 times each by one speaker, and 17 utterances (and their RS imitations) spoken at least 10 times by a second speaker. The data from the second speaker was collected in two sessions about 6 months apart; the first speaker's data was collected in three sessions. (Some of this same material was used in Liberman & Streeter, 1976.) In each recording session, the speaker being recorded read a target sentence from a card, using a normal speaking rate and intonation pattern, and then after a suitable pause, imitated the target sentence by substituting a [ma] for each of its syllables, while attempting to preserve the original rhythm and intonation. After all the utterances in the experimental set had been produced, the cards were shuffled and the process repeated a total of 10 times to obtain the 10 tokens of each target sentence and each *mama* imitation to be averaged.

Durations in the target utterances were measured by means of a computer wave-form editor. Duration of the RS versions were measured automatically by a computer pattern-recognition technique, based on the voice/unvoiced/silence decision algorithm described in Atal and Rabiner (1976), and modified to decide among the three categories [m], [a], and silence.

Prosodic Feature Set

Nine binary features were chosen as a means of encoding prosodic structure. These features cover three general areas: stress, boundary location, and rhythmic grouping. Binary features were used in order to permit the model to take a maximally simple form, as described in the following subsection.

Before being coded in terms of these features, an utterance is divided into **feet,** which generally run from main word stress to main word stress. Normally, then, foot boundaries are inserted in front of the main stress of every content word, and nowhere else. There are two exceptions: (*a*) In sequences of monosyllables such as *new blue boat,* where the stress pattern would be classically described as 2 3 1, the medial monosyllable is not given as a separate foot boundary, resulting in the division | *new blue* |*boat;* and (*b*) a function word which is a stress maximum is taken to begin a foot, as in *the* |*cat is* |*on the* |*mat.* Also, it is assumed that feet are interrupted by major phrase boundaries.

Our nine prosodic features can now be described as follows:

1. *Stress.* This feature is assigned to every stressed syllable.
2. *Main foot stress.* This feature is assigned to the stressed syllable at the beginning of each foot.
3. *Main phrase stress.* This feature is assigned to stressed syllables which have a major pitch accent. Typically there is one such syllable in each phrase. Obviously, every main phrase stress must also be a main foot stress.
4. *End of word.* This feature is assigned to the last syllable of each lexical word.
5. *End of phrase.* This feature is assigned to the last syllable of each major phrase (where there is a noticeable pause or pseudopause). All but one of the utterances in the data set used for this chapter consisted of exactly two phrases.
6. *Start of trochee.* This feature is assigned to those main foot stresses which are followed by at least one syllable within the same foot. Since two or more following syllables are also consistent with this feature, the word trochee must be taken in a loose sense.
7. *Start of dactyl.* This feature is assigned to those main foot stresses which are followed by at least two syllables within the same foot.
8. *Second position in dactyl.* This feature is assigned to the syllable immediately following the main foot stress of a dactylic foot.
9. *Third position in dactyl.* This feature is assigned to the last syllable in a dactylic foot.

Features 1–3 encode information about stress level; features 4 and 5 encode boundary information; features 6–9 provide information about rhythmic grouping. These features were chosen with two ends in view: (*a*) to include some representation of factors known or alleged to influence duration; and (*b*) to be definable with minimum opportunity for disagreement regarding their values in a particular case. Note that no theoretical or practical validity is being claimed for the details of this feature set—it is simply a conveniently definable set of features, which is likely to be highly correlated with whatever the "true" feature set is.

Assumptions of the Model

For a first attempt, I adopted a rather simple view of the function mapping prosodic feature specifications into durations. We assume n well-defined prosodic features. Each element in the data set (syllable, segment, or whatever) is marked either $+$ or $-$ for each such feature. Then the predicted duration for a given syllable or segment is determined by adding, to a fixed base duration, a fixed quantity (which can be positive or negative) for each prosodic feature which is present.[3] Thus the influences of the various features are assumed to be additive and independent. Symbolically, we assume that

$$(1) \qquad D = B + a_1 f_1 + a_2 f_2 + \cdots + a_n f_n$$

where D is the predicted total duration of a given segment or syllable; B is the (invariant) base duration; a_i is 1 if the ith feature is present, 0 if the ith feature is absent; and f_i is the durational increment (plus or minus) attributed to the ith feature.

Since we have a list of observed durations, and specification of a prosodic feature vector for each one, multiple linear regression will give us values for the base duration and feature-associated durations which minimize the (squared) prediction error.

RESULTS

In order to see how successful this procedure is at predicting novel data, the data set for each of the two subjects was divided into two subsets

---

[3]Of course, when different phonetic elements are examined, a different base duration and set of feature-associated durations is assumed in each case. One would like the feature-associated duration values to be predictable, at least for a given type of phonetic element, either by being invariant or by being some function of that element's base duration. Since the only phonetic element considered in this chapter is the syllable [ma], we avoid such questions for the present.

of 10 utterances each in the case of the first speaker, and of 8 and 9 utterances in the case of the second speaker. Since the average number of syllables per utterance was 10, each subset contained about 100 syllables. The parameter values resulting from regression on one of the data subsets for each of the speakers are given below:

(2)

Features:	Base	1	2	3	4	5	6	7	8	9
Subject A:	179	18	33	34	13	48	−7	−15	−12	10
Subject B:	174	27	30	22	16	55	5	−22	−21	8

Figure 2 shows some superimposed plots of predicted versus observed durations for three utterances, using the parameter values given for Subject A in (2) and taking the observed durations from the same data subset that was used to generate those parameters. These cases were chosen as fairly typical of their kind. For the data subset in question, the percentage of variance accounted for by the model was 88%, and the mean absolute deviation (average of the absolute value of prediction versus observation) was 11 msec. Percentage of variance accounted for is not a very meaningful measure in this kind of situation, but it will serve for rough comparison with the other conditions described below.

In the data subset for which Subject B's parameters were obtained, the percentage of variance accounted for was 92%, and the mean absolute deviation was 9 msec. Because of the nonorthogonality of the feature set, it is difficult to compute the significance of these results, but we can offer for comparison the results of running the same regression, with the same prosodic feature matrix, using durations from the original target utterances, or using the set of RS durations randomly permuted. Using the target utterance durations, 63–68% of the variance was accounted for by the model, with mean absolute deviations of 38–44 msec. Using randomly permuted RS durations, approximately 5–15% of the variance was accounted for.

Figure 3 shows a similar set of plots for the case in which parameters derived from the first subset of data were employed to predict durations in the second subset. For the second subset as a whole, duration prediction on the basis of parameters derived from the first subset accounted for 85% of the variance in the case of one subject, and 82% in the case of the second subject. The mean absolute deviations were 12 and 18 msec, respectively.

It is worth noting that the data subsets were not selected randomly, but rather tended to respect the boundaries of different data collection ses-

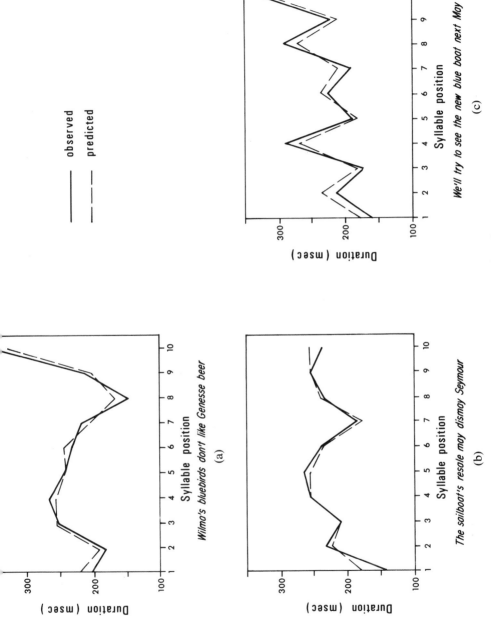

Figure 2. Prediction within a data set.

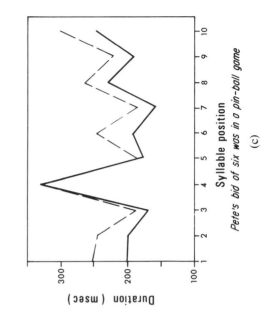

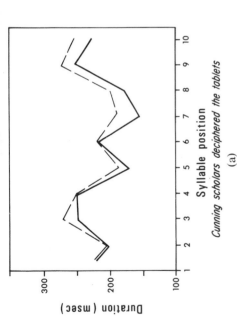

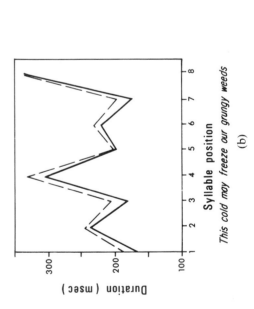

Syllable position

Cunning scholars deciphered the tablets

(a)

This cold may freeze our grungy weeds

(b)

Pete's bid of six was in a pin-ball game

(c)

Duration (msec)

—— observed
– – – predicted

Fig. 2. Predictions versus data sets.

136

sions. In the case of the data represented in Figure 3, the speaker in question spoke somewhat faster in the session represented in the second data subset, an effect which is especially noticeable in Figure 3(c). This last case has the highest mean absolute deviation of any of the across subset predictions (nearly 30 msec).

To help clarify the modeling method, the duration prediction for the utterance in Figure 3(a), *cunning scholars deciphered the tablets,* is given in Table 1.

DISCUSSION

When I began this study, I viewed it as a *reductio ad absurdum,* a trial of a model which was so simpleminded that it had no hope of any substantial success, but which might provide some lessons in the details of its failure. I remain convinced that the feature set employed is inadequate for the general case. Specifically, it seems unlikely that only two degrees of boundary strength are sufficient, and perhaps in general one should regard prosodic features (stress, boundary, and rhythmic group-

TABLE 1

Duration Prediction for *Cunning Scholars Deciphered the Tablets*

Parameters of the model	Syllable position									
	1	2	3	4	5	6	7	8	9	10
Base	179	179	179	179	179	179	179	179	179	179
1	18		18			18			18	
2	33		33			33			33	
3			34						34	
4	-7		-7			-7			-7	
5		13		13			13			13
6				48						48
7						-15				
8								-12		
9									10	
Total	223	192	257	240	179	208	180	189	257	240
Observed	224	192	240	238	167	209	151	172	241	217

ing) as being hierarchically defined, along the lines suggested in Liberman (1975) and Liberman and Prince (1977).

Although the present study shows little evidence of any interaction among the various prosodic features employed (e.g., different values of phrase boundary for stressed and unstressed syllables), it is hard to believe that such interactions do not exist. Furthermore, when different segments are mixed together, as in natural speech, interactions between segmental and prosodic effects may well arise which would complicate the model even for the treatment of a specific syllable such as [ma]. Finally, it is possible that reiterant speech itself produces a prosodically unnatural (though lawful) style of speech, whose spurious regularities are lacking in more normal linguistic activity. Even if this were true, however, the laws governing reiterant speech would retain some theoretical interest, since they must somehow be generated by more ordinary linguistic knowledge and skills.

There are various other ways of looking at the results of this modeling attempt, and many other questions about such modeling in general, which will not be discussed here. The main point of this chapter is simply that the prognosis is favorable—even the simplest kind of model, assuming that it embodies a sensible set of features, appears to have substantial predictive value.

REFERENCES

Atal, B. S., & Rabiner, L. R. A pattern-recognition approach to voiced-unvoiced-silence classification with applications to speech recognition. *IEEE Transactions on Acoustics, Speech and Signal Processing* (Vol. ASSP-24), 1976, 201–212.

Liberman, M. The intonational system of English. Unpublished Ph.D. dissertation, Massachusetts Institute of Technology, 1975.

Liberman, M., & Prince, A. On stress and linguistic rhythm. *Linguistic Inquiry* 1977, 8, (2), 249–336.

Liberman, M., & Streeter, L. Use of nonsense-syllable mimicry in the study of prosodic phenomena. Talk given at the 92nd meeting of the Acoustical Society of America, San Diego, November 1976.

Lindblom, B., & Rapp, K. *Some temporal regularities of spoken Swedish.* Publication No. 21. Institute of Linguistics, University of Stockholm, 1973.

Nakatani, L. H., & Schaffer, J. A. Hearing "words" without words: Speech prosody and word perception. Talk given at the 92nd meeting of the Acoustical Society of America, San Diego, November 1976.

10

Cross-Language Study of Tone Perception

Jackson T. Gandour / Richard Harshman

INTRODUCTION

One of the aims of modern linguistic theory is to develop a set of linguistic-phonetic features that are universally applicable to all languages of the world. The precise number and nature of the features that should be included in this universal set are still very much in dispute. The present study represents an attempt to bring fresh experimental data to bear on the number and nature of phonetic features or dimensions related to **tone** (see Wang, 1967); to determine the dimensions underlying the perception of tone, and also the degree to which an individual's language background influences his tonal perception.

Multidimensional scaling turns out to be a useful tool for measuring human perception in the tonal domain. Briefly, multidimensional scaling procedures spatially represent the underlying structure of a matrix of data values that generally correspond to subjective distances between stimulus objects (**stimulus space**), based on judgments of different individuals. Individual differences multidimensional scaling procedures (PARAFAC: Harshman, 1970; INDSCAL: Carroll & Chang, 1970) additionally provide information about the relative importance of each dimension to every individual (**subject space**). This information about the weights of the dimensions can be used to assess variation in perceptual structures across individuals or subgroups. With respect to the tonal domain, is it the case that all individuals, regardless of language background, share a common perceptual space, or rather, is it the case that the weight or perceptual saliency of a dimension(s) for an individual depends on its linguistic (or nonlinguistic) function in his native language?

EXPERIMENTAL DESIGN

We chose three languages that differ from one another in the way pitch is used to mark linguistic distinctions—Thai, Yoruba, and (American) English. Both Thai and Yoruba, in contrast to English, use pitch to distinguish minimally meanings of individual lexical items. This particular linguistic use of pitch, commonly referred to as tone, leads to the classification of Thai and Yoruba as **tone languages,** English as a nontone language. Thai and Yoruba, although both are tone languages, differ in the number and kind of underlying contrastive tones. Thai is traditionally analyzed (Henderson, 1949) as having five contrastive tones: three **level** tones: high, mid, low; two **contour** tones: falling and rising. For description of fundamental frequency trajectories associated with the Thai tones, see Abramson (1962). Yoruba, on the other hand, is traditionally analyzed (Ward, 1952) as having three contrastive level tones: high, mid, and low. For a description of fundamental frequency trajectories associated with the Yoruba tones, see Hombert (1976). Although Yoruba does not have lexically contrastive falling and rising contour tones, they do surface phonetically as a result of rules of tonal assimilation. Thus, both Thai and Yoruba have phonetic contour tones, but from different sources in the grammar. In the case of Thai, the lexicon; in the case of Yoruba, the output of phonological rules. It was our aim to investigate the degree to which such differences in the phonological and/or phonetic structure of a sound system may influence one's tonal perception.

The set of stimulus tones used in the experiment is presented in Figure 1. We included three level tones ($11\ 33\ 55$), five falling tones ($53\ 31\ 51\ \overline{53}$ $\overline{31}$), and five rising tones ($35\ 13\ 15\ \overline{35}\ \overline{13}$). All the fundamental frequency trajectories associated with the tones were linear ($5 = 150\ \text{Hz}, 3 = 125\ \text{Hz}, 1 = 100\ \text{Hz}$).

Synthetic speechlike syllables were constructed by imposing these fundamental frequency trajectories on [wa], using a line analog speech synthesizer (Rice, 1971). The durations of the syllables for the nine long tones and four short tones were 312 msec and 156 msec, respectively. The amplitude curve was fixed to display a sharp rise followed by a gradual fall.

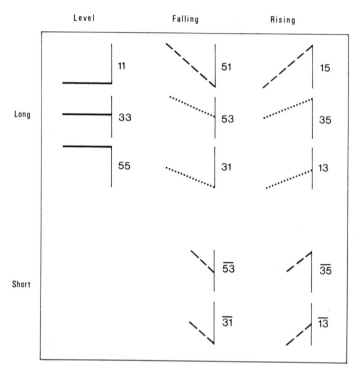

Figure 1. Numeric and graphic representations (after Chao, 1930) of the 13 stimulus tones used in the experiment. The ordinate represents a 5-step pitch scale ranging from 5 (highest point) to *1* (lowest point), and the abscissa represents time. A superscript horizontal bar distinguishes the numeric representations of the **short** contour tones from their **long** counterparts. The solid, dashed, and dotted horizontal lines differentiate the 13 stimuli by magnitude of slope.

Subjects were asked to rate the degree of dissimilarity between pairs of the stimulus tones on an 11-point scale. Their scores were accumulated into dissimilarity matrices, one for each subject. The value of a cell in the matrix represents the subjective distance between a pair of tones. The data for 140 subjects (101 Thai; 15 Yoruba; 24 English) served as input to the combined group PARAFAC multidimensional scaling analysis.

RESULTS AND DISCUSSION

Stimulus Space

Results of the PARAFAC combined group analysis indicate that five dimensions provide the best summary representation of the perceptual structures underlying the subjects' dissimilarity ratings. Figure 2 shows the order and position of the 13 stimulus tones on each of the five interpretively labeled dimensions. As the labels suggest, four of the dimensions can be related to the fundamental frequency, and one to the duration of the stimulus tones.

Dimension 1:   **Average pitch** places the *11* and *55* tones at either end of the axis, and *33* near the middle. The *15* and *51* tones cluster with *33*. With the other two clusters of tones (*35 53 $\overline{35}$ $\overline{53}$; 31 13 $\overline{31}$ $\overline{13}$*), average pitch values may be assigned as follows: *55* = 5; (*35 53 $\overline{35}$ $\overline{53}$*) = 4; (*33 15 51*) = 3; (*$\overline{13}$ $\overline{31}$ 13 31*) = 2; *11* = 1. For pairs of tones of the same pitch range and duration, we may further note that rising tones are perceived to be higher than falling tones. Within such pairs, the end point is always higher for the rising tone, indicating that overall pitch height is weighted by the ending component of the stimulus tones.

Dimension 2:   **Direction** places the five rising (*15 13 35 $\overline{13}$ $\overline{35}$*) and five falling (*$\overline{53}$ $\overline{31}$ 53 31 51*) stimulus tones at opposite ends of the axis, and the three level (*55 11 33*) tones somewhat near the middle, but closer to the falling than rising tones. Neither the rising nor falling tones cluster according to beginning or end point. This suggests that subjects perceived direction of pitch movement in the stimulus tones, not as movement **from** a fixed point A **to** a fixed point B, but instead as movement in a direction **away from** A and **toward** B. We further note that the degree of similarity of tones opposite in direction of movement depends in part on the size of the pitch range, the larger the pitch range, the more dissimilar the tones.

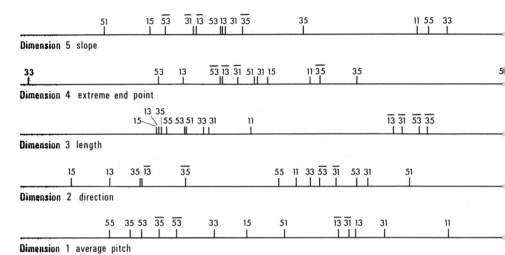

Figure 2.   Stimulus coordinates on the five PARAFAC dimensions.

Dimension 3:   **Length** separates the nine long tones (*15 13 35 55 53 51 33 11*) from the four short tones ($\overline{13}$ $\overline{31}$ $\overline{53}$ $\overline{35}$).

Dimension 4:   **Extreme endpoint** appears to separate those tones that have a *1* or *5* endpoint from those that have a *3* endpoint. Contour tones, however, are not judged to be as dissimilar from one another as level tones. According to our interpretation, tones at the opposite ends of the physical pitch continuum are judged to be more similar psychologically than one would predict from their distances to tones in the middle of the continuum. This fourth dimension is an attempt of PARAFAC to represent such curvature in the perceptual space.

Dimension 5:   **Slope** orders the tones according to magnitude of slope: Those tones with steepest slope (*51 15* $\overline{53}$ $\overline{31}$ $\overline{13}$) at one end of the axis, those with zero slope (*11 55 33*) at the other end, and those with intermediate slope (*53 13 31 35*) near the middle. On this interpretation, $\overline{35}$ is the only tone slightly out of position.

Subject Space

The mean subject weights for each language group on each dimension are displayed in Figure 3. The differences in weights on the five dimensions indicate to what extent the perception of tone depends on an individual's language background.

Subjects, regardless of language background, placed more relative importance on the first dimension—**average pitch**—than any of the other four dimensions. We do find, however, that the relative perceptual saliency of the **average pitch** dimension compared to the other dimensions is significantly higher for the nontone language group, English, than for the tone language groups, Thai and Yoruba (as determined by a one-way analysis of variance with planned comparisons). Regarding the second dimension—**direction**—the Thai and Yoruba groups attach significantly greater importance to this dimension than does the English group. These differences in the relative perceptual saliency of the direction of pitch movement can be related to linguistic function. In both Thai and Yoruba, pitch movement carries a considerable amount of linguistic information; in English, it does not.

It is the Thai group that places significantly greater emphasis on the third dimension—**length**—than either the English or Yoruba groups. These differences in relative perceptual saliency of duration properties of the stimulus tones across language groups may also be related to linguistic function. Vowel length is contrastive in Thai, noncontrastive in Yoruba and English. It is the English group that places significantly greater emphasis on the fourth dimension—**extreme endpoint**—than either of the

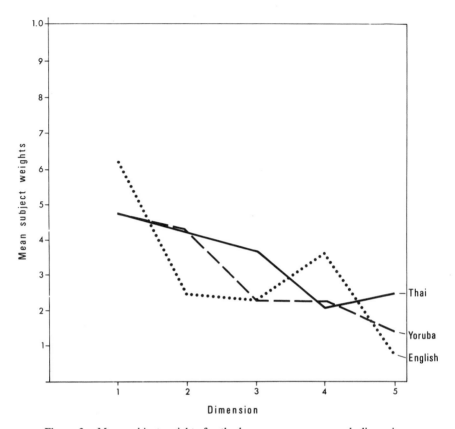

Figure 3. Mean subject weights for the language groups on each dimension.

tone language groups, Thai and Yoruba. The lesser importance attached
to this dimension by the Thai and Yoruba groups may reflect its lack of
relevance to the phonetic and/or phonological structure of these two tone
languages. Regarding Dimension 5—slope—however, the tone language
groups, Thai and Yoruba, placed relatively greater emphasis on this
dimension than the nontone language group, English. The linguistic function of a slope-related dimension in both Thai (lexical component) and
Yoruba (phonological rule component) might possibly account for the
heightened sensitivity of Thai and Yoruba speakers to differences in
magnitude of slope between the stimulus tones.

The relevance of linguistic information has been amply demonstrated
by the differences in relative degree of importance attached to particular
dimensions across language groups. It is not simply the case that we find
group differences, but moreover, we find that these differences in relative

perceptual saliency of dimensions can be related in a plausible way to linguistic experience. It is surely not accidental, for example, that the Thai and Yoruba groups place more relative emphasis on those dimensions more closely related to linguistic structure than the English subjects.

Individual differences in subject weights on particular dimensions, however, did result in considerable overlap between the language groups. To find out how well **individual** subjects could be classified into their respective language groups based on the pattern of subject weights for the combination of dimensions, we performed several discriminant analyses. In the Thai–English analysis, only 4% of the subjects were misclassified, 5 English subjects. In the Yoruba–English analysis, 10% of the subjects were misclassified, 1 Yoruba and 3 English subjects. In the Thai–Yoruba analysis, 9 of the 15 Yoruba individuals were incorrectly classified into the Thai group; 5 Thai individuals were incorrectly classified into the Yoruba group. In the Thai–Yoruba–English combined group analysis, 86% of the subjects were correctly classified into their respective language groups.

In general, the discriminant analysis results indicate that, within the five-dimensional perceptual space, we can fairly effectively distinguish a speaker of a tone language (Thai or Yoruba) from a speaker of a nontone language (English), but much less effectively speakers of typologically and genetically distinct tone languages. Figure 4 dramatizes the extent of variation between the tone language groups, Thai and Yoruba, and the nontone language group, English, on three of the five dimensions.

The particular clustering patterns of the stimulus tones **and** the differences in patterns of relative saliency on the dimensions across language groups lead us to suggest that **direction** and **slope** primarily reflect linguistic–phonetic distinctions; **average pitch** and **length** reflect either linguistic–phonetic or nonlinguistic–auditory distinctions (or both) depending on the language group and the individual subject, whereas **extreme endpoint,** while a little difficult to interpret, probably reflects simply nonlinguistic–auditory properties of the stimulus tones.

SUMMARY

An individual differences multidimensional scaling analysis of paired-comparison dissimilarity ratings of 13 tones for 140 subjects revealed that five dimensions—**average pitch, direction, length, extreme endpoint,** and **slope**—best summarize the perceptual structure underlying the dissimilarities data. Language subgroup variation in relative importance of these dimensions appears to be primarily related to differences in the way pitch is used to convey linguistic information. Discriminant analysis

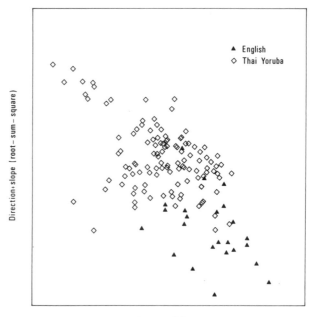

Average pitch

Figure 4.   Plot showing the relative importance of Dimension 1 versus Dimensions 2 and 5 for 140 subjects. The projections of subject points on the horizontal axis indicate the weights on Dimension 1—**average pitch**; the projections of subject points on the vertical axis show the combined (root–sum–square) weights on Dimensions 2—**direction** and 5—**slope.**

showed that most individual speakers of a tone language (Thai or Yoruba) can be easily distinguished from speakers of a nontone language (English) on the basis of their distinctive patterns of perceptual saliency for these five dimensions.

REFERENCES

Abramson, A. S. The vowels and tones of Standard Thai: Acoustical measurements and experiments. *International Journal of American Linguistics,* 1962, *28*(2), Part II.

Carroll, J. D., & Chang, J. J. Analysis of individual differences in multidimensional scaling via a *n*-way generalization of "Eckart-Young" decomposition. *Psychometrika,* 1970, *35*(3), 283–319.

Chao, Y. R. A system of tone letters. *Le Maître Phonétique,* 1930, *45,* 24–27.

Harshman, R. A. Foundations of the PARAFAC procedure: Models and conditions for an "explanatory" multidimensional factor analysis. *UCLA Working Papers in Phonetics, 16,* 1970.

Henderson, E. J. A. Prosodies in Siamese, a study in synthesis. *Asia Major* (New Series), 1949, *1*, 189–215. Reprinted in F. R. Palmer (Ed.), *Prosodic analysis*. London: Oxford University Press, 1970.

Hombert, J. M. Consonant types, vowel height and tone in Yoruba. *UCLA Working Papers in Phonetics*, 1976, *33*, 40–54.

Rice, L. A new line analog speech synthesizer for the PDP-12. *UCLA Working Papers in Phonetics*, 1971, *17*, 58–75.

Wang, W. S.-Y. Phonological features of tone. *International Journal of American Linguistics*, 1967, *33*, 93–105.

Ward, I. C. *Introduction to the Yoruba language*. Cambridge: Heffer and Sons, 1952.

11

Multidimensional Analysis of Vowel Variation[1]

Robert Berdan

MULTIVALUED VARIABLES

The early work by Labov (1963, 1966) on the quantification of linguistic variation dealt with both **dichotomous** and **multivalued** variables. Dichotomous variables included such things as the phonetic realization of postvocalic /r/ as either a "definitely constricted /r/-like sound" or the lack of the constriction (Labov, 1966, p. 50). Vowel variation, on the other hand, has frequently been discussed by relating three or more phonetic variants (phones or surface realizations) to a single variable (phoneme or underlying representation).

[1]The work on which this paper is based was supported in part by SWRL Educational Research & Development under contract NE-C-00-3-0064 with the National Institute of Education, Department of Health, Education and Welfare. Computing assistance obtained from the Health Sciences Computing Facility, UCLA, sponsored by the National Institutes of Health Special Research Grant No. RR-3. I am grateful to Professor Ronald Macaulay for access to his very rich corpus of Scottish English phonology and for his helpful criticism. The participants at the MSSB Conference provided many useful comments, most of which have now been incorporated into the paper. I am particularly grateful to J. B. Kruskal, who pointed out the applicability of principal component analysis to this problem, and to S. E. Legum for discussion of many problems.

As the emphasis of sociolinguistic research has shifted to the development of variable rules within probabilistic grammars, the concentration on dichotomous variables has become greater (e.g., Labov, Cohen, Robins, & Lewis, 1968; Cedergren & Sankoff, 1974; Rousseau & Sankoff, this volume). Statistical and computational methodology is not yet available for extending variable rule procedures, based on binomial probabilities, to the trinomial and multinomial probabilities inherent in multivalued variables. Thus, in Cedergren's analysis of the spirantization and deletion of /s/ in Panamanian Spanish (Cedergren, 1973), the three variants [s, h, ø] are treated by two dichotomous rules: one rule of spirantization relating [s] and [h], and another rule of deletion which applies only to [h].

Any multivalued variable could in theory be treated as a series of dichotomous variables in this fashion, a procedure which requires the specification in the grammar of probabilities associated with each step, or minimally, one specification fewer than the number of surface variants being generated. There are two types of problem connected with this. From the linguistic point of view, it is often difficult, or arbitrary, to specify the steps or the order in which variants are generated. Second, the parameters associated with the various variants may be mathematically related, so that it is redundant or misleading to specify more than one or two of them. The procedures compared in this chapter allow for the **simultaneous** prediction of all probabilities associated with the variants of a multivalued variable. The number of parameters which must be specified for the individual grammar may be as few as one, and is determined by how well the observed variation is predicted, and how well these parameters can be interpreted within conventional linguistic theories.

DATA SET

The data presented here are drawn from a larger data base of Scottish English assembled and analyzed by Ronald Macaulay (1977, 1978). Macaulay tape-recorded interviews with 48 speakers of Scottish English in Glasgow. The speakers constitute a stratified sample of males and females from four social groups and three age groups (10-year-olds, 15-year-olds, and adults). For each of the vowels in which Macaulay was interested, 40 tokens were transcribed from the first half of each speaker's interview, and 40 more tokens from the second half.[2] Only examples of stressed vowels were used, and instances with following /r/ were excluded

[2]For some speakers there were substantially fewer tokens of /ɪ/ in the interview.

from this analysis. To reduce possible lexical bias, no more than 3 tokens of any single lexical item were transcribed for any speaker.

From the full set of data collected by Macaulay, only the vowel /ɪ/ will be considered here. Trained transcribers categorized vowel tokens into the following five conventional perceptually determined phonetic categories:

$$[\mathrm{I}], \quad [\mathrm{I}^{\vee},\varepsilon^{\wedge}], \quad [\varepsilon^{\flat}, \ddot{\imath}_{\downarrow}], \quad [\partial^{\wedge}], \quad [\Lambda^{\wedge}]$$
$$\mathrm{I}_1 \qquad \mathrm{I}_2 \qquad \mathrm{I}_3 \qquad \mathrm{I}_4 \qquad \mathrm{I}_5$$

Mean proportions of each phonetic category for each social group are shown in Table 1.

VARIABILITY AND COMMONALITY

While aggregated data from individuals within sociolinguistic groupings may well reflect the differences between the groups, as in Table 1, they do not take into account variation within the groups, which may be considerable. This is the case for the /ɪ/ data, even when both age and social level are criteria for grouping. The high degree of diversity observed within groups could only be partially reduced if other social criteria were used, even if allowance were made for effects of the phonetic environment on the realization of /ɪ/.

Failing to find absolute linguistic homogeneity among members of sociologically defined language groups, one might simply proceed to create a separate grammar for each individual. Obviously, this is possible in the case of /ɪ/; observed relative frequencies of each phonetic variant for each speaker are interpreted as estimates of the probability that those variants are generated by the speaker's grammar. The sociolinguist, however, seeks not only to describe individual grammars, but also to describe the commonality observed among speakers who have shared highly simi-

TABLE 1

Mean Proportions of / I / Variants by Social Group

Social group	I_1	I_2	I_3	I_4	I_5
1	.231	.548	.182	.037	.001
2	.052	.529	.313	.094	.001
3	.022	.334	.450	.173	.021
4	.016	.298	.472	.171	.044

lar language acquisition and language use experiences, in the search for constraints on the sets of possible grammars that can occur in natural language communities (Berdan, 1975). The application of variable rules to individual grammars can be viewed as one such expression of commonality: Probabilities associated with rule features are assumed to be common for grammars of all members of the group; only input probabilities vary for individual grammars. In the following section we investigate other statistical approaches toward characterizing commonalities, particularly as pertain to multivalued variables.

THE WEIGHTED INDEX

The early quantified treatment of multivalued linguistic variables such as Scottish English /ɪ/ employed a unidimensional index. In his early studies in New York, Labov (1966) arranged the phonetic variants of each variable on an ordinal scale on the basis of articulatory criteria. Each variant was assigned an integer weight 1 to n for each of the n categories of the variable. Multiplying the proportion of tokens in each category by their respective weights and summing across categories, an index was computed for each individual. This procedure has been used in numerous other treatments of multivalued vowel variation (e.g., Trudgill, 1974; Callary, 1975), and was applied to the present data by Macaulay (1977, 1978).

The following weights were assigned to each of the phonetic categories of /ɪ/ in the Scottish English data to derive an index for each of the 48 speakers as described above.

$$100 \; [\text{ɪ}]$$
$$200 \; [\text{ɛ}^\wedge] \; [\text{ɪ}\,]$$
$$300 \; [\text{ɛ}'] \; [\text{ï}\,]$$
$$400 \; [\text{ə}^\wedge]$$
$$500 \; [\text{ʌ}^\wedge]$$

The means and standard deviations for the indices assigned to speakers in each social group are shown in Table 2.

The mean index increases for each social group, ranging from 203 for Social Group 1 to 293 for Social Group 4. Pairwise comparison of the means shows all groups to be significantly different (by two-tailed t test, $p < .02$), except Groups 3 and 4. The weighted index thus provides a useful mechanism for discussing the social differentiation of language use in Glasgow.

TABLE 2
Mean /I/ Index for Four Scottish English Social Groups

	Social group			
	1	2	3	4
Mean	203	248	284	293
Standard Deviation	38.4	36.4	27.8	29.1

Similar differentiation has been shown in the other studies cited earlier. None of these studies, however, attempted to incorporate this social group difference or the index itself within a formal grammar. The problem in trying to do so is that no method has yet been presented for recovering or generating the probability of each of the several variants from the single index value for each speaker.[3] Unless this can be done it is difficult, if not impossible, to test whether or not the representation of the data as a unidimensional variable preserves the essential characteristics of the data set.

MULTIDIMENSIONAL SCALING

Multidimensional scaling provides an alternative technique for analyzing these data.[4] It also provides some measure of how well one or more dimensions preserve the characteristics of the multivalued data set. To use multidimensional scaling with these linguistic data, an underlying vowel, with n phonetic categories, is defined in n-dimensional space, with each phonetic category represented on an axis orthogonal to each of the other phonetic categories. For each individual, the proportion of tokens falling in each phonetic category is interpreted as a coordinate for that axis. Each person in the data set is thus represented as a point in the n-dimensional space.[5] The Euclidean distance is calculated between each

[3]Kruskal (personal communication) suggests a procedure for doing this based on the assumptions that the phonetic categories represent the segmenting of a continuous variable on which the tokens are normally distributed (cf. Snell, 1964).

[4]Multidimensional scaling has been used somewhat differently in a number of linguistic studies, for example, Black (1976), Sankoff and Cedergren (1976), Terbeek (1973), and Wexler and Romney (1972).

[5]Actually, the points lie in a $(n - 1)$-dimensional subspace, since the sum of an individual's variant proportions is always 1.

pair of points. These distances can be interpreted as a measure of dissimilarity between persons for input to multidimensional scaling analysis (cf. Kruskal, 1964a, 1964b). Each data point, or individual, is represented by the 47 distances between that point and all others in the data set.

In this study the nonmetric scaling algorithm of KYST (Kruskal, Young, & Seery, 1973) was used. The function of the algorithm is to attempt to maintain the same rank ordering of the distances between the points as they are projected in a space defined in fewer and fewer dimensions. The extent to which the relationship among the points is maintained is expressed as a function **stress,** the value of stress decreasing as the fit improves. The values of stress for the /ɪ/ data reduced to one, two, and three dimensions by the scaling algorithm are graphed in Figure 1.

The unidimensional scaling output by the program is in a sense comparable to the conventional weighted index discussed in the preceding section which typically has been reported for data of this type. For both, proportions of each of the five variants for an individual have been reduced to a single value. The two methods use very different properties of the data set, however. The weighted index procedure assigns weights to each of the phonetic variants and assumes some ordering among them. The scaling procedure does not make these assumptions. Scaling looks only at the relative differences among the individuals in the use of each of the variants. Despite these differences in assumptions, the two procedures yield virtually identical results. The Pearson product-moment correlation coefficient for the values assigned to each of the 48 speakers by the two procedures is $r = .970$.

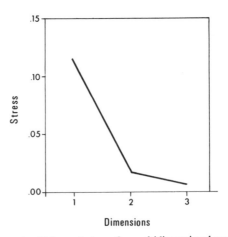

Figure 1. Values of stress for multidimensional scaling.

Unlike the use of the weighted index, the scaling procedure allows some measure of how well the reduction to a single linear variable maintains the information in the original five-dimensional data set. The value of stress calculated by KYST (Formula 1) for one dimension is .130, high enough to suggest that forcing the data into a single dimension has resulted in some distortion of the original five-dimensional data set (cf. Kruskal, 1964a, 1964b).

The value of stress drops markedly when two dimensions are retained (.033), and very little more with three dimensions (.012). This **elbow** in the graph of stress (Figure 1) at two dimensions suggests that two dimensions provide the most parsimonious representation of the data; the goodness of fit is improved very little by increasing the number of dimensions further. The two-dimensional distribution of the speakers is shown in Figure 2.

Examining this graph, the two dimensions seem to correspond largely to vowel height (vertical axis) and front–backness (horizontal axis). Individuals in Social Group 1 vary chiefly along the dimension of vowel height; members of the other social groups vary chiefly in the use of variants differentiated by relative front–backness. It should be noted that even though each of the phonetic variants is describable with respect to

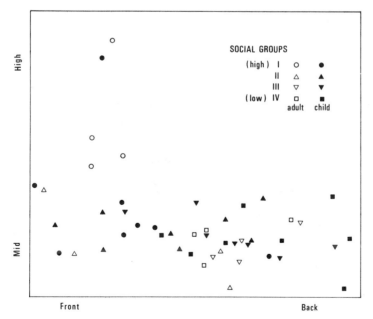

Figure 2.   Two-dimensional plot of /ɪ/ by speaker.

these two parameters, this fact is not input for the program, and there is no necessary reason for the results of a two-dimensional scaling analysis to be interpretable as the same parameters. That they are in this case is a function of the distribution of variants across individual speakers. For example, there are no speakers with high relative frequencies of Variant 1, [ɪ], and Variant 5, [ʌˆ], but low relative frequencies of the intermediate variants. A preponderance of speakers with such bimodal distributions of tokens would have resulted in dimensions which would be much more difficult to interpret in conventional linguistic terms.

The use of multidimensional scaling does allow some characterization of the dimensionality of the data set, without assuming that it must be linear. This is a distinct advantage. In this case, at least, the unidimensional analysis provides essentially the same information about the data as does the weighted index. Also, like the weighted index, however, values generated by the scaling procedure are not interpretable as parameters of generative grammars. There is no way to recover from the coordinates on each of the several dimensions the individual probabilities of each of the phonetic variants. As Sankoff and Cedergren (1976) concluded on the basis of using multidimensional scaling with rather different linguistic data sets, multidimensional scaling provides a valuable heuristic tool that makes few assumptions about the nature of the data, but is frequently rather difficult to interpret.

PRINCIPAL COMPONENT ANALYSIS

Principal component analysis is somewhat similar to multidimensional scaling in that it allows reduction of the multidimensional data set to any predetermined number of dimensions. It has the distinct advantage, however, that it allows recovery of predictions of the probability of each of the original variants.[6] Principal component analysis is a special case of factor analysis, the properties of which are well described in Harman (1967). The advantage of principal component analysis over other types of factor analysis for this application is the very direct and readily interpretable expression of the components in terms of the observed variants.

As with the multidimensional scaling, principal component analysis looks at the individual speakers as points in a five-dimensional space, coordinates on each dimension being the relative frequency of each of the five phonetic variants. The property of the data set used for the analysis is the correlation across speakers for each pair of variants. In geometric

---

[6]This advantage was pointed out to me by Kruskal (personal communication).

TABLE 3
Correlations of the Phonetic Variants with the Principal Components·

Variant	One component analysis	Two component analysis	
	First component	First component	Second component
I_1	-.724	-.906	-.017
I_2	-.875	-.520	-.756
I_3	.917	.856	.394
I_4	.870	.704	.513
I_5	.588	.064	.873

terms, the first principal component can be conceived of as the single straight line through the five-space which comes closest to each of the points. Similarly, two principal components define the plane which best fits all of the data points. For this analysis the SPSS factoring procedure PAl was used, with orthogonal axis and orthogonal rotation (Nie, Hull, Steinbrenner, & Bent, 1975). The location of each individual on the principal components is determined by multiplying the standardized form of the proportion on each variant by the respective coefficients in Table 3, and summing across all variants. These coefficients are the correlations of the values on each of the phonetic variants with the principal components.

When only one principal component is extracted from the data set in this way, the data are reduced to a unidimensional variable, as was the case with the weighted index or the single dimension with the scaling procedure. Values for individuals on this principal component are very similar to those found with the other two procedures. The Pearson product-moment correlation coefficient for the first principal component and the weighted index is $r = .987$; between the first principal component and the unidimensional scaling it is $r = .975$. In other words all three procedures differentiate among the individual speakers in highly similar ways.

The advantage of the principal component analysis over the other approaches is that the orientation of this line with respect to the original axes defined by the phonetic variants is known. Coordinates on these axes for the point estimates for each individual are interpretable as predictions of the probability of using each phonetic variant for each individual.[7] That

[7]Actually they are interpreted here as relative probabilities because of the possibility that some values could be negative. Negative values were arbitrarily set at 0 and the probabilities of the other variants adjusted to maintain the same relative magnitude.

TABLE 4
Coefficients for Computing Predicted Values of the Phonetic Variants

Variant	One component analysis First component	Two component analysis First component	Second component
I_1	-.224	-.576	.373
I_2	-.270	-.012	-.424
I_3	.283	.383	-.029
I_4	.269	.234	.138
I_5	.182	-.332	.718

is, all five values of the variants of /ɪ/ may be predicted from the single value derived above for each individual. In practice the predicted proportions of each phonetic variant for each individual are computed by multiplying the coordinates on the principal components by the coefficients in Table 4, and in the case of two or more principal components, summing across them.

The estimation of separate coordinates for each speaker ensures that for virtually all individuals these predictions are substantially better than those based on the five mean values for his or her social group, and predictions based on two principal components are generally better than those based on only the first principal component.[8]

The linguistic, or phonological interpretation of the principal component analysis is fairly straightforward in terms of the perceptual phonetic categories. No attempt has been made here to extend this interpretation to the use of binary distinctive features, if indeed a binary system is most appropriate for expressing these fine phonetic distinctions. In articulatory terms these categories are distinguished chiefly in terms of height and front–backness. It is clear from the correlations in Table 3 that the two-component analysis is not interpretable directly in these two articulatory dimensions.

[8]The first principal component accounts for 65.7% of the variance in the data. That is a substantial proportion of the difference among speakers but allows the potential for considerable difference between observed values and those predicted by the location of speakers on the principal component. The first two principal components together account for 81.5% of the variance, which suggests that the two-component analysis will provide a substantially more adequate prediction of the observed distribution.

The sociolinguistic interpretation of the principal component analysis is substantially different from that usually associated with the reporting of group means. When group means are reported, one is led to infer that persons differ in a linguistically significant way only when they also differ along sociological or demographic parameters. Thus linguistic commonality is absolute within social groups.

In the principal component analysis much less is assumed: namely, that two things are common across speakers. The first is phonetic space. That is, the set of possible surface variants for the single underlying form is the same for all speakers, whether or not any particular speaker uses all of the surface forms. For purposes of the principal component analysis this commonality was expressed as the five-dimensional space in which indi-·vidual speakers were plotted.

The second commonality is the location within that space of the principal components. That is, there is single linear variable, or set of variables (two, in the case of the two-component analysis) by which the use of all five variants of /ɪ/ may be predicted. The coefficients in Table 4 used for computing those individual predicted values are common across all speakers. The differences among individuals are described only in terms of different values on the principal components.

SUMMARY

The assumption of linguistic homogeneity within sociolinguistic groups, as reflected in the reporting of group means does not adequately represent the variation among individuals found in this set of Scottish English /ɪ/ data. The use of a weighted index or multidimensional scaling to reduce the dimensionality of the data makes more apparent some of the social differentiation among the groups but neither of these procedures can be readily adapted to the construction of sociolinguistic grammars. The principal component analysis allows similar reduction of dimensions. It also allows prediction of the full set of phonetic variants from a limited set of values for each individual. This is analogous to saying that the set of variants may be **generated** in the sense that term is used in conventional generative theory. The theoretical formalisms for exploiting this capability have not been developed here,but the potential for them exists with the principal component analysis in a way that it does not for the other procedures. Further development along the lines suggested here offers the potential that multivalued linguistic variables can be handled within sociolinguistic grammars much as dichotomous variables are.

REFERENCES

Berdan, R. On the nature of linguistic variation. Unpublished Ph.D. dissertation, University of Texas, 1975.

Black, P. Multidimensional scaling applied to linguistic relationships. *Cahiers de l'Institut de Linguistique de Louvain,* 1976, *3*(5–6), 43–92.

Callary, E. Phonological change and the development of an urban dialect in Illinois. *Language in Society,* 1975, *4,* 155–169.

Cedergren, H. The interplay of social and linguistic factors in Panama. Unpublished Ph.D. dissertation, Cornell University, 1973.

Cedergren, H., & Sankoff, D. Variable rules: Performance as a statistical reflection of competence. *Language,* 1974, *50,* 333–355.

Harman, H. H. *Modern factor analysis.* Chicago: University of Chicago Press, 1967.

Kruskal, J. B. Multidimensional scaling by optimizing goodness of fit to a nonmetric hypothesis. *Psychometrika,* 1964, *29,* 1–27. (a)

Kruskal, J. B. Nonmetric multidimensional scaling: A numerical method. *Psychometrika,* 1964, *29,* 115–129. (b)

Kruskal, J. B., Young, F., & Seery, J. How to use KYST, a very flexible program to do multidimensional scaling and unfolding. Murray Hill, N.J.: Bell Laboratories, 1973.

Labov, W. The social motivation of a sound change. *Word,* 1963, *19,* 273–309.

Labov, W. *The social stratification of English in New York City.* Washington, D.C.: Center for Applied Linguistics, 1966.

Labov, W., Cohen, P., Robins, C., & Lewis, J. A study of the non-standard English of Negro and Puerto Rican speakers in New York City. Final Report, Cooperative Research Project 3288, 2 vols. Washington, D.C.: Office of Education, 1968.

Macaulay, R. K. S. *Language, social class and education: A Glasgow study.* Edinburgh: Edinburgh University Press, 1977.

Macaulay, R. K. S. Variation and consistency in Glaswegian English. In P. Trudgill (Ed.), *Sociolinguistic patterns in British English.* London: Arnold, 1978.

Nie, N. H., Hull, C. H., Steinbrenner, K., & Bent, D. H. *Statistical package for the social sciences* (2nd ed.). New York: McGraw-Hill, 1975.

Sankoff, D., & Cedergren, H. J. The dimensionality of grammatical variation. *Language,* 1976, *52,* 163–178.

Snell, E. J. A scaling procedure for ordered categorical data. *Biometrics,* 1964, *20,* 592–607.

Terbeek, D. Six dimensions of vowel quality. In C. Corum, T. Smith-Clark, & A. Weiser (Eds.), *Papers from the Ninth Regional Meeting of the Chicago Linguistic Society.* Chicago: Chicago Linguistic Society, 1973, 672–678.

Trudgill, P. J. *The social differentiation of English in Norwich.* Cambridge: University Press, 1974.

Wexler, K., & Romney, A. K. Individual variations in cognitive structures. In R. Shepard, A. K. Romney, & S. Nerlove (Eds.), *Multidimensional scaling: Applications.* Vol 2. New York: Seminar Press, 1972.

12

Approaches to Vowel Normalization in the Study of Natural Speech

Donald Hindle

VARIATION AND NORMALIZATION

In recent years, progress has been made in applying the tools of experimental phonetics to problems of phonological change and variation.[1] For the analysis of vowel variation and change, the problem which is the focus of this chapter, estimates of the first and second formant frequencies of a vowel reflect its quality, and therefore differences in the frequencies of the first two formants correspond to differences in vowel quality. This relationship has been exploited in studies of linguistic change in the speech community such as the work reported by Labov, Yaeger, and Steiner (1972). One example of the importance of precise measures of phonetic variants is the case of near mergers, where it is shown that speakers can consistently maintain slight differences in formant values for two phonemes while they cannot be shown to differentiate the two phonemes in their reactions (Labov *et al.*, 1972: Chapter 6). Current research in Philadelphia indicates that the first syllable of *Murray* and of

[1]This is a preliminary report of an investigation of vowel normalization supported by National Science Foundation grant SOC 75-00245, entitled "The Quantitative Study of Linguistic Change and Variation," William Labov, principle investigator.

merry are heard by Philadelphians as the same on labeling and subtle performance tasks, but a consistent difference is maintained, *merry* having a higher second formant. A second case showing the need for attention to small differences in formant values is found in vowel shifting conditioned by situational factors (Yaeger, 1975).

These two examples involve the examination of differences within the vowel system of a single individual. In a study of linguistic change in its social context, addressing the problems outlined by Weinreich, Labov, and Herzog (1968), including the embedding of change in the community and in linguistic structure, the transition from one speaker to another, and the constraints which govern change, it is necessary to compare the vowel systems of different individuals. Impressionistically, comparisons can confidently be made, at least at a broad level. For example, when a 12-year-old Philadelphia girl says [fəⁱt], we can hear that it is different from a 64-year-old man who says [faⁱt]. The difference in the vowel nucleus reflects a change currently going on in the Philadelphia community in which the nucleus of /ay/ is raised before voiceless consonants. When we turn to the formant measurements used to characterize differences in vowel quality, however, we may find that this difference has disappeared. Vowels spoken by different individuals that sound different may have the same formant measurements, and conversely, vowels of different speakers that sound the same may have different formant values; in general, the vowel systems of different individuals represented by measured formants cannot be superimposed.

This is a well-known problem, often illustrated through the mean formant values for men, women, and children reported by Peterson and Barney (1952). In their study, the 33 men, 28 women, and 15 children were asked to produce two tokens of each of 10 vowel phonemes embedded in the environment of preceding /h/ and following /d/. Figure 1(a) shows the mean first and second formant values of the 10 vowels, with the men represented by filled-in circles, the women by lined circles, and the children by open circles. Focusing on the filled-in circles, it is easy to see that the total area occupied by the men's vowels is small compared with the area taken up by the children's vowel system. For each phoneme, the values for the women fall intermediate between the men and the children. The noteworthy feature in this figure is that for each phoneme, the formant values for different speaker groups differ widely.

This dispersion clearly presents a problem: What is a speaker doing when he equates two vowels spoken by different speakers and having different formant values? This is the psychological aspect of the normalization problem. In this chapter, we consider normalization rather as a technical problem: How can the measured formant values for different speakers be transformed so that different speakers' versions of the same phoneme coincide in the normalized systems?

NORMALIZATION PROCEDURES AND THEIR RATIONALES

A number of solutions to the normalization problem have been proposed in the literature. Here we will investigate three of these. The first to be considered, the vocal tract length procedure, starts from the hypothesis that formant frequency for a given vowel phoneme is inversely proportional to vocal tract length: The longer the vocal tract, the lower the formant frequencies. This relationship is apparent in Figure 1(a), where the men, who have the longest vocal tracts, also have the lowest formants, and the children, with the shortest vocal tracts, have the highest formants. To normalize a group of speakers then, their formants are multiplied by a speaker-dependent scale factor proportional to vocal tract length. Several methods have been proposed for finding the vocal tract length from acoustic measurements (Nordström & Lindblom, forthcoming; Wakita, 1975). In the procedure proposed by Nordström and Lindblom, the estimate of the vocal tract length is based on an experimentally observed curve relating vocal tract length to mean third formant for the low vowels (their Figure 6). For each individual to be normalized, the mean third formant of the low vowels is found, and then the vocal tract length is estimated from the Nordström–Lindblom empirical curve. The normalization scale factor is defined as the tract length divided by a constant reference length. For the present study, the constant reference length used is the mean estimated vocal tract length of all the individuals normalized.[2]

Figure 1(b) shows the Peterson and Barney means normalized by the Nordström and Lindblom vocal tract length procedure. It is clear that this normalization has had its intended effect—namely, an increase in clustering and separation of the different vowel phonemes. There is no perfect clustering, but the phonemes do occupy separate, definable spaces.

The second normalization procedure considered here also involves a linear transformation of the formants by a single scale factor, but in this case without the intervention of vocal tract length. This method of nor-

---

[2]Fant (1975) points out that the Nordström–Lindblom formula leaves out the end correction for lip rounding, and suggests that a more realistic formula would be $k = \sqrt{\dfrac{VT + 1}{VT_{ref} + 1}}$ rather than $k = \dfrac{VT}{VT_{ref}}$ where k is the scale factor, VT the individual vocal tract length, and VT_{ref} the reference length. There is then a small systematic error in the Nordstöm–Lindblom normalization used here, but this does not significantly affect the results (cf. Nordström, 1977).

F₂ (kHz)

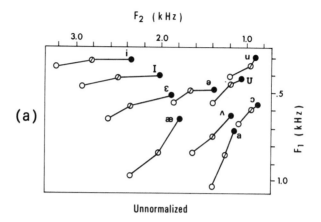

(a)

Unnormalized

F₂ (kHz)

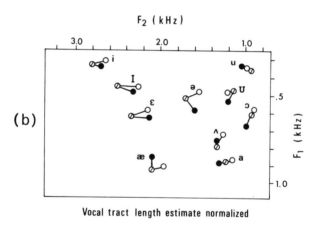

(b)

Vocal tract length estimate normalized

● Men   ⊘ Women   ○ Children

Figure 1. Peterson and Barney means. (a) Unnormalized. (b) Vocal tract length esti-mate normalized. Parts (c) and (d) are on facing page.

malization is based on Nearey (1977),who observes that the hypothesis that a group of speakers can be normalized by multiplying the formants by a single, speaker-dependent scale factor is equivalent to assuming that the logarithms of the formants can be normalized by the addition of a speaker-dependent constant. If the normalized formant is equal to the original formant multiplied by a scale factor k, then the logarithm of the

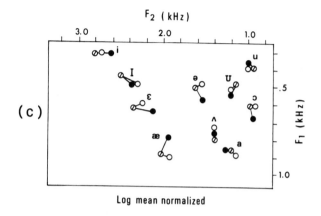

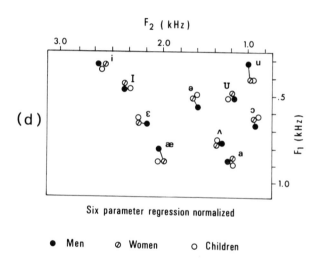

● Men   ⊘ Women   ○ Children

Figure 1 (continued). (c) Log mean normalized. (d) Six-parameter regression normalized.

normalized formant is equal to the logarithm of the original formant plus the logarithm of k. Hypothetically, this relationship would hold for the logarithms of any first and second formant. Therefore, it will hold for the mean of the logarithms of all first and second formants, and this mean can be used to calculate the scale factor. The first step in this procedure is to find the mean of the logarithms of all first and second formants for each individual. The logarithm of the scale factor is then defined as the difference between the individual log mean and the average log mean for the group being normalized. The multiplicative scale factor for each individual is the antilog of this quantity.

Figure 1(c) shows the results of the log mean normalization. While the relative positions of the normalized Peterson and Barney means differ slightly from the vocal tract length estimate normalization (Figure 1[b]), the effect can be seen to be generally the same, with similar relations produced within each phoneme for the different speaker groups. Overall, the normalization is successful in that it produces separation and clustering.

The third normalization procedure differs from the preceding two in that instead of a single-scale factor, six parameters are used in the normalization transformation, three for each formant. In this method, devised by Sankoff, Shorrock, and McKay (1974), the normalization depends on first finding the means for each phoneme word class for each individual and for the group overall, and then regressing the group means on each individual's means. The parameters used to transform an individual's formant space are found by inverting the transform resulting from this regression. For each formant then, the normalized formant is the sum of a constant and some scaling of the first and second formants:

$$F_1^* = a_1 + b_1 F_1 + c_1 F_2$$
$$F_2^* = a_2 + b_2 F_1 + c_2 F_2$$

In general, for the normalized first formant, the parameter c_1, and hence the effect of the second formant, will be small, and conversely, the parameter b_2, the effect of the first formant on the normalized second formant, will be small. Figure 1(d) shows the results for the Peterson and Barney data. Since this approach is more powerful than the single-scale factor approach, it is expected to produce greater clustering and greater separation of vowel classes, and that is what we find.

Thus, while all three normalization procedures are seen to be successful with respect to the Peterson and Barney data, the regression normalization is, as predicted, most successful in producing clustering and separation.

A SOCIOLINGUISTIC CRITERION

Although the two single-scale factor normalizations have their intended effect, they do not work perfectly, and in fact, no single-scale factor could yield a perfect normalization for the Peterson and Barney data. It is apparent from the unnormalized values in Figure 1(a) that the scale factor relating men's and women's values for /ɔ/ must be very different from that relating their values for /ʌ/, since their untransformed values are close together for the first vowel, and far apart for the second. In general, if the unnormalized data were uniformly scalable, the lines connecting the speaker groups would be straight and would converge at the origin. Fant (1966) suggests that physiological differences between men, women, and children, in addition to differences in overall vocal tract length, can account for the discrepancies. However, studies of formants produced by simulated vocal tracts indicate that a large part of the deviation from uniform scaling is due to factors other than vocal tract shape (Nordström & Lindblom, forthcoming; Nordström, 1977). Another possible source of the discrepancies is that there are genuine differences between the speaker groups in the articulation of vowels. Nordström and Lindblom note that the Peterson and Barney study was based on speakers from a variety of dialects, including some who were not native speakers of English, which surely affected the results. For example, Peterson and Barney treat /ɔ/ and /a/ as separate phonemes, but for about half the geographic United States, these phonemes are merged, and therefore are expected to have the same formant values (Labov *et al.*, 1972, p. 119).

This brings us to the heart of the normalization problem as it pertains to the study of variation in the community, for here it is essential to have a transformation that will minimize formant differences between individuals due to inherent physiological factors, but will preserve distinctions that correspond to perceptibly different vowels. This need suggests a third criterion in addition to clustering and separation to evaluate normalization: namely, that a successful normalization will reveal socially significant differences. For example, in a speech community where there are perceptible differences between the vowels of young and old speakers, a situation in which change is going on, the normalization must preserve this relation.

TWO STUDIES

We will use data gathered in the Philadelphia community to test the normalization procedures. The first set of data is from a study of speakers from one neighborhood in South Philadelphia. Interviews of 2 to 4 hours were made by Anne Bower, and the acoustic analysis was carried out by Elizabeth Dayton and Bruce Johnson. The sample consists of 19 speakers, 9 men and 10 women, ranging in age from 12 to 84 years. For each speaker, 100 to 200 vowel nuclei were measured, with a minimum of three tokens for each vowel class, taken from the stressed vowels of running conversation. When the mean phoneme values of the unnormalized vowel systems are superimposed, there is, as expected, considerable overlap. Normalizations applied to the 19 speakers produce increased clustering and separation as was seen with the Peterson and Barney mean values. The vocal tract length estimate normalization produces somewhat less clustering than the log mean normalization, and the regression normalization results in the greatest clustering and separation. For the phonological variable /ay°/, the vowel which occurs before voiceless consonants as in *fight, life,* these results are summarized in Figure 2(a), which shows the standard deviations for the two formants for the unnormalized version (*U*), the vocal tract length normalization (*T*), the log mean normalization (*L*), and the regression normalization (*R*). The decrease in standard deviation is here taken as a measure of the increase in clustering, and patterns similar to the pattern for /ay°/ are observed for the other vowel classes.

The variable /ay°/ has been selected here because it is known to be the locus of large-scale phonetic changes, the nucleus moving from [a] to [ə]. This change only affects /ay/ before voiceless consonants. Our knowledge of ongoing change is based on convergent observations of speakers of different ages in the Philadelphia community. Impressionistic ratings of the quality of /ay°/ for different speakers, and the position of the measured formants of /ay°/ relative to other vowels of the same individual's system both indicate that the older speakers have a nucleus close to [a] and the younger speakers close to [ə]. Acoustically, the differentiation and change is reflected by a relatively higher first formant for older speakers. While comparisons across speakers using unnormalized formants are misleading, we expect that once the formants have been normalized, there will be a positive correlation between F_1 and age, and a regression of F_1 on age will show a positive regression coefficient.

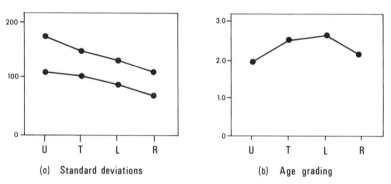

(a) Standard deviations   (b) Age grading

Figure 2. Normalization for neighborhood study for /ay°/, 19 speakers. *U* = unnormalized; *T* = vocal tract length estimate normalization; *L* = log mean normalization; *R* = regression normalization.

To test the success of the normalization procedures in revealing the known social differentiation with respect to /ay°/, we have regressed the first formant on age for the various normalizations. Figure 2(b) shows the regression coefficients for age. For the unnormalized data, the age coefficient is 2.0 indicating that as age increases, the first formant increases two times. However, this regression is not statistically significant. For the vocal tract length estimate, the age coefficient increases to 2.5, significant at the .05 level. This means that the normalization produces not only the clustering desired, as indicated in the decreased standard deviations, but a clustering in which the individual speakers are ranked more closely by age as predicted. A similar effect is evident for the log mean normalization, and the revealed age grading is slightly stronger. For the six-parameter regression, however, while clustering is enhanced as indicated by the decrease in standard deviations, the age grading, though better than the unnormalized versions, is not as good as the single-scale factor normalizations. That is, the normalization has normalized away some of the variation we are interested in.

A second set of data comes from a random survey of the Philadelphia community encompassing 60 speakers. The survey is a brief, formal telephone questionnaire designed to give a representation of all phoneme classes, in addition to other sociolinguistic variables. These 60 speakers were analyzed acoustically, and the nuclei of the vowel phonemes measured, as for the neighborhood study. The telephone has properties which present some special problems for normalization. The frequency range is limited, and as a result, the third formant is often missing for speakers with small vocal tracts. Thus, the estimation of the vocal tract length by

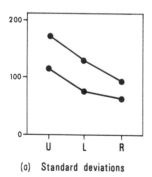

(a) Standard deviations

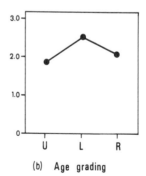

(b) Age grading

Figure 3. Normalization procedures for telephone survey for /ay°/, 60 speakers. U = unnormalized; T = vocal tract length estimate normalization; L = log mean normalization; R = regression normalization.

mean third formant is precluded. Nevertheless, the first two formants are clear, and acoustic analysis can be successfully accomplished.

The two normalization methods, log mean and regression, were performed on these 60 speakers, with results similar to the neighborhood study. Figure 3(a) shows the standard deviations as measures of increased clustering in /ay°/. As in the neighborhood study, the normalizations produce increased clustering. Figure 3(b) shows the age grading revealed for /ay°/ by the same measure used above. Here the age coefficient for the unnormalized data is significant at the .05 level, but both normalizations produce age grading significant at the .01 level. Again, we see that the expected age grading peaks for the log mean normalization, and is reduced for the regression normalization.

CONCLUSION

Thus, while the clustering produced by the single-scale factor normalizations is by no means perfect, the fact that they reveal known social differentiation more clearly than either the unnormalized version or the six-parameter regression version is strong evidence for their usefulness. In continuing the investigation of normalization techniques, transformations other than by a single-scale factor may be found to be more useful, but any procedure will have to be evaluated in terms of its effect on socially significant differentiation.

REFERENCES

Fant, G. A note on vocal tract size factors and non-uniform F-pattern scalings. *Speech Transmission Laboratory-Quarterly Progress and Status Report,* 1966, *4,* 22–30. Stockholm: Royal Institute of Technology.

Fant, G. Non-uniform vowel normalization. *Speech Transmission Laboratory-Quarterly Progress and Status Report,* 1975, *2*(3), 1–19. Stockholm: Royal Institute of Technology.

Labov, W., Yaeger, M., & Steiner, R. *A quantitative study of sound change in progress.* Philadelphia: U. S. Regional Survey, 1972.

Nearey, T. M. Phonetic feature systems for vowels. Unpublished Ph.D. dissertation, University of Connecticut, 1977.

Nordström, P.-E. Female and infant vocal tracts simulated from male area functions. *Journal of Phonetics,* 1977, *5,* 81–92.

Nordström, P.-E., Lindblom, B. A normalization procedure for vowel formant data. In *Proceedings of the 8th International Congress of Phonetic Sciences,* Leeds, forthcoming.

Peterson, G. & Barney, H. Control methods used in a study of vowels. *Journal of the Acoustical Society of America,* 1952, *24,* 175–184.

Sankoff, D., Shorrock, R. W., & McKay, W. Normalization of formant space through the least squares affine transformation. Unpublished program and documentation, 1974.

Wakita, H. An approach to vowel normalization. Paper presented at the 89th meeting of the Acoustical Society of America, 1975.

Weinreich, U., Labov, W., & Herzog, M. Empirical foundations for a theory of language change. In W. P. Lehman & Y. Malkiel (Eds.), *Directions for historical linguistics.* Austin: University of Texas Press, 1968, 97–195.

Yaeger, M. Speaking style: Some phonetic realizations and their significance. *Pennsylvania Working Papers on Linguistic Change and Variation I-1.* Philadelphia: U.S. Regional Survey, 1975.

13

Diphthongization in Montreal French

Laurent Santerre / Jean Millo

THE PHONOLOGICAL SYSTEM OF QUEBEC FRENCH

The phonological system of Quebec French includes pairs of vowels which contrast with respect to length and quality (Santerre, 1974); they are as follows:

Short		Long	
/ɛ/	*faite, mettre*	/ɜ/	*fête, maître*
/a/	*patte, tache*	/ɑ/	*pâte, tâche*
/ɔ/	*notre, votre, coq, cote*	/o/	*nôtre, vôtre, coke, côte*
/œ/	*jeune, veulent*	/ø/	*jeûne, émeute*

Long vowels have diphthongized variants. Short vowels can also have the same diphthongized variants as the corresponding long vowels, when lengthened by following /ʀ/:

fer [fa^{e}ʀ]   *l'or* [lɔ^{u}ʀ]
l'art [lɑ^{o}ʀ]   *l'heure* [la^{ø}ʀ].

All stressed /a/s change to [ɑ] in word final position or before a word final /ʀ/.

(1) $/a/{\to}[\alpha]/{-}\begin{Bmatrix} \# \\ R\# \end{Bmatrix}$, except if /w—

Canada	[kanadɑ]
part	[pɑʀ]
par	[paʀ]
mois	/mwɑ/ → [mwɑ]
soir	[swaʀ] → [swɛʀ]
moi	/mwa/ → [mwa] ~ [mwɛ].

All short vowels change with respect to length and quality before /z/; short vowels are lengthened when followed by /v/, but their quality is not altered since /v/ has an extrabuccal point of articulation.

$$\textit{rêve} \quad /R3v/ \to [Ra^e v]$$
$$\textit{lève} \quad /\text{lɛv}] \to [\text{lɛ:v}] *[\text{la}^e\text{v}]$$

All the /ɛ/s have been changed to /з/ when followed by /ʒ/; on the other hand, the quality of /ɔ/ has not been altered by the same lengthening: for example, *horloge* /ɔʀlɔʒ/ *[ɔʀlɔ°ʒ].

The a/ɑ opposition remains when these vowels are followed by /ʒ/: for example, *étage* /etaʒ/, *l'âge* /lɑʒ/; we observe, however, a strong tendency for /a/ to become [ɑ] before /ʀ/ as in rule (1). Diphthongization is possible once the /ɑ/ quality has been reached: for example, *voyage* /vwajaʒ/ → [vwajɑʒ] → [vwajɑ^{u}ʒ].

We transcribed and counted the diphthongs of /з/ and /ɛ/ together, and studied separately the diphthongs of each of /ɑ/, /o/, /ø/, /œʀ/, /ɔʀ/, /wa/, and /aʒ/. In examining oral vowels we excluded high vowels which do not present diphthongized variants but only a variation in quality, as in *rire* /ʀiʀ/ → [ʀi^{i}ʀ], for example.

THE SPEAKERS

We selected 32 tapes of 30 minutes each from the Sankoff–Cedergren corpus (Sankoff & G. Sankoff, 1973); the speakers are divided equally according to sex, two age groups (30 years and under and 40 years and over) and two language levels corresponding roughly to working class and middle class speakers. The working class group includes secretaries, laborers, some students, and some unemployed men. The middle class group consists of professionals, wives of professionals, actors and university graduate students, and one exceptional woman in her fifties, neither highly educated nor from a middle class milieu, but who speaks what is clearly a cultivated variety of French.

THE TREATMENT OF THE CORPUS

The first 10 minutes of each one of the 32 recordings were first transcribed phonetically by a team of five linguistics students, corrected by another team of three students, then rechecked and recorrected at least twice; the next 20 minutes were transcribed by one of the students who had participated in the first stage and checked by two phoneticians who had also participated in the transcription of the first 10 minutes of each recording. Hundreds of spectograms were made in order to establish the acoustic parameters which aid the ear in determining the nature and the range of the diphthong. We did not succeed, however, in accounting for the auditory recognition of diphthongs in terms only of changes in the formants. Thus, in the course of the transcription, unless there was unequivocal instrumental proof to the contrary, we relied on the auditory evidence. Our results then are based on a very detailed phonetic transcription (Santerre, 1976).

Inherent in this kind of transcription is the difficulty in distinguishing among a large number of closely related variants. In this chapter, however, we have grouped many variants together in order to have statistically meaningful amounts of data which will be pertinent to the perceptual impressions of the inattentive listener. The average Montreal French speaker who is unaware of the diphthongization phenomenon in his language would find our percentages excessive; we believe in fact that although these results are meaningful as objective measurements under laboratory conditions they do not necessarily have implications for subjective impressions in everyday conversation. Our treatment classifies the diphthongs separately according to three types of stress: The first type is found at the end of a syntactic group or in word-final position followed by a pause (*une grosse tête*); the second type falls in word-final position within a syntactic group (*une tête folle*); and the third type is found word internally (*entêté*).

OVERALL RATES OF DIPHTHONGIZATION

Table 1 depicts overall tendencies for diphthongization of the various phonemes in the three stress environments while Table 2 presents a breakdown by speaker category.

Among working class speakers, men and women diphthongize to the same extent, whereas among middle class speakers women diphthongize slightly more than men. Although these results may seem surprising, they are clearly confirmed by the data. This phenomenon is not recent since

TABLE 1

Number of Diphthongs per Total Occurrence of Each Phoneme and Relative
Frequency for Each Stress Type

Phoneme	Stress 1		Stress 2		Stress 3		Total	
ø	18/65	(.28)	0/11	(0)	0/12	(0)	18/88	(.20)
œʀ	405/829	(.49)	22/479	(.05)	0/76	(0)	427/1384	(.31)
з	1514/2811	(.54)	293/1844	(.16)	14/428	(.03)	1821/5083	(.36)
aʒ	56/239	(.23)	8/26	(.31)	0/97	(0)	64/362	(.18)
wa	150/466	(.32)	45/432	(.10)	1/44	(.02)	196/942	(.21)
ɑ	282/612	(.46)	50/322	(.16)	22/475	(.05)	354/1409	(.25)
ɔʀ	209/631	(.33)	20/482	(.04)	0/164	(0)	229/1277	(.18)
o	366/1173	(.31)	18/558	(.03)	0/390	(0)	384/2121	(.18)
Total	3000/6826	(.44)	456/4154	(.11)	37/1686	(.02)	3493/12666	(.28)

women are usually conservative about their language and are unaware of
the fact that they diphthongize high vowels. Note as well that young
middle class speakers diphthongize less than their elders.

THE VARIANTS

In Figure 1, note that there are variants of /ɑ/ with both [ɑ] and [a] as
nuclei. This stems from the fact that some [ɑ]s have an underlying
phonological form /a/ and change to [ɑ] in environments where poste-

TABLE 2

Number of Diphthongs per Stress 1 Occurrences of Each Phoneme, and
Relative Frequency by Language Level, Age, and Sex

	Working class	Middle class	Total
Young	1309/1892 (.69)	342/1836 (.19)	1651/3728 (.44)
Old	975/1469 (.66)	374/1629 (.23)	1349/3098 (.44)
Women	1304/1921 (.68)	407/1789 (.24)	1711/3710 (.46)
Men	980/1440 (.68)	309/1676 (.18)	1289/3116 (.41)
Total	2284/3361 (.68)	716/3465 (.21)	3000/6826 (.44)

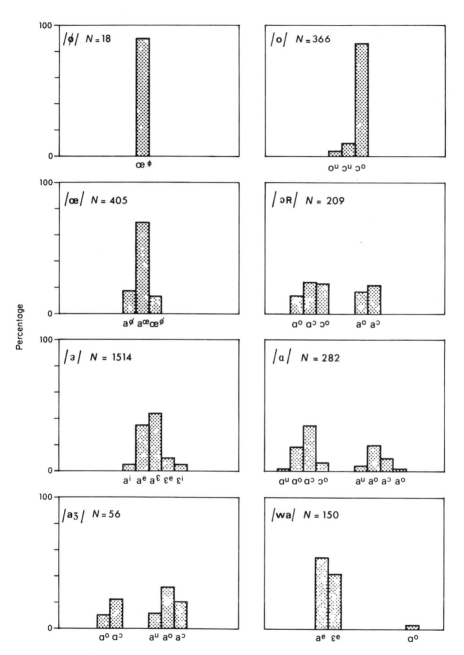

Figure 1. Principal diphthongized variants of each phoneme.

riorization rule (1) applies, giving rise to the occasional fronting of /ɑ/s to [a] in environments where (1) cannot have applied. This same reasoning explains the variants of /ɔʀ/, since in Montreal French the quality and the length of /ɔ/ and /ɑ/ followed by /ʀ#/ are exactly the same: There is no difference in the pronunciation of *tort* and *tard*. As for /aʒ/ in working class speech the most frequent words evidence a tendency toward posteriorization, but usage varies even for individual speakers, sometimes even for the same words, depending upon the stylistic situation. For /wa/ we find some posterior diphthongization when followed by /ʀ/: for example, *soir* /swaʀ/ → [swaᵉʀ] ~ [swɑᵓʀ].

SPEAKER GROUPS AND INDIVIDUAL VOWEL
DIPHTHONGIZATION RATES

As seen in Figure 2, working class speakers generally diphthongize more than middle class speakers. We notice that they diphthongize the low vowels more than the high ones. Furthermore, the diphthongization of /aʒ/ is a characteristic of working class speakers only.

The older working class speakers differentiate more between the long low vowels and the phonetically lengthened low vowels. The same older working class speakers diphthongize the /o/ much less than their younger counterparts, and this difference in age carries over to the middle class

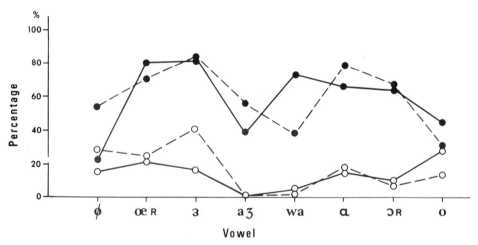

Figure 2. Diphthongization percentages for young (———●———) and old (---●---) working class speakers and young (———○———) and old (---○---) middle class speakers under Stress 1.

group as well. Taking into account the small number of tokens for /ø/ and /aʒ/, we can conclude from Figure 2 that diphthongization is slightly in progress among the working class speakers and that it is regressing except for /o/ among middle class speakers.

In Figure 3, we note that the diphthongization of /aʒ/ which is a characteristic of working class speech is used more often by men than women. Women are known to be more careful about their language than men, but this does not prevent a higher rate of diphthongization for certain vowels. Note that diphthongization is due not to laxness of articulation, but rather to a greater expenditure of energy. Montreal French speakers can be heard correcting themselves when, after having initially pronounced [meʀ], they pronounce distinctly the diphthongized form [maeʀ], which is stylistically perceived as being fancier by working class speakers.

In the next section we will examine in more detail the differential behavior of our age, sex, and class groups with respect to diphthong variant choice.

A CLOSER LOOK AT VARIANT PREFERENCES

Table 3 shows that the variant involving the larger change of quality [ae] is the one most used by working class speakers (40.1%). The middle class speakers (64.4%) use mostly the variant with the lesser change of quality

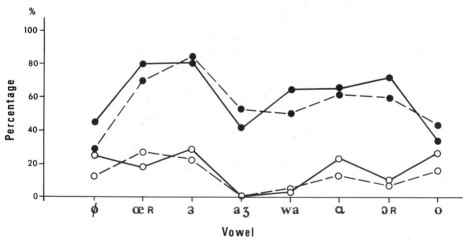

Figure 3. Diphthongization percentages for women (————●————) and men (---●---) working class speakers, and women (————○————) and men (---○---) middle class speakers under Stress 1.

TABLE 3

Most Frequent Variants of /ɜ/, as Percentages of Total Diphthongs

| | Working class | | | Middle class | | |
	a^e	a^ε	Total diphthongs	a^e	a^ε	Total diphthongs
Young	33.6	43.7	631	9.1	81.7	142
Old	48.3	30.7	501	28.7	54.2	240
Women	40.6	33.4	625	27.9	60.5	215
Men	39.4	43.6	507	13.2	72.4	167
Total	40.1	38.0	1132	21.3	64.4	382

[a^ε]. Within the working class it is only the older speakers who favor the larger range variant, the younger ones preferring the smaller one. Among the middle class speakers, the small range variant is used by both the old and, overwhelmingly, the young speakers. We also observe that even if diphthongization were to disappear with time, the long /ɜ/ could remain low, since the articulation of its two variants begins with /a/; the smaller range variant is achieved by a lesser closure at the end of the diphthong.

In comparing men and women among the working class speakers, we observe that women prefer the larger range variant (40.6% for [a^e] against 33.4% for [a^ε]), while men favor the smaller range variants [a^ε] (43.6% of the diphthongizations). Among the middle class speakers women as well as men prefer using the smaller range variant, though the difference in rates is maintained.

We conclude that the young male working class speakers will impose their pronunciation of the /ɜ/. Women behave in the same way as older speakers.

Turning to the diphthongized forms of /œ/, we see in Table 4 that the reduced form [$a^œ$] is becoming more and more important. The distribution of allophones is more scattered with the older working class speakers. Middle class women use the reduced form in 92.9% of the cases; they are probably not aware that they are diphthongizing the vowel.

We notice that this articulation begins with a larger aperture before reaching the [œ].

In Table 5, we see that the reduced form [ɔ°] is the most frequent one for all the groups in the sample. The target /o/ is reached only after articulation has passed a stage of larger aperture.

TABLE 4

Most Frequent Variants of /œ /, as Percentages of Total Diphthongs

	Working class				Middle class			
	$a^{\emptyset}$	$a^{œ}$	$œ^{\emptyset}$	Total diphthongs	$a^{\emptyset}$	$a^{œ}$	$œ^{\emptyset}$	Total diphthongs
Young	16.7	72.2	10.0	180	11.8	78.4	9.8	51
Old	26.2	54.0	18.2	126	4.2	83.3	12.5	48
Women	20.5	65.8	12.1	190	2.4	92.9	4.8	42
Men	20.7	62.9	15.5	116	12.3	71.9	15.8	57
Total	20.5	64.7	13.4	306	8.1	80.9	11.1	99

From Table 6, we can affirm that the young speakers of both middle and working classes use the reduced form [$\alpha^{ɔ}$] more than any other allophone of /ɑ/, a tendency more noticeable for men than for women. The target /ɑ/ is reached first, followed by overshooting the closure of the articulation.

We present no detailed results on the allophones of /ɔʀ/ since their distribution is rather scattered. The highest percentage of use by working class speakers is only 26.7% in the case of [ɔ°ʀ]. The scattering seems to result from the fact that ʀ causes posteriorization of /a/s and the assimilation of [ɑ] to [ɔ].

TABLE 5

Most Frequent Variants of /o/, as Percentages of Total Diphthongs

	Working class			Middle class		
	$ɔ^{u}$	$ɔ^{o}$	Total diphthongs	$ɔ^{u}$	$ɔ^{o}$	Total diphthongs
Young	13.7	81.4	161	0	94.5	91
Old	14.8	80.2	81	9.1	81.8	33
Women	16.5	77.9	127	2.6	94.8	77
Men	11.3	84.3	115	2.1	85.1	47
Total	14.0	80.9	242	2.4	91.2	124

TABLE 6

Most Frequent Variants of /ɑ /, as Percentages of Total Diphthongs

	Working class					Middle class				
	$ɑ^o$	$ɑ^ɔ$	a^o	$a^ɔ$	Total diphthongs	$ɑ^o$	$ɑ^ɔ$	a^o	$a^ɔ$	Total diphthongs
Young	21.1	40.3	17.4	9.2	109	16.1	41.9	12.9	9.7	31
Old	19.0	27.6	24.1	3.4	116	11.5	38.5	19.2	3.8	26
Women	20.8	33.3	20.0	1.5	120	17.5	27.5	20.0	5.0	40
Men	19.0	34.3	21.9	11.4	105	5.9	70.6	5.9	11.8	17
Total	20.0	33.8	20.9	6.2	225	14.0	40.4	15.8	7.0	57

The reduced form [wa^ɛ] is overshadowed by the extended form [wa^e] at least for the working class speakers and even more so for women (see Table 7).

For the middle class speakers the data are sparse. They suggest that young speakers, in contrast to the older speakers, use the extended form. Note that the pronunciation of *moi, toi* [mwe,twe] is in current use, though in this chapter, we focus only on closed syllables (ending in a consonant); in fact closure of the vowel is a necessary condition for diphthongization in Quebec French.

For /aʒ/, the most frequent allophone is [a^{o}ʒ] (34% for young working class speakers and 29.2% for old working class speakers). The second

TABLE 7

Most Frequent Variants of /wa/, as Percentages of Total Diphthongs

	Working class			Middle class		
	wa^e	$wa^ɛ$	Total diphthongs	wa^e	$wa^ɛ$	Total diphthongs
Young	47.6	39.8	103	66.6	0	6
Old	57.9	34.2	38	0	66.6	3
Women	60.9	32.6	92	50.0	25.0	4
Men	30.6	49.0	49	40.0	20.0	5
Total	50.4	38.3	141	44.4	22.2	9

most frequent is [ɑᵓʒ] (21.9% for the young speakers and 16.7% for the old speakers).

Diphthongization of /aʒ/ does not seem to occur among the young or the old middle class speakers.

All the words involved end with /aʒ/, except for *âge* /ɑʒ/. To diphthongize, the /a/ must change to [ɑ], which explains why there are allophones beginning both with [a] and with [ɑ].

The most frequent allophone of /ø/ in our data is [œᵊ] (90% for the working class and the middle class speakers). The number of diphthongs is too small to distinguish the tendencies of different age and sex groups.

SUMMARY AND CONCLUSIONS

1. Working class speakers diphthongize Stress 1 vowels at an overall rate of 68%, while middle class speakers diphthongize in 21% of the cases. Among the latter, the young speakers diphthongize less (19%) than the older speakers (23%), and women diphthongize more (24%) than men (18%). Hence, middle class women tend to behave like older speakers with respect to this aspect of Montreal French.

2. The diphthongization of /aʒ/ is a characteristic of working class speech only.

3. The highest rates of diphthongization occur for /ɜ/, lengthened /œ/, and /ɑ/.

4. The intensity and duration concomitant to Stress 1 affect the rate of diphthongization considerably since the total percentage of vowels diphthongized drops from 43.9% under Stress 1 to 10.9% under Stress 2. This could not be so if diphthongization were conditioned solely by the surrounding phonological segments.

5. For the different vowels, the allophones occurring most frequently are:

/ɜ/	:[aᵋ]	44%
/œ/	:[aᵒᵉ]	69%
/o/	:[ɔᵒ]	86%
/ɑ/	:[ɑᵓ]	35%
/ɔʀ/	:[ɔᵒʀ]	24%
/aʒ/	:[aᵒʒ]	32%
/wa/	:[waᵉ]	55%
/ø/	:[œᵊ]	90%

We notice great variation not only in rates of diphthongization of the phonemes, but also in which allophones are used.

6. Except in the case of [aᵒʒ] and [waᵉ], the most reduced forms are the most frequently used.

7. For the majority of the population, which corresponds to our working class group, it can be affirmed that diphthongization is not decreasing; but it appears to have been checked among the middle class. When we look at individual types of diphthongization, there is an indication in some cases of a reduction in the degree of diphthongization.

8. The same general articulatory pattern applies for all diphthongs: There is always an overshooting of the phonological target whenever further opening is allowable (for all vowels except /ɑ/), after which the target is reached, often followed by some degree of closure. This model cannot be used for vowels in open syllables (i.e., not closed by a consonant).

REFERENCES

Sankoff, D., & Sankoff, G. Sample survey methods and computer assisted analysis in the study of grammatical variation. In R. Darnell (Ed.), *Canadian languages in their social context*. Edmonton: Linguistic Research, Inc., 1973, 7–64.

Santerre, L. Deux E et deux A phonologiques en français québécois. Etude phonologique, articulatoire et acoustique des oppositions de timbre et de durée. *Cahiers de linguistique de L'Université du Québec*, 1974, *4*, 117–146.

Santerre, L. Les diphtongues dans le français québécois. In M. Boudreault & F. Möhren (Eds.), *Actes du XIIIᵉ Congrès international de linguistique et philologie romanes*, Québec: Les Presses de L'Université de Laval, 1976, 1183–1199.

14

The Relation between Oral and Written Comprehension[1]

Stanley E. Legum / Kong-On Kim / Harvey Rosenbaum

INTRODUCTION

In this study we ask what effect partial mastery of the alphabetic system has on comprehension of the written language. In other words, how much of the orthographic system needs to be mastered before written comprehension comes to approximate oral comprehension? In studying these questions we have also had to investigate the nature of oral comprehension among English-speaking elementary school children.

PARTICIPANTS AND PROCEDURES

In a study of 391 children from grades 1 to 7 of Southern California elementary schools, we studied the acquisition of 15 decoding skills (e.g., letter recognition, consonant clusters, short vowels, and long vowels) and 30 syntactic and semantic constructions.[2] We hypothesized that good

[1]Portions of this work were conducted pursuant to Contract NE-C-00-3-0064 with the National Institute of Education, Department of Health, Education and Welfare.
[2]These were chosen to sample most of the decoding tasks and most types of complex syntax.

decoders would be able to comprehend simple to moderately complex sentences equally well in both the written and oral modes. To test this hypothesis, we first tested all students' written comprehension. Six months later we retested children who were apparent counterexamples to the hypothesis, that is, children who did well on our decoding measures and relatively poorly on at least some of our comprehension measures. These children were first tested on their oral comprehension on a subset of the same or similar material as they had originally received, and several days later were retested on the same material in written form.

MATERIALS

Rather than give a detailed description of all 45 subtests, we will simply name the areas we tested and present a general summary of our testing procedures. All our test items are multiple choice with either two or three alternatives to choose among. Subtest criteria are set so that there is a less than 5% chance of passing by answering randomly. For example, the criterion is seven out of eight items for the two-choice tasks and six out of eight on the three-choice tasks. Each of the decoding subtests consisted of eight items, samples of which are given in Figure 1.

The letter recognition task involved the matching of upper and lower case letters, a task that correlates well with letter naming ability. The decoding tasks for consonants and vowels in monosyllabic words require the child to choose one of three real words that represents a pictured object. The distractors form minimal or near minimal pairs with the correct answer and with each other. The ability to divide compound words, the ability to recognize roots and affixes, the ability to determine the full form of contractions, and the ability to identify stress-determined pronunciation differences were tested by similar items with real words or sentences replacing the pictures.

The six easiest comprehension subtests dealt with the dimensional adjective pairs, *big–small, high–low, long–short, wide–narrow,* and *thick–thin.* All of these subtests were of the same form: Eight pairs of numbered pictures and a question such as *Is car 1 big or small?* or *Which car is big?* (see Figure 2). Two subtests measuring comprehension of *if* and *unless* each contained eight pictures of stars and commands of the form *If the star is not black, put an X in the box* (see Figure 3). The remaining 22 comprehension subtests all had the form of a sentence followed by a question and a set of possible answers. These tests included five measures of factive and implicative verbs, two measures of subjoined clauses, four measures of active and passive sentences, four measures of

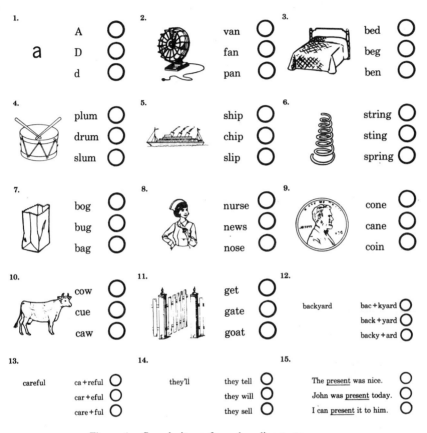

Figure 1. Sample items from decoding tests.
1. Letter recognition
2. Initial consonants
3. Final consonants
4. Consonant clusters (2 elements)
5. Consonant digraphs
6. Consonant clusters (3 elements)
7. Short vowels (CVC)
8. Vowel + *r*
9. Diphthongs
10. Vowels with multiple pronunciations
11. Long vowels (-e final)
12. Compound words
13. Affixes
14. Contractions
15. Stress governed pronunciations.

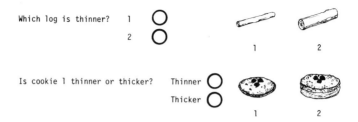

Which log is thinner? 1 ◯

                  2 ◯

                               1   2

Is cookie 1 thinner or thicker?   Thinner ◯

                            Thicker ◯

                               1   2

Figure 2. Sample from dimensional adjective test.

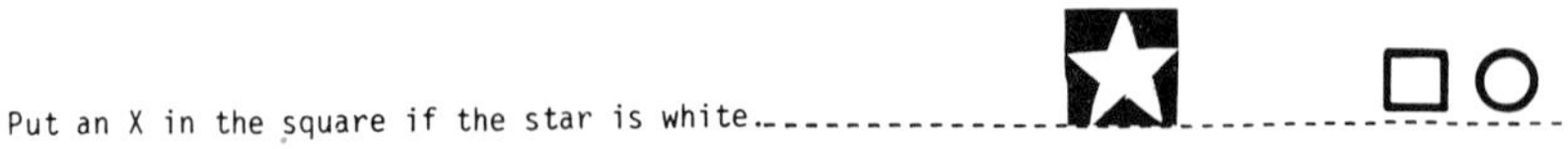

Put an X in the square if the star is white ------------ ★ ------------- ☐ ◯

Figure 3. Sample from *if* and *unless* test.

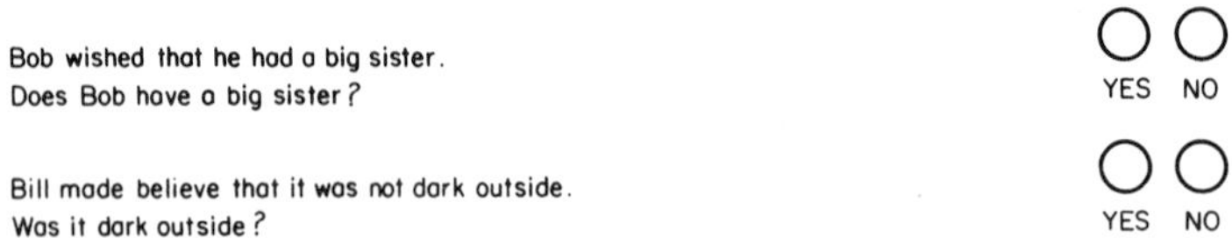

Bob wished that he had a big sister.   ◯ ◯
Does Bob have a big sister?   YES NO

Bill made believe that it was not dark outside.   ◯ ◯
Was it dark outside?   YES NO

Figure 4. Sample items from tests of factive and implicative verbs.

relative clauses, and seven measures of temporal connectors (*before, after, until, since, when,* and *while*). Figure 4 is a sample from the factive and implicative test booklet.

Not all tests were given at each grade level. The number of children in each grade taking each test is indicated in Table 1.

RESULTS

The following general results were obtained:

1. Three-quarters of the first graders and 97% of the second and third graders show no difficulty in recognizing the letters of the alphabet (see Table 2).

2. Consonants are still very difficult by the end of first grade with initial consonants in monosyllabic words being the only subcategory of consonants on which more than a third of the children reach criterion. By second and third grade consonants are of only minor difficulty. By the end of second grade only consonant digraphs and three-letter consonant clusters still present substantial difficulty, with 58 and 59% reaching criterion. By

TABLE 1
Number of Children Taking Each Test by Grade: Domain

Grade	Consonant	Vowel	Polysyllabic	If/Unless	Subjoined clauses	Active/ passive	Relative clauses	Temporal terms	Dimensional adjectives	Factive/ implicative
1	56	46	62	48	48	62	39	26	50	60
2	59	61	50	45	45	46	46	46	62	47
3	49	45	73	72	72	57	66	68	46	
4			9	54	54	53	53	53		
5										55
6							16			
7							49	56		53
Total	184	152	194	219	219	218	269	249	158	215

189

TABLE 2

Percentage Reaching Criterion on Letter Recognition and Consonant
Subtests by Grade

Grade	N	Letter[a] (1)	Initial (2)	Final (3)	2 Cluster (4)	Digraph (5)	3 Cluster (6)
1	56	73	68	34	16	9	4
2	59	97	95	86	81	58	59
3	49	98	94	90	96	82	80
Total	154	89	85	70	63	48	46

[a]Parenthentical numbers refer to sample items in Figure 1.

third grade, the oldest group taking the consonant test, 80% demonstrate
the ability to decode digraphs and three-letter consonant clusters, and 90
to 96% are able to decode initial consonants, final consonants, and two-
letter consonant clusters. In fact, 84% of the third grade children control
at least four of the five consonant subtests.

3. Vowels, however, are another matter, as can be seen from Table 3.
No more than 20% of the first graders we tested were able to reliably
decode any specific vowel subtest. In second grade the only vowel subtest
that more than half the children were able to decode was short vowels in
CVC monosyllabic words. Sixty-two to 80% of the third graders were able
to decode each of the vowel subtests.

4. Looking at the performance of individual second and third grade
children, we find an interesting result. As indicated in Table 4, 94% of the
children who can decode four or five of the vowel subtests can decode all
or all but one of the consonant subtests. Doing well on the consonant test
does not, however, predict how well a child will do on the vowel test.

5. Decoding four or more vowel types appears to be a necessary
condition for being able to comprehend simple written sentences. Tables 5

TABLE 3

Percentage Reaching Criterion on Each Vowel Subtest by Grade

Grade	N	CVC[a] (7)	Vr (8)	VV (9)	Mlt (10)	VCe (11)
1	46	13	20	15	11	13
2	61	65	41	44	48	36
3	45	78	80	71	62	69
Total	152	53	46	44	41	39

[a]Parenthetical numbers refer to sample items in Figure 1.

TABLE 4

Distribution of Second and Third Grade Children Reaching Criterion on
Vowel and Consonant Decoding Tests

		Number of vowel subtests on which criterion was reached					
		1	2	3	4	5	Total
Number of	0	0	0	1	0	0	1
consonant subtests	1	0	0	0	0	0	0
on which	2	0	0	0	0	0	0
criterion was reached	3	2	0	1	0	1	4
(including	4	6	2	0	2	0	10
letter recognition	5	1	4	7	2	4	18
subtest)	6	0	6	4	12	26	48
	Total	9	12	13	16	31	81

and 6 indicate the number of children reaching criterion on specific numbers of factive-implicative subtests by the number of vowel subtests on
which they reached criterion. Table 5 includes the second graders taking
both tests and Table 6 includes the third graders taking both tests. Almost
all third graders who reached criterion on any factive-implicative subtest
also reached criterion on all five vowel subtests. The results for second
graders are similar though less clear-cut.

6. Children who can decode all five vowel types seem to comprehend in
writing the same material that they can comprehend in speech. As one
indication of this, consider the following four contingency tables from the
oral and written retesting. Twelve second graders, eight third graders, and
six fourth graders are represented on these charts. Six months earlier all
the second and third grade children reached criterion on all five vowel
subtests and all the fourth grade children reached criterion on all four
polysyllabic subtests. These were not all the children who satisfied these
criteria, but rather, just those who seemed by inspection to be doing
poorly on the comprehension subtests when originally tested. In other
words, these are good decoders whose written comprehension appears to
be poorer than we know oral comprehension to be at these grade levels.

Tables 7 through 10 show matches between oral and written test scores
ranging from 58 to 92%. A number of the children in the two testings
reached criterion with a score of 7 on one test and missed criterion by a
score of 6 on the other. If we reclassify such children as matches, the

TABLE 5

Distribution of Second Grade Children Reaching Criterion on Vowel and
Factive-Implicative Subtest

		Number of vowel subtests on which criterion was reached						
		0	1	2	3	4	5	Total
Number of factive- implicative subtests on which criterion was reached	0	9	6	3	2	2	1	23
	1	1	0	0	0	1	0	2
	2	0	0	0	0	0	1	1
	3	0	0	0	1	0	1	2
	4	0	0	0	1	0	1	2
	5	0	0	1	1	0	1	3
	Total	10	6	4	5	3	5	33

agreement between the oral and written testing on these four subtests
ranges from 73 to 96%. Similarly, summing across the 13 different variables and 31 different speakers on which we have oral–written comparison data, we find that the oral and written data are the same 78.1% of the
time, the oral test scores are higher 13.8% of the time, and the written test
scores are higher 8.0% of the time.

TABLE 6

Distribution of Third Grade Children Reaching Criterion on Vowel and
Factive-Implicative Subtests

		Number of vowel subtests on which criterion was reached						
		0	1	2	3	4	5	Total
Number of factive- implicative subtests on which criterion was reached	0	2	1	1	0	4	1	9
	1	0	0	0	0	0	0	0
	2	0	0	0	0	0	0	0
	3	0	0	0	0	1	1	2
	4	0	0	0	0	0	2	2
	5	0	0	0	0	0	9	9
	Total	2	1	1	0	5	13	22

TABLE 7

Comparison of Oral and Written Comprehension of *If*

	Written		
	Reached criterion (7 or 8)	Random[a] (2 to 6)	Total
Oral Reached criterion (7-8)	22	3	25
Random[a] (2-6)	0	1	1
Total	22	4	26

[a]No children received scores of 0 or 1.

7. Large numbers of children appear to still be acquiring commonplace syntactic and semantic features as late as the seventh grade. This fact is illustrated by the data in Figure 5 on the written comprehension of relative clauses. We do not have decoding measures on any of the children in the fifth and seventh grades, so the possibility remains that what we are seeing here is the indirect effect of poor decoding skills. This seems unlikely because less than 30% of the seventh graders reached criterion on the SS (center embedded, subject relativized) relative clauses while twice

TABLE 8

Comparison of Oral and Written Comprehension of *Unless*

	Random[a] (2-6)	*Unless* treated to mean *if* (0-1)	Total
Oral Random (2-6)	6	5	11
Unless treated to mean *if* (0-1)	6	9	15
Total	12	14	26

[a]No children received scores of 7 or 8.

TABLE 9

Comparison of Oral and Written Comprehension of Single-Action Subjoining Complementizers

	Written		
	Reached criterion (7-8)	Random[a] (2-6)	Total
Oral			
Reached criterion (7-8)	24	2	26
Random (2-6)	0	0	0
Total	24	2	26

[a]No children received scores of 0 or 1.

TABLE 10

Comparison of Oral and Written Comprehension of Two-Action Subjoining Complementizers

	Written			
	Reached criterion (7-8)	Random (2-6)	Treated as single action (0-1)	Total
Oral				
Reached criterion (7-8)	1	0	0	1
Random (2-6)	0	2	4	6
Treated as single action (0-1)	0	4	15	19
Total	1	6	19	26

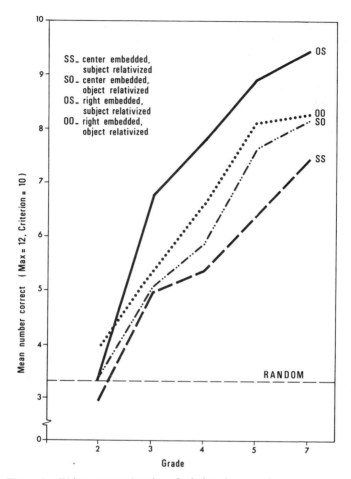

Figure 5. Written comprehension of relative clauses at five grade levels.

that number, almost 60%, reached criterion on the OS (right embedded, subject relativized) relatives.

CONCLUSION

We would like to emphasize the following points:

1. The critical factor in learning to read seems to be the range of vowel types that a child can decode.

2. Once a child has mastered the five types of vowels we measured, oral comprehension and written comprehension of sentences in isolation appear to covary.
3. A good deal of language acquisition, as measured by improvements in both written and oral comprehension, is still occurring at the end of elementary school.

15

How Do Babies Learn
Grammatical Categories?

John Macnamara

THE COGNITIVE AND THE LINGUISTIC

Benjamin Lee Whorf (1956, p. 215) claimed that Nootka, an Amerindian language of Vancouver Island, does not distinguish between nouns and verbs. He claimed further that this linguistic fact portrayed "a monistic view of nature," one in which there was no distinction between "temporary events" like actions and "longlasting and stable events" like objects. Thus, Whorf took the absence of a noun/verb distinction as evidence that Nootka Indians did not, as we do, distinguish in reality between objects and actions. I would like to claim, on the contrary, that in all languages one can refer to objects and be understood as referring to them.

To begin with, Whorf's claim is justified at the linguistic level—see Hockett (1958, p. 224). The basic division in Nootka is between stems which are inflected and those which are not. However, many stems when without inflection have "nounlike syntactical uses"; when certain inflections are added the same stems "are used syntactically in verblike ways [Hockett, 1958, p. 225]." Elsewhere Hockett (1963) remarks that Nootka shows "something very much like the noun/verb contrast." It is possible to refer to a man as an object, /qu'?as/. By adding the suffix /-ma/ the word acquires verblike functions. Closer to home, many English words can surface in different form classes. We can *police the house* or *house the police*. This does not in any way impair our ability to speak of either a house or a policeman as an object. And I do not see how a similar linguistic flexibility on the part of the Nootka Indians should impair theirs. The conclusion from these examples is well known: Linguistic arguments lead to linguistic conclusions, not to conclusions in cognitive psychology.

In this chapter I will discuss a number of matters relating to the parts of speech into which names fall. I will discuss modern definitions of **noun** and study their implication for the description of infant language learning. After all, the infant must come to place his words in the appropriate form classes and subclasses: nouns, verbs, adjectives, and the like. I will be particularly interested in possible connections between linguistic form classes and classes of physical objects. Any correspondences between the two would constitute an obvious advantage to the child. The chapter concludes with a discussion of three subdivisions of nouns: those based on gender in Indo-European languages; those based on classifiers in many languages; and finally the distinction between count and mass nouns, found in many languages including English.

NAMES AND NOUNS

Whorf's mistake was to equate the linguistic and the cognitive. It is true that in English we often use nouns when we refer to objects: *house, man, dog, cat.* We also use nouns for other purposes. We speak about *a walk, a talk,* which are activities; we speak about *the red* on a wall, which is an attribute; we speak about *the outside* and *the inside,* relational terms, and so on. English does not set up a one–one correspondence between nouns and objects.

The traditional definition of noun—"the name of a person, place, or thing"—leaked in several places. One found persons' names, like *Ford* and *Hoover,* which had become names for classes of objects. The Welsh are a group of people, but one can *welsh on* one's friends. *Canada* is the name of a place, yet it serves a function very like that of an adjective in such an expression as *Canada goose.* "Thing" in the definition was the leakiest of all; it embraced every word which was a noun and was not the name of a person or place. That made the definition vacuous. Modern linguistics confronts the circularity squarely and defines a noun as any word which fits into a noun slot in a sentence! It follows from this approach that: (*a*) The notion sentence is logically prior to noun, and (*b*) in effect the class "noun" effectively becomes an intuitively given one.

There is much to be said for this, because despite the lack of defining characteristics, there is surprisingly little disagreement on which words are nouns. Nouns are not all and only the two-syllable words of English, nor anything like that; the concept noun is a purely mental descriptor, yet one which is applied with great accuracy and stringency.

From the point of view of infant learning there may be some difficulty in making "sentence," a complex structure, logically prior to "noun." The difficulty would disappear if the notion sentence were innately given in its entirety, but it does not seem to be. In English, the description of sentence must include reference to noun. Yet there are languages (Nootka being one) which do not have nouns, or do not have any resembling English nouns; so they cannot have sentences like English sentences, though they do have some sort of sentences. All this leads us to conclude that nouns and sentences, like almost all mental structures, are the output of innate factors working on environmental input. There seems to be a strong innate tendency, though, to create a sentence structure which includes nouns.

Seeing that the notion, noun, involves some learning on the part of the child, can we suggest any strategy which he might employ? A likely one was proposed by Roger Brown (1957), although it might also have been suggested by the medieval doctrine of modes of meaning (see O'Mahony, 1964). The suggestion is simply that children are aided in learning the form classes, noun and verb, by the correlation with objects and actions, respectively. Brown examined the vocabularies of children aged about 4 or 5 years (investigating their sentence use) and found that their nouns referred more often than those of adults to concrete objects, like sticks and stones (as distinct from truth or justice). Their verbs referred more often than those of adults to actions. However, about 33% of the children's nouns did not name objects which have "a characteristic visual contour," and about 33% of their verbs did not name actions.

I have pursued this line of investigation in two directions: (a) by studying the vocabularies of adults and (b) by also studying the vocabularies of children who were much younger than those studied by Brown.

First the study of adults, which was carried out some time ago in Dublin and is reported here for the first time. The idea behind the experiment was that even for adults a noun tends to denote an object, whereas a verb tends to denote an action. A list of 40 words, chosen in no principled way, all of which could be either a noun or a verb, was shown to 72 adult English speakers who were simply asked to indicate with an N or a V whether the word struck them at first sight as a noun or as a verb. The hypothesis predicted that words like cup would be classed as nouns because cups are subsisting objects; on the other hand words like *run* would be classed as verbs because while one can speak of *a run*, the word does not usually refer to an object.

Table 1 compares the results of this experiment with those of West (1953), who specifies for the majority of the words on our list the relative frequency (for written English) with which each word occurred as a noun and as a verb. In the right-hand column the major grammatical classifications mentioned in *The Pocket Oxford Dictionary* are given in the order in which they appear. The first portion of the prediction is well confirmed: The first 10 words on the list, and 4 others, can denote a subsistent object, and all except *tug* were marked as nouns by a great majority of judges. The remaining 26 words do not denote subsistent entities, and all but 6 were marked as verbs. Of those 6, 4 denote relatively lasting bodily states: *fear, ache, lust,* and *thirst.* Two others fall into no obvious category: *comment* and *escape.* Subsequent work at McGill has revealed no strong tendency for bodily states to be classified as nouns rather than verbs, though it does bear out the main prediction that words which can be either nouns or verbs usually strike judges as nouns if they denote a subsisting object, as verbs if they refer to an activity. Moreover these judgments are relatively stable. The 72 original subjects were asked to judge the list of 40 words a second time, and the number who changed their minds was under 10 for most words, the highest being 22.

One judge suggested that the frequency with which the word is used as a noun or verb in speech or writing determines how it is classified in the experiment. Table 1 demonstrates that the explanation fits the data very well indeed. It is interesting to note how closely *The Pocket Oxford Dictionary* is consistent with the two other sources of information listing the category noun first in the same instances that the others do; likewise for the category verb. The single clear exception is *ache.*

In support of the frequency explanation is the fact, long known, that persons can accurately rank words in order of relative frequency of occurrence—cf. Howes (1954), Shapiro (1969), and Underwood (1966, p. 223). It would not be surprising if they, and the compilers of *The Pocket Oxford Dictionary,* were able to rank for frequency the grammatical categories in which a word is used. However, the frequency figures also stand in need of explanation; they explain nothing in and of themselves. My belief is that *cup* is used more frequently as a noun because there are subsisting entities denoted by that name, and that *run* is used more frequently as a verb because as a verb the word normally refers to an activity, not to a subsisting entity.

Weinreich (1966) wrote: "We intend the distinguishing feature of each major morpheme class, e.g. [+ Noun], to be taken as semantic in the full

TABLE 1

Classification of Words as Nouns and Verbs ($N = 72$)[a]

Word	First testing		West relative frequency (%)		Pocket Oxford Dictionary
	N	V	N	V	
arm	70	2	80	20	N/tr/int
back	76	5	72	28	N/tr
bed	72	0	100	0	N/tr
cup	72	0	95	5	N/tr
hand	71	1	94	6	N/tr
line	72	0	98	2	N/tr/int
pen	72	0	100(?)	0(?)	N/tr
point	46	26	70	30	N/tr/int
soap	72	0	97	3	N/tr/int
shoe	72	0	96	4	N/tr
act	35	37	68	32	N/tr/int
build	1	71	0	100	tr/int/N
call	15	59	7	93	int/tr/N
fear	58	14	52	48	N/int/tr
feed	4	68	19	81	tr/int/N
feel	6	66	2	98	tr/int/N
find	6	66	2	98	tr/N
hit	1	71	16	84	tr/int/N
kick	15	57	12	88	int/tr/N
look	3	69	12	88	int/tr/N
push	2	70	6	94	tr/int/N
read	0	72	1	99	tr/int/N
run	2	70	10	90	int/tr/N
save	0	72	0	100	tr/int/N
shave	9	63	22	78	tr/int/N
tug	10	62	-	-	tr/int/N
twist	4	68	22	78	tr/int/N
wash	1	71	10	90	tr/int/N
ache	62	10	16	84	int/N
blush	21	51	-	-	int/N
comment	37	35	-	-	N/int
cost	63	9	75	25	tr/N
escape	36	36	23	77	int/tr/N
harp	70	2	-	-	N/int
fall	16	5€	17	83	int/N
lust	65	7	-	-	N/int
rebel	62	10	-	-	N/int
struggle	28	44	67	33	int/N
thirst	62	10	100(?)	0(?)	N/int
tremble	3	69	17	83	int/N

[a] N = noun; V = verb; tr = transitive verb; int = intransitive verb.

sense of the word; more revealing names might be 'thingness' or 'substantiality'; 'quality' (for [+ Adjective]), and so on [pp. 432–433]." While this strikes one as an exaggerated claim, the work just reported shows that it is not without foundation. I now wish to ask whether a child would be helped if he were guided by the correlation between object and noun.

CHILDREN'S VOCABULARIES

To see if our hypothesis is sustained, I studied a number of the baby vocabularies that have been published in the last decade or so, suspecting that in the vocabularies of young children there are words that refer to objects and words that refer to actions, but no words that refer to both. Insofar as this can be tested from studying the vocabularies it appears to be true. Katherine Nelson (1973) provides the most comprehensive account, reporting the first 50 words from 18 children. She discovered no hint of a semantic crossover; no word referred now to an action, now to an object. She lists 114 different words under what she calls "general nominals," that is words which she judges as headed for (though not necessarily already belonging to) the form class noun as their primary linguistic category. All 114 words refer to subsisting entities. None was used by a child to refer to an action, and none referred to an unstable object like smoke or steam. Some of the objects referred to were due to disappear, like milk and juice, but even these are stable until one consumes them.

Among the first 50 words Nelson lists a small number which refer to or demand action: for example, *bye–bye, hi, please, up, out, go, want,* and *know*. Not one in and of itself refers to an object. Some are elliptical for *please do, pick up, take out,* and so on. In other words, the child has omitted the verb.

Braine's monograph (1976) warns us of the danger of self-deception in all of this. Nelson might in effect have divided babies' words into those referring to objects and those referring to actions. Why try to relate the two classes to syntactic form classes? Indeed, many of the words will end up in two or more form classes. We would agree that before the age of 2 years (and perhaps even later), there are no grounds in children's utterances for calling some words nouns and some verbs. Semantic categories, such as object and action names, are preferable. Nevertheless, were we to show Nelson's list of words to adults and ask them to indicate whether a word or expression (cf. the fuller versions of the elliptical action words) was primarily a noun or a verb, our results in the second section of this chapter indicate that they would make exactly the same division that Nelson does when she uses a semantic criterion.

At the two-word stages studied by Braine (1976) and by Bloom, Light-bown, and Hood (1975) the two classes of words will begin to separate from one another syntactically. Although, as Braine notes, the different positions of words have semantic correlates, we take word order as a syntactic matter, and see it as leading on toward more fully developed syntactic form classes.

Apart from Nelson (1973) we examined a number of sources: Brown, Fraser, and Bellugi (1964), Bloom (1970), Braine (1963), Gruber (1967), Menn (1976), and Nelson (1972). These studies present complete lists of babies' vocabularies, each containing about 50 words. There seem to be only two exceptions to the rule which relates objects to words that will function primarily as nouns and actions to words that will function primarily as verbs. Brown *et al.* include *jump* in their list of "nouns." Nelson (1972) gives *cookoo* as an action word. Both must be special uses, word games perhaps, in the children's world. Menn's study is particularly interesting because it lists 30 words which were understood by a 15½-month-old boy named Jacob. All the words fit the general rule. The other studies deal with words which the children actually said.

From what we can see of their vocabularies, then, babies make matters easier for themselves semantically and syntactically by generally confining words to a single function, and by using certain words to refer exclusively to objects while others refer exclusively to actions. On the assumption that their minds present the environment to them in two major categories, objects and events, we can begin to see how meaning can help children in forming the two major grammatical categories of their mother tongue. If that is the case, they may be guided by meaning in setting up these grammatical categories initially, and so in establishing the structure of a sentence. Once that is done, they can allow a greater flexibility at both the syntactic and semantic levels. They will be able to allow a single word to serve in several form classes and to relax the rule which relates nouns to objects and verbs to actions.

SUBDIVISIONS OF NOUNS

Many languages make linguistic subdivisions of nouns which the child must cope with. In this section I will discuss by way of illustration three such divisions: gender in Indo-European languages; classifiers (of nouns) as found in a great many languages; and count and mass nouns as found in

English as well as in many other languages worldwide. Not very much is known about acquisition in these connections, but we may make certain deductions based on phenomena intimately related to naming. A fourth distinction, that between proper and common nouns, has been dealt with elsewhere (Katz, Baker, & Macnamara 1974).

Gender

Many Indo-European languages like French, Spanish, and Irish, divide nouns into two classes, masculine and feminine. To these classes many like Latin and German add a third, neuter. Whatever the origin of these distinctions in Proto-Indo-European, the divisions are entirely linguistic today. That is, they do not relate in any convenient manner to any known cognitive or perceptual divisions of objects. Certainly the notions of masculinity and femininity will not carry the learner far. In French, for example, *homme* 'man' is masculine and *femme* 'woman' is feminine. But then *personne* 'person' which can refer to either sex is itself feminine. When we enter the asexual world of most objects, the terms masculine and feminine seem to be little more than fiction. *Pied* 'foot' is masculine, whereas *main* 'hand' is feminine. *Roc* 'outcrop of rock' is masculine, and *roche* 'rock' is feminine. To make matters worse, in German *fräulein* 'young woman' and *mädchen* 'girl' are both neuter. And as though it were the ultimate in perversion, in Irish *cailín* 'girl' is masculine. In the last three examples, the true nature of the distinction is revealed by the source of the gender in morphology. In German all words which end in -*lein* or in -*chen,* diminutive suffixes, are neuter; while in Irish all words which end in -*ín,* also a diminutive suffix, are masculine. The objects referred to make no difference.

The learner of such genders must rely on what linguistic clues he can and for the rest commit a prodigious amount of detail to memory. Tucker, Lambert, and Rigault (1977) studied the manner in which native French speakers set about the task. They composed a set of nonsense words which meet the phonological rules of French but do not exist per se as French words. To these they affixed examples of all the common endings of French words and asked young native speakers of French to tell them whether these words were masculine or feminine (by indicating whether they should be preceded by *le* or *la*). It was found that they had a very accurate appreciation of the correlation between ending and gender. Apparently, French children note carefully the regular covariations. When ending is no help they must simply learn, one by one, which words belong to which gender.

Classifiers

Many languages require nouns (and sometimes verbs) to be marked with classifiers. Of these the most important one refers to extendedness, and we will take it as our example. According to Friedrich (1970) the relevant factor which governs the choice of classifier is a semantic one, and it is the extendedness of an object in one, two, or three dimensions, not its overall shape.

First, consider a few examples drawn from a paper of Peter Denny (in press). In Ojibway, an Algonquian language, *makkakkōnss akāči— minak—at* is glossed as 'the box, it—three dimensional—is small'. There the classifier is *minak* which means significantly extended in three dimensions. Another example from the same language is: *napak-āpīk—at,* an expression referring to anything like a ribbon which Denny glosses as 'flat—two dimensional—it is'.

To exemplify how classifiers function in those languages, Denny (1976) cites the contrast which English speakers make between *who* and *which.* As relatives, *who* refers to humans and *which* to nonhumans. Actually both words come from the same root, but *-līc,* meaning 'like' was added to the root to form *which.* The early suffix, then, came to act much like a classifier signifying nonhuman.

Denny (in press) finds such classifiers indicating dimensionality in a wide variety of languages: Eskimo; the Athabascan languages, Chirichua Apache and Western Apache, Chipewyan and Koyukon; the Algonquian languages, Ojibway and Cree; Tzeltal (Mayan); Tarascan (Mexico); Bantu (Africa); Ponapean, Gilbertese, and Trukese (Pacific); Burmese; Malay; Iban; and Australian. This is quite impressive evidence for a universal in the visual representation of objects, a universal which is so important in many cultures that it gives rise to a set of linguistic markers. Presumably, the child's cognitive representation of objects guides him in learning the appropriate classifiers for his language. Such classifiers, then, present a sharp contrast to gender in Indo-European which, typically, is without semantic classificatory force.

Count/Mass

A very common distinction among nouns across the world's languages is that between count and mass. English makes it, and so it is easy to illustrate. Words like *cup, spoon,* and *hand* are commonly called count nouns; we say *a cup, several cups, ten cups.* Words like *milk* and *porridge* are called mass nouns; one does not usually speak about *a porridge* or *ten porridges*. At first sight, then, it seems that the distinction can be made on syntactic grounds. As a first approximation one might say that nouns which occur in the plural are count; those which do not are mass. However, there are such words as *oats* which is plural; but it gives evidence of being mass, because it does not normally permit of the singular. Contrast it with *wheat*, which does permit of the plural, normally. *Oats* is one of those special forms called *pluralia tantum* (plural only). On the other hand we find that even the clearest examples of mass nouns can be used in the plural in special circumstances. One can imagine a waiter telling the kitchen: "Three milks and two porridges." The same is true of every mass noun in the language. The opposite is true of words that pass as strong count nouns. Take *books* and *shelves;* when used in the plural they are clearly count nouns. Yet one can imagine a philistine discussing their respective merit as fuel for a fire and saying: "You should always mix a little shelf with book." And again the same is true of all the count nouns in the language. Indeed Gleason (1965) makes just this point. He goes on to argue that the basis for the distinction is not semantic, instancing *gravel* (mass) as opposed to *pebbles* (count). "Pebbles are no more countable than gravel. . . . It is simply a convention of English that *pebble* is a count noun, usually plural, whereas *gravel* is a mass noun [p. 135]."

I would like to argue that the distinction is semantic: that count nouns name things which have a characteristic form, and mass nouns do not. If a substance is referred to in such a manner that it is given a characteristic form, its name becomes a count noun. Hence, *milks* and *porridges* because they mean *glasses of milk* and *bowls of porridge*. On the other hand when things are referred to in such a manner that their characteristic form is either irrelevant or misleading, their names become count nouns. Hence when referred to as fuel we can get, *you should add a little shelf to book*. Gleason's counterexamples can very easily be seen to fit these rules. Gravel consists of pebbles, but gravel has no characteristic form, while pebbles do. However, one can imagine a truck driver saying: "I delivered two gravels this morning," meaning loads of gravel. On the other hand one could imagine a man who ground rocks for some chemical enterprise saying: "Slate does not yield as good a product as pebble."

"Nothing is perfect," says the philosopher in the *Crock of Gold*, "the porridge has lumps in it." So it is with the thesis I am propounding. It seems to account for most uses. Yet certain words which are normally mass nouns can become count nouns, though no characteristic form is intended. If a scientist speaks of *wheats* he most probably means varieties of wheat. But this is not a very large lump. It merely means that an appropriate rider should be attached to the general rule, to the effect that the plural of a mass noun signifies variety when no characteristic form or container is intended. There will have to be other riders to indicate such facts as that nouns which refer to something which cannot possibly be given a characteristic shape, like justice, honor, and love (unless it means persons loved), will always be mass nouns. Truth is a formless thing; *truths* refers to statements which are true, and they have a characteristic form when made either orally or in writing.

From all this it seems that the mass/count distinction is basically a semantic one, and rather similar to the dimensionality distinctions of which Denny (in press) speaks. Denny's dimensionality classifiers make subdivisions of characteristic shapes; the count/mass distinction indicates whether or not there is a characteristic shape (or form if it is sound). Grammatical distinctions which map onto semantic ones are relatively easy for a child to learn, probably. The two systems support each other.

There is a study of Roger Brown's (1957) which shows that young children spot the covariation of semantics and linguistics related to count and mass nouns. He tested 16 children in preschool between the ages 4 and 6 years, showing each child several sets of pictures. In one set the first picture showed a pair of hands kneading (action) a formless substance like spaghetti (mass) in a colored vessel (count). Each of the other three pictures in that set illustrated one of the three features: the hands kneading, the spaghettilike substance, or the container; it did not show the other two features. Brown then selected some nonsense words with which to describe the pictures and said to a child, for example: "Do you know what it is to sib? In this picture (No. 1) you see sibbing. Now show me another picture of sibbing." If he was testing a count noun, the question was "Do you know what a sib is?" and went on appropriately. For a mass noun he began: "Have you ever seen any sib?" and continued accordingly. Naturally each child was not tested twice with the same nonsense word.

The contrast between noun and verb was quite evident. Of the 15 responses for verbs, 10 revealed that the child had fastened on the action; of the 29 responses for nouns, 28 indicated that the child had selected an object rather than an action. The contrast between count and mass nouns was just as marked. With a count-noun probe, 11 of the 14 responses chose the appropriate picture; with a mass-noun probe, 12 of the 15 responses did likewise. There were a small number of "no responses." The differences in response frequencies were statistically significant.

These results indicate that the children were sensitive to the semantic differences between verbs, count nouns, and mass nouns. They were relatively senior children, the youngest being 4 years. We suspect that at a much earlier age these children had noticed the differences and used them to learn the appropriate syntactic signaling. In Nelson's (1973) study cited earlier 94 of the 114 "nominals" are words that refer to substances that have a characteristic form while 16 are not. Four are ambiguous. Thus the great majority of these words will end up functioning primarily as count nouns. Yet some very common words in baby talk, like *water, butter,* and *meat,* will end up functioning primarily as mass nouns. So the child is familiar with objects and words for objects which will lead him to the mass/count distinction from his earliest beginnings in language. I believe that his knowledge of the objects referred to will help to guide him to the associated linguistic rules.

SUMMARY

What does all this add up to? I have drawn attention to the fact that children must not only learn words for things but they must assign those words to syntactic categories. There are probably some universal properties of mind involved, because every language provides means for referring to objects. But the properties are likely to be general and abstract. Even the form class, noun, is not found in every language. And while these are undoubtedly objects which receive a name in every language, the number is not large. The general properties of mind, then, are likely to be like this: Expect that the words you hear will fall into classes that will be indicated by the possible combinations of words (phrase structure); expect that there will be words for objects as a whole, particularly objects which are important in the life of the people with whom you live. In a similar vein, nature must somehow instruct the young not to be surprised if they encounter subclasses of nouns which are based on no corresponding subclasses of objects—for example, gender in Indo-European. On the other hand, it probably instructs them to be on the lookout for correspondences between words and objects. And when they occur, as they do for classifiers in many languages, and for the mass/count distinction (as I have argued), then the correspondence can aid in both ways, in spotting syntactic regularities and important perceptual aspects of objects.

It was argued that at least English-speaking children in the early stages of language learning confine the words that will later function primarily as nouns, and those that will function primarily as verbs, each to a single semantic function. An examination of published vocabularies suggests that children do not use a word like *hand* to signify a part of the body and at the same time the action of handing. Moreover, the evidence suggests that the words that will become primarily nouns almost always refer to objects, while those that will become primarily verbs almost always refer to actions. Imagine that the semantic difference may help to establish the syntactic difference between nouns and verbs. That in itself would help the child to discover the principal forms of sentences (declaratives, questions, commands) in his language. Once he has mastered these, he can afford to relax the rule that states that nouns refer to objects and verbs to actions. He can also relax the rule that allows each word to belong to only one form class.

REFERENCES

Bloom, L. *Language development: Form and function in emerging grammars.* Boston: M.I.T. Press, 1970.

Bloom, L., Lightbown, P., & Hood, L. *Monographs of the Society for Research in Child Development,* 1975, *40,* Serial no. 160.

Braine, M. D. S. The ontogeny of English phrase-structure: The first phase. *Language,* 1963, *39,* 1–13.

Braine, M. D. S. Children's first word combinations. *Monographs of the Society for Research in Child Development,* 1976, *41,* Serial no. 164.

Brown, R. Linguistic determinism and the part of speech. *Journal of Abnormal and Social Psychology,* 1957, *55,* 1–5.

Brown, R., Fraser, C., & Bellugi, U. Explorations in grammar evaluation. In U. Bellugi & R. Brown (Eds.), *The acquisition of language.* Monograph of the Society for Research in Child Development, 1964, *29,* 79–92.

Denny, J. P. What are noun classifiers good for? In *Papers from the Twelfth Regional Meeting of the Chicago Linguistics Society.* Chicago: Chicago Linguistic Society, 1976, 122–132.

Denny, J. P. The "extendedness" variable in classifier semantics. In M. Mathiot (Ed.), *Boas, Sapir & Whorf Revisited,* an issue of the *International Journal of the Sociology of Language.* In press.

Friedrich, P. Shape in grammar. *Language,* 1970, *46,* 379–407.

Gleason, H. A. *Linguistics and English grammar.* New York: Holt, Rinehart & Winston, 1965.

Gruber, J. S. Correlations between the syntactic constructions of the child and the adult. Paper presented at the biennial meeting of the Society for Research on Child Development, New York, 1967.

Hockett, C. F. *A course in modern linguistics.* New York: Macmillan, 1958.

Hockett, C. F. The problem of universals in language. In J. H. Greenberg (Ed.) *Universals of language.* M.I.T. Press, 1963, 1–29.

Howes, D. H. On the interpretation of word frequency as a variable affecting the speed of recognition. *Journal Experimental Psychology,* 1954, *48,* 106–112.

Katz, N., Baker, E., & Macnamara, J. What's in a name? A study of how children learn common & proper names. *Child Development,* 1974, *45,* 469–573.

Menn, L. Pattern, control, and contrast in beginning speech: A case study in the development of word form and word function. Unpublished Ph.D. thesis, University of Illinois at Urbana-Champaign, 1976.

Nelson, K. Semantic structures of the earliest lexicons. Paper delivered to the Eastern Psychological Association, Boston, 1972.

Nelson, K. Structure and strategy in learning to talk. *Monographs of the Society for Research in Child Development,* 1973, *38* (1–2, Serial number 149).

O'Mahony, B. E. *The mediaeval doctrine of modes of meaning with special reference to Martin of Denmark*. Unpublished Ph.D. dissertation, Catholic University of Louvain, Institut Supérieur de Philosophie, 1964.

Shapiro, B. J. The subjective estimation of relative word frequency. *Journal of Verbal Learning and Verbal Behaviour*, 1969, *8*, 248–251.

Tucker, G. R., Lambert, W. E., & Rigault, A. *French speakers' skill with grammatical gender*. The Hague: Mouton, 1977.

Underwood, B. J. *Experimental psychology* (2nd ed.). New York: Appleton, 1966.

Weinreich, U. Explorations in semantic theory. In T. A. Sebeok (Ed.), *Current trends in linguistics*, Vol. 3. The Hague: Mouton, 1966, 395–477.

West, M. *A general service list of English words: With semantic frequencies and a supplementary word-list for the writing of popular science and technology* (rev. and enlarged ed.). London: Longmans, Green, 1953.

Whorf, B. L. *Language, thought and reality*. M.I.T. Press, 1956.

16

Scalar Variation in Comprehension among Aphasics

Margaret Seguin

INTRODUCTION

Even limited experience with a number of people with aphasia leads to fairly reliable expectations about the speech of other aphasics. The rhythm, vocabulary, and syntax of the several syndromes become familiar, predictable, and imitable. This predictability suggests that the language features characterizing the various syndromes are parallel to dialect features; it suggests that an aphasic dialect may be rule governed and describable in the way that normal language is. Yet the general sense of familiarity is not confirmed by an analysis of the output of even an individual aphasic. In fact, remarkable fluctuations in performance are characteristic. Even within the same conversation an aphasic may produce a word or construction in one utterance, and block it in another.

One way to predict behavior which is inherently variable is to assign a probability to the occurrence of particular variants. That is the manner in which variation theory gives a unified account of the use of more and less formal variants of the sound system of a language. The study reported here is an attempt to discover the structure of variation in one aspect of aphasic language. The specific behavior to be examined is the performance of aphasics on some words from the Peabody Picture Vocabulary

Test (PPVT), which measures word recognition by selection of the correct choice from four pictures for each word spoken by the examiner (Dunn, 1959, 1965).

The null hypothesis for this entire study is that the performance of aphasics on the PPVT will be undifferentiated from the performance of the standardization population except for quantitative reductions. The standardization population showed a pattern of roughly linear decreasing success through the test. It is not possible to begin this study by a direct test of the null hypothesis. A substantial portion of the literature on aphasia begins with the premise that there are several distinct syndromes of aphasia (e.g., Adams & Mohr, 1970; Geschwind, 1970; Goodglass, Quadfasel, & Timberlake, 1964; Green, 1969; Whitaker, 1972). Though this premise has been challenged both theoretically and empirically (e.g., Marie, 1906; Penfield & Roberts, 1959; Schuell, Jenkins, & Jimenez-Pablon, 1964; Smith, 1971, 1972), the existence of such claims makes it necessary to examine the performance of subgroups of the aphasic population in order to ensure that disparate patterns will not cancel each other. The following divisions will be used here:

1. Hemiplegic versus nonhemiplegic aphasics.
2. Mild, moderate, and severe comprehension impairment groups.

If any of these subgroupings of the aphasic population display qualitatively different patterns of performance on the PPVT, then an analysis of the nature of the words missed by the separate subgroups may reveal correlations between types of aphasia and linguistic features. The number of linguistic features and combinations of features that could be tested is huge. This study focuses on an ad hoc measure of participation in derivational morphological paradigms called **intersection.** Intersection is one way of referring to the number of connections a word has with other items in the lexicon. If a word has a large number of intersections, the number of "wrong turns" possible is greater. The choice of the feature of intersection size for this study was motivated by recurrent observation of conversations like the following actual interchange in a therapy group:

Therapist:	Now, where is the light?
Patient 1:	Ah, above, over
Therapist:	Where?
Patient 2:	On top of, up, there
Patient 3:	Below the ceiling
:	

The high overlap in semantic features, category, and distribution among prepositions appears to contribute to the word-finding problems displayed in this conversation. A formalism which explicitly studies such connections may contribute to our understanding of these phenomena. Although there are studies of the effect of derivational status and word class on various sorts of performances by aphasics, there is no previous study which focuses on the number of connections of various sorts which words have within the lexicon.

This chapter will first discuss the characteristics of the aphasic population whose performance is studied and then discuss the organization and administration of the Peabody Picture Vocabulary Test. Next, PPVT performance of several groups of the population will be presented. Finally, the notion of intersection will be formalized and the patterns of PPVT performance of the several groups of aphasics will be analyzed for words which intersect with many morphological sets and for words which intersect with few morphological sets.

THE SAMPLE

The 123 aphasics whose PPVTs were studied were chosen from the patients tested at the Aphasia Division of the Speech Clinic at the University of Michigan. The tests used were in all cases the first administration, so that none of the patients had as yet received therapy at the Residential Aphasia Program of the Speech Clinic. Many of the patients, however, had received less intensive therapy through other agencies.

Only patients with initial cerebrovascular lesion (stroke) were included in this study. Possible confounding factors associated with differences in the various types of aphasiogenic lesions (e.g., tumors, traumatic, and other lesions) are avoided by restricting the population in this way. Demographic, educational, and further clinical details on the sample are reported in Seguin (1977).

Right-sided paralysis accompanies the onset of aphasia in most cases. Geschwind (1970) presented a concise summary of two qualitatively distinct syndromes of aphasia associated with lesions to specific brain areas. (See top of p. 214 for a tabular summary.)

Despite the clinical picture of distinct syndromes, careful analysis of performance on specific linguistic tasks has not generally revealed reliable qualitative differences in performance pattern between groups of aphasics (see Goodglass, 1968). In order to observe the effect of the presence of hemiplegia, the results of the 92 right hemiplegics are tabulated separately from the results of the 31 nonhemiplegics in this population below. In order to test the claim that qualitatively distinct syndromes of aphasia are specific defects in speech comprehension and speech production, the

Broca's aphasia	Wernicke's aphasia
Little speech	Much speech, many filler words
Emitted slowly, with great effort	Rapid and effortless
Poor articulation	Normal rhythm and melody
Omits small grammatical words and endings	Grammatical skeleton is preserved
Comparable written disorder	Writing preserved, but written content distorted
May have good comprehension	Profound failure to comprehend
Associated with right paralysis (hemiplegia)	Usually no paralysis
Correlated with damage to Broca's area of the brain (adjacent to the motor cortex)	Correlated with damage to Wernicke's area of the brain (adjacent to sensory cortex)

results of three categories of patients based on severity of residual comprehension deficit, as measured by selected subtests of the Minnesota Test for Differential Diagnosis of Aphasia (Schuell, 1965), are separately tabulated below (34 patients with a mild comprehension deficit, 56 patients with a moderate comprehension deficit, and 33 patients with a severe comprehension deficit).

THE PPVT

The PPVT is designed to estimate verbal intelligence through measurement of hearing vocabulary. It consists of 150 test words with a plate of four drawings for each word. As the examiner reads each word, the patient selects one of the four pictures. Words 60–110 inclusive were analyzed for this study and are listed below in Table 1, which reports success rate by word for the entire aphasic sample population.

The words in the PPVT (Form A) were drawn from an original pool of 3885 picturable words selected from *Webster's New Collegiate Dictionary*. The words most effective in discriminating age levels were empirically determined by administering forms of the test to sample populations. There were 16 categories for plates including: man-made objects, animals, birds, human actions (gerunds), plants, adverbs, adjectives, and occupations. All four pictures on each plate were of equal size, equal intensity, and equal appeal. The final order of words was the empirical order of increasing difficulty for a standardization population.

The PPVT was standardized by administering the test to 4012 white children and youths aged 2–18 years, residing around Nashville, Tennes-

TABLE 1

Success Rates on Words 60-110 of the PPVT (123 Aphasics)

Number	Word	Success rate	Number	Word	Success rate
60	bronco	.92	86	hovering	.69
61	directing	.88	87	bereavement	.85
62	funnel	.94	88	crag	.62
63	delight	.76	89	tantrum	.68
64	lecturer	.81	90	submerge	.68
65	communication	.82	91	descend	.84
66	archer	.96	92	hassock	.87
67	stadium	.96	93	canine	.77
68	excavate	.92	94	probing	.78
69	assaulting	.93	95	angling	.77
70	stunt	.85	96	appraising	.92
71	meringue	.96	97	confining	.61
72	appliance	.80	98	precipitation	.63
73	chemist	.92	99	gable	.43
74	arctic	.72	100	amphibian	.77
75	destruction	.75	101	graduated	.75
76	porter	.93	102	hieroglyphic	.56
77	coast	.89	103	orate	.79
78	hoisting	.90	104	cascade	.63
79	wailing	.73	105	illumination	.62
80	coil	.96	106	nape	.68
81	kayak	.85	107	genealogist	.56
82	sentry	.82	108	embossed	.53
83	furrow	.86	109	mercantile	.79
84	beam	.73	110	encumbered	.42
85	fragment	.82			

see, in April–June, 1958. The fact that the PPVT was standardized on subjects 18 years and younger obliges us to be cautious in the interpretation of the performances of the adult brain-injured population studied here. If the test order is associated with difficulty of association between a word and a specific picture, then adults may have the same order. If the test order is associated more with obscurity of the higher numbered words, then adults, who have wider experience, may show very different patterns than the standardization group.

The starting point of the PPVT varies from subject to subject. It is usual to begin the test with item 100 for adults. A basal number is established by requiring that eight consecutive correct responses be obtained. In the modified testing procedures for the aphasic testing reported here, testing is ordinarily started at item 60. Some patients had lower basals than 60, some considerably higher.

The examiner stops the test when the subject misses six out of any eight consecutive items, and the final item tested is the ceiling for that subject. This testing procedure creates a situation in which all items are not attempted by all subjects. In order to minimize that problem in the interpretation of this data, only items 60 (by which time 76.4% of subjects had reached base) to 110 (by which time only 30.8% of subjects had reached ceiling) were included in the analysis. This still gives a too-high success rate for each word since subjects who have previously reached their ceiling are not considered. For each subject the basal, ceiling, and correctness of each response between base and ceiling were recorded. Data on other test scores and characteristics of each subject were also recorded. These data were sorted in various ways to test the following specific predictions:

1. The population of diagnosed adult aphasics will not differ from the standardization population in relative order of success on the list of words of the PPVT.
2. The presence of hemiplegia will not be associated with any significant difference in pattern of performance on the PPVT.
3. The degree of severity of comprehension deficit of subjects will not be associated with any significant difference in pattern of performance on the PPVT.
4. The morphological relations of words in the vocabulary of English will not be associated with level of difficulty of words for subjects on the PPVT.

RESULTS—PATTERNS OF THE SUBGROUPS

Table 2 presents results of tests of Hypotheses 1–3, that neither the massed aphasic sample, nor any subgroup would show a qualitatively distinct pattern from the standardization population on the PPVT.

TABLE 2

Rank-Order Correlations

Between	Spearman rank
Normals^a and aphasics	+.68
Normals^a and hemiplegics	+.65
Normals^a and nonhemiplegics	+.66
Hemiplegics and nonhemiplegics	+.86
Mild comprehension deficit group to severe comprehension deficit group	+.66
Normals^a and mild comprehension deficit group	+.73
Normals^a and moderate comprehension deficit group	+.64
Normals^a and severe comprehension deficit group	+.70

^{a}As determined by word order on the PPVT.

The mean Peabody score is 101.43 (standard deviation 24), which compares to a score of 109 for adults of IQ 100. For the entire sample of 123 aphasics, the success rate through the test items analyzed (60–110 inclusive) ranged from 96% on word 71, *meringue* to a low success for the entire subject population of 42% on word 110, *encumbered*.

As measured by rank-order correlation between aphasics and normals, the massed performance of the entire aphasic sample displays the expected decrease in success rate through the test. Words most out of order are word 88, *crag,* on which 62% succeeded, and word 96, *appraising,* on which 92% of subjects succeeded. In interpreting this, as with all results below, it is important to caution that the number of comparisons involved is very large, and random variation may be expected to operate to produce occasional apparent patterns in a few cases.

Separation of the aphasic subjects into a group with residual hemiplegia and a group without residual hemiplegia showed no qualitative difference in pattern between the two groups. There appears to be a tendency toward a quantitative difference, with the hemiplegic group showing fewer high ($\geq$ 90% success rate) success words (11, compared to 15 for the nonhemiplegics) and more low ($\leq$ 65% success rate) success words (10, compared to 5 for the nonhemiplegic group). A chi-square test showed no words which had significantly different success rates for the two groups.

Table 3 below summarizes some of the characteristics of the hemiplegic and nonhemiplegic groups separately. There are no differences between the groups which might account for leveling of underlyingly distinct patterns of performance between the two groups, but the nonhemiplegic

TABLE 3

Characteristics of Hemiplegia Groups

Education group	(92) Hemiplegics	(31) Nonhemiplegics
Mean	12.68	13.20
Standard deviation	2.64	2.86
Comprehension group		
Mild	22 (24%)	12 (39%)
Moderate	42 (46%)	14 (45%)
Severe	28 (30%)	5 (16%)
Speech group		
Mild	7 (8%)	11 (35%)
Moderate	39 (42%)	11 (35%)
Severe	46 (50%)	9 (30%)

group does have a greater proportion of less severely impaired members than does the hemiplegic group.

Insofar as the PPVT is a measure of aphasics' comprehension ability, the results observed are not consistent with report of qualitative differences between two syndromes of aphasics associated with the presence of hemiplegia. Separation of the aphasics into three groups by severity of their comprehension impairment revealed a very clear scalar difference between the three groups. The severe comprehension impairment group had only seven words in the high success category. Of these 7, 5 were among the 13 words on which the moderate comprehension group had high success. Of those 13, 12 were among the 30 words on which the group with mild impairment of comprehension had high success.

The pattern on low success words was almost completely the reverse. The mildly impaired group had only 3 low success words, all of which were among the 13 low success words of the moderately impaired group. Of those 13, 12 were among the 30 low success items for the severely impaired group.

The chi-square test yielded 11 words with different patterns of success rates between the three groups ($p \leqslant .0099$). In every case, the more severely impaired groups had lower success rates than the less impaired groups. Generally, the pattern observed was a Guttman scale. Insofar as performance on the PPVT measures an aspect of comprehension, the results do not agree with reports of qualitatively distinct syndromes between groups with more and less severe impairment of comprehension.

INTERSECTIONS

Students of aphasia have reported correlations between various linguistic features and aspects of aphasic word recognition and production. Though frequently studied, no clear results are available on the effect of simple versus complex morphology on aphasic performance. Words which are morphologically simple, are, in that respect at least, like islands in the vocabulary. Complex "derived" words like *communication* intersect with several classes of other words in the vocabulary (the other *-tion* words, the other *com-* words, etc.). Speakers of a language may be aware of such **intersections,** or they make not make the connection at any level, conscious or unconscious. Insofar as morphology is a formalization of intersections of words and sets of words, there are two aspects of difficulty for words according to the two polar types of morphological structure. Highly connected words are difficult to isolate in the lexicon because of the multiplicity of connections, and **island** words are difficult to reach in the lexicon because of the poverty of connections.

Intersection is an aspect of the relations between a particular word and a number of other words in the vocabulary of a speaker and can be used in thinking about a number of levels of language organization. For example, the word *angling:*

1. Has morphologically simple stem *angle,* but is inflected *-ing.*
2. Shares the feature of grammatical class with all other verbs in the language, and is related to words in other grammatical classes (*angler*).
3. Has formal relationship to *an angle* (they are homonyms).
4. Has semantic relationship to *fishing* (they are synonyms).
5. Shares the predication class feature "activity," with two required arguments, with a subset of English verbs.

Figure 1 presents a visual analogy to an intersection which includes not

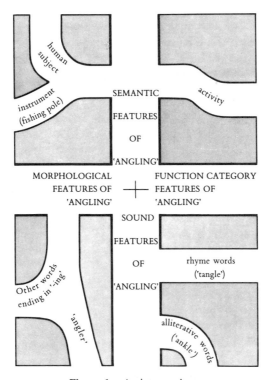

Figure 1. An intersection.

only the streets which actually intersect as *angling*, but a number of wrong-turn streets which intersect as well. The wrong-turns in Figure 1 are not all associated with the intended form/meaning target in the same way. Without pushing the metaphor any further, I suggest two polar types of words distinguished by their intersection behavior at the morphological level:

Islands	Corners
Monomorphemic words which take only the inflections of the appropriate form class. *Example:* Word 99 *gable*.	Derivationally complex words which share morphemes with a great many other words in the vocabulary. *Example:* Word 105 *illumination*.

In the next section of this chapter lists of words which are least difficult and most difficult for all aphasics and for comprehension impairment groups will be analyzed in terms of this polarity. It is important to point out that the classification proposed is ad hoc. It is much more common for linguists to focus on category membership than on the sorts of connections between words highlighted here. Criteria of assignment are specified more fully in Seguin (1977) where the words to be analyzed are assigned to a class for each intersection feature.

Table 4 presents the intersection classes of words 60–110 on the PPVT.

RESULTS: THE EFFECT OF INTERSECTION

The results just presented provide no evidence that there are qualitatively different patterns of performance on the PPVT among selected groups of the aphasic population studied here. It remains to be determined if the linguistic feature discussed is predictive of the performance as it was observed. Two sets of results will be presented in Table 5.

1. The matching of the intersection values of the words and the pattern of performance of the whole population of high and low success words.
2. Matching of the intersection values of the words and the pattern of performance of each of the three comprehension groups on high, moderate, and low success words.

The effect of intersection classes can be seen by comparing the proportion of islands which are high success with the corresponding proportion

TABLE 4

Morphological Intersection Classes of Words 60-110

Islands		Corners		Not Classified[a]	
60	bronco	61	directing	76	porter
62	funnel	63	delight	79	wailing
66	archer	64	lecturer	85	fragment
67	stadium	65	communication	93	canine
69	assaulting	68	excavate	94	probing
70	stunt	72	appliance	100	amphibian
71	meringue	73	chemist	102	hieroglyphics
74	arctic	75	destruction		
77	coast	87	bereavement		
78	hoisting	90	submerge		
80	coil	91	descend		
81	kayak	96	appraising		
82	sentry	97	confining		
83	furrow	98	precipitation		
84	beam	101	graduated		
86	hovering	103	orate		
88	crag	105	illumination		
89	tantrum	107	genealogist		
92	hassock	108	embossed		
95	angling	109	mercantile		
99	gable	110	encumbered		
104	cascade				
106	nape				
23 (45%)		**21 (41%)**		**7 (14%)**	

[a]The seven words which were not classified were omitted for two sorts of reasons. For example *porter* is related to a number of other items in the lexicon morphologically, but the derivation is not productive: *Porter* is not *one who ports* as its form would predict. *Wailing,* on the other hand, is related to only a few marginal items *(bewail)* and does not clearly belong in either class.

of corners and similarly the proportion of words in each class which are low success.

The hypothesis proposed earlier predicts that the proportion of the islands and corners which are in each success category should be roughly the same. Consistent deviations from that pattern such as in Table 5 may be evidence against the hypothesis that intersection categories do not influence success patterns.

As reflected in the high Spearman rank correlations of the aphasics and normals, the islands tended to be in the higher range of words. This "explains" the aphasics' performance, but raises a more general question concerning language categories. (See Gamkrelidze, 1974.)

TABLE 5

The Effect of Morphological Intersections — Summary

	High success words		Low success words	
	Percentage of islands which are high success	Percentage of corners which are high success	Percentage of islands which are low success	Percentage of corners which are low success
All aphasics	35	14	13	29
Mild comprehension deficit	61	57	4	10
Moderate comprehension deficit	48	5	22	29
Severe comprehension deficit	22	10	35	57

LIMITATIONS OF THE STUDY

A number of factors limit the significance which can be attached to the conclusions to be drawn from this study. Before conclusions are suggested, those limiting factors will be briefly reviewed.

The sample population of aphasics was drawn from a select group of referral patients. The Speech Clinic requires that patients considered for admission to the Residential Aphasia Program be mobile and self-sufficient in daily needs. Furthermore, the performance of this group of adult aphasics was compared to the order of the PPVT, which was established with a pool of subjects between 2 and 18 years.

The entire sample population did not attempt each word, so that comparison of success rates by word is somewhat obscured, except as rank ordered. The wrong answers were not analyzed, so that some difference in error rates might well be due to the relative sensibleness of the alternative pictures.

The various sortings of the population into groups by the factors of hemiplegia and severity of comprehension deficit are resortings of the same group of individuals, rather than separate random samples. Furthermore, some of the groups had small numbers of subjects in them.

Finally, the usage frequency of the words was not controlled for, nor were a number of other factors such as semantic domain, abstractness, and saliency in the test situation.

CONCLUSIONS

This report has presented two factors by which a sample of 123 aphasics could be classified in order to observe any qualitatively distinct syndromes. A linguistic distinction by which the words of the PPVT could be classified was then presented. The effects of both these variables were matched against data on the performance of the aphasics studied to test four specific hypotheses on variation in aphasic language comprehension. Those can be summarized in the following two general predictions:

1. Aphasics' patterns of performance on the PPVT would not be qualitatively distinct from the performance of the standardization population, with no qualitative differences between any groups of aphasics (Hypotheses 1–3).

2. Intersection class assignment would not predict the pattern of performance on the PPVT (Hypothesis 4).

The results reported were consistent with the first set of hypotheses. The massed aphasic sample did not show a qualitatively different pattern than predicted from the standardization population. While performance from word to word is quite variable, the overall pattern is gradually decreasing success through the test. Qualitatively distinct patterns are not observed between groups of aphasics based on the subject variables tested. In particular, the category of hemiplegia, which is the most frequently commented on indicator of type of aphasia, does not correlate with qualitative pattern differences.

Severity of comprehension deficit did not correlate with a qualitative difference in performance pattern. The pattern was rather an implicational scale.

Insofar as performance on the PPVT measures an aspect of comprehension, the results presented in this chapter do not agree with reports of qualitatively distinct syndromes between groups of aphasics associated with presence of hemiplegia or severity of language deficit.

The results of the test of the linguistic variable of intersection class were not consistent with the second hypothesis. The linguistic factor tested, the distinction between words which are morphologically isolated in the lexicon and words which are highly integrated morphologically into the lexicon, was a good predictor of success patterns. However, this is also true of the standardization population as reflected in the rank-order of the words in the standard test.

The results and conclusions of this study have implications both for theories of aphasia and for theories of language which hope to integrate data from aphasia. With respect to aphasia, the evidence presented here bears on the issue of the representation of language in the brain. Insofar as the limited PPVT data bear on or reflect the status of language functions, there was no evidence of discrete, qualitatively distinct syndromes.

For the study of language, the results presented here suggest the possibility of integrating data from aphasia by studying the structure of variation. The results of this study do not help linguists to select between alternative formalisms, since any adequate theory of language must predict that there are connections between words at the morphological level.

The apparent tendency towards significant predictiveness of the notion of "intersection" does suggest that the study of aphasia in languages of different morphological types may be an important project for linguists. English has a relatively impoverished derivational system. The study of word recognition and other tasks in aphasics in languages with very productive morphological systems may help in understanding how the processes of derivation and lexicalization interact.

The methodological implications of the present study are perhaps of greater heuristic value than the specific findings described above. The design and execution of this study indicate that the merger of the unique approaches of linguistic theory with those of the clinical sciences concerned with language can be productive for both.

REFERENCES

Adams, R. D., & Mohr, J. P. Affectations of speech. In I. M. M. Wintrobe, G. W. Thron, R. D. Adams, I. L. Bennet, E. Braunwaid, K. Isselbacher, & R. G. Petersdorf (Eds.), *Harrison's principles of internal medicine*. New York, McGraw-Hill, 1970, 172–185.

Dunn, L. *The Peabody Picture Vocabulary Test*. American Guidance Service, Inc., 1959.

Dunn, L. *Manual for the Peabody Picture Vocabulary Test*. American Guidance Service, Inc., 1965.

Gamkrelidze, T. V. The problem of 'l'arbitraire du signe'. *Language*, 1974, *50*, 102–110.

Geschwind, N. The organization of language and the brain. *Science*, 1970, *170*, 940–944.

Goodglass, H. Studies on the grammar of aphasics. In S. Rosenberg & J. H. Koplin (Eds.), *Developments in applied psycholinguistics research*. New York: Macmillan Company, 1968.

Goodglass, H., Quadfasel, F. A., & Timberlake, W. H. Phrase length and the type and severity of aphasia. *Cortex*, 1964, *1*, 135–153.

Green, E. 1969. Phonological and grammatical aspects of jargon in an aphasic patient: A case study. *Language and Speech*, 1969, *12*, 103–118.

Marie, P. The third left frontal convolution plays no special role in the function of language. *Semaine médicale*, 1906, *26*, 241–247.

Penfield, W., & Roberts, L. *Speech and brain mechanisms*. Princeton: Princeton University Press, 1959.

Schuell, H. *Booklet for the Minnesota Test for Differential Diagnosis of Aphasia*. Minneapolis: University of Minnesota Press, 1965.

Schuell, H., Jenkins, J. J., & Jimenez-Pablon, E. *Aphasia in adults*. New York: Harper and Row, 1964.

Seguin, M. Linguistic factors in word recognition in aphasia. Unpublished Ph.D. dissertation, University of Michigan, Ann Arbor, 1977.

Smith, A. 1971. Objective indices of severity of chronic aphasia in stroke patients. *Journal of Speech and Hearing Disorders*, 1971, *36*, 167–207.

Smith, A. *Diagnosis, intelligence and rehabilitation of chronic aphasics*. Ann Arbor: The University of Michigan Press, 1972.

Whitaker, H. A. Unsolicited nominalizations from aphasics: The plausibility of the lexicalist model. *Linguistics*, 1972, *78*, 62–71.

17

Variation and Change in Patterns of Speaking: Language Shift in Austria

Susan Gal

INTRODUCTION

The hypothesis that linguistic change has its source in synchronic variation in the speech community (Weinreich, Labov, & Herzog, 1968), is now supported by empirical work on phonological change (e.g., Labov, 1965), syntactic change (Bickerton, 1973a; Sankoff & Laberge, 1972) and lexical semantic change (reported in Kay, 1975). While there is controversy about the precise way linguistic variation and change should be conceptualized (cf. Sankoff, 1973; Bickerton, 1973b), there is agreement on several basic points. Linguistic change is neither so fast nor so slow as to be unobservable; new forms which eventually replace older forms can first be located in synchronic variants in the speech of subgroups within the community; and changes observed over time are the result of the redistribution of synchronic variants to different linguistic environments, to different social situations, and to different speakers. The aim of this chapter is to demonstrate that language use, or more specifically, the pattern of language choice in a bilingual community, also undergoes change according to these same general principles.

Although it has often been noted that rules for speaking are subject to change (cf. most recently Bauman & Scherzer, 1974, p. 11), most ethnographies of speaking have been synchronic and have not provided descriptions of such change. A particularly salient case of change in patterns of speaking is language shift. Weinreich defined this as "the change from habitual use of one language to that of another [1953, p. 68]." Note that shift does not necessarily refer to change in competence to speak either language. An elaboration of Weinreich's definition distinguishes stable, long-term bilingual communities from "unstable" ones in which shift takes place as one of the languages is abandoned (Fishman, 1964).

This chapter will concentrate on the way in which a new linguistic form, German, is spreading through a community and on the changes in stylistic function it undergoes as it spreads. It will be shown that in this community the use of either Hungarian or German is first a sign of ethnicity, that is, of membership in one of two hierarchically ranked social groups. However, in the course of the change from the habitual use of Hungarian in all interactions to the habitual use of German in all interactions, the two languages come to be utilized by speakers not only for demonstrating group solidarity but also simultaneously for expressing the kind of rhetorical stylistic meanings which had previously been communicated through variation within each language. This use of the same linguistic means for what had previously been separately expressed communicative functions may well be a general characteristic of socially motivated linguistic change, since it occurs in phonological change (Labov, 1965) as well as in language shift.

THE COMMUNITY AND ITS REPERTOIRE

Oberwart (Felsőőr), an Austrian town located near the Hungarian border, contains a Hungarian–German bilingual community that has been surrounded by German monolingual villages for about 400 years. In 1921 it was transferred from Hungary to Austria. Approximately one-fourth of Oberwart's 5000 residents are bilingual and are the descendants of the original Hungarian peasant community founded almost 1000 years ago. In contrast to the rest of the population, which is German monolingual, the peasants have been bilingual in Hungarian and German for several centuries.

Until World War II this peasant community considered itself different from its neighbors because of its language, ethnicity, and religion. In contrast to the largely monolingual sections of town, the peasants remained land- and kin-oriented; higher prestige went to those who had large land holdings and were willing to work hard in agriculture.

After World War II Austria's industry and commerce grew quickly and the industrialization of the countryside reached Oberwart. Well-paying jobs in light industry and government administration became available in and around Oberwart. Although there had long been some Oberwarters who worked in industry in neighboring cities, it was not until after World War II that wage work became more attractive than peasant agriculture. By 1964 only one-third of the bilingual population was still engaged in agriculture full time. Many former peasants had become part-time peasants; others went to work and stopped tilling their land altogether.

Briefly, Oberwart's linguistic repertoire consists of varieties of German and Hungarian. Both languages have what natives perceive as local and standard forms. The local-standard differences are best characterized as bundles of covarying linguistic variables. Given appropriate social situations, it is possible for most Oberwarters to move along a continuum from more standard to more local speech in either of their languages. The language shift to be described here has been going on for approximately 50 years, but seems to have sped up during the postwar period.

For Oberwarters, each of the two languages available to them can be said to symbolize a social group and its values; but the relative prestige of the groups and languages has changed in recent years. Hungarian symbolizes peasant identity and today is deprecated because peasant identity is no longer respected. Peasant (Hungarian: *paraszt*, German: *Bauer*) is used here and in the rest of the chapter as an Oberwart cultural category which includes all agriculturalists. While still respected by the old, it carries a negative connotation for young people. The preferred status for young people is worker. The world of work is a totally German-speaking world, and the language itself has come to represent the worker. The peasant parents of young workers often say about their children *Ü má egisz nimet* 'He/she is totally German already'. This is not a reference to citizenship, nor to linguistic abilities. Oberwarters consider themselves Austrians, not Germans, and even young people are considered bilingual, often using Hungarian in interactions with their elders. The phrase indicates, rather, the strong symbolic relationship between the young people's status as workers and the language which they use at work.

German also represents the money and prestige available to those who are employed, but not available to peasants. German therefore carries more prestige than Hungarian. The children of a monolingual German speaker and a bilingual speaker never learn Hungarian, regardless of which parent is bilingual. In addition, while in previous generations the ability simply to speak both German and Hungarian was the goal of Oberwarters, today there is a premium not just on speaking German but on speaking it without any interference from Hungarian. Parents often boast that in their children's German speech, *Nem vág bele e madzsar* 'The Hungarian doesn't cut into it'. That is, passing as a monolingual German speaker is now the aim of young bilingual Oberwarters.

SYNCHRONIC VARIATION IN LANGUAGE USE

The general statements about symbolic associations between languages, social statuses and evaluations already discussed do not, in themselves, predict informants' choice of language in particular situations. For instance, although Hungarian is negatively evaluated by young bilinguals, they nevertheless use it in some interactions. In addition, those who are workers do not always use German, and peasants do not always use Hungarian.

In any interaction between bilingual Oberwarters a choice must be made between German and Hungarian. (For the present purposes variation within each language can be ignored. We will return to it later.) While in many interactions one or the other is chosen for the entire event, there are some situations in which both are used by the same speakers even in one short exchange. One version of this consists of very old speakers interacting with very young ones, the old speaker using Hungarian and the young speaker using German. The other version, rapid alternation between codes, is a common phenomenon in many bilingual communities and has been termed **conversational code switching** (Gumperz, 1976). When both languages may appropriately be used, Oberwarters say that they are speaking *ehodzan dzsün* 'as it comes'. For any interaction, then, there are three possibilities, German (*G*), Hungarian (*H*), or the use of both (*GH*).

To predict an individual's choices among the three possibilities, the role relationship between the participants in the interaction is the most important factor. Since aspects of the situation such as locale or occasion were largely irrelevant, specification of the identity of the interlocutor was sufficient to predict choices. (Table 1 contains a list of the main interlocutors distinguished by Oberwarters.)

However, informants differed from each other in their habitual choices. To describe the pattern of synchronic language use we can rank informants along a vertical axis and interlocutor types along the horizontal axis as in Table 1. The data in Table 1 come from questionnaires administered to 32 informants. The habitual language choices of these and of 36 additional informants were also systematically observed during the year of fieldwork. This observation yielded results very similar to those in the questionnaires. Since the average agreement between observation and

TABLE 1

Choice of Language in Oberwart by Men and Women (Questionnaires)[a]

Informants	Age of informant	Interlocutors										
		1	2	3	4	5	6	7	8	9	10	11
A	14	H	GH		G	G	G			G		G
B	15	H	GH		G	G	G			G		G
C	17	H	GH		G	G	G			G		G
D	25	H	GH	GH	GH	G	G	G	G	G		G
E	27	H	H		GH	G	G			G		G
F	25	H	H		GH	G	G			G		G
G	42		H		GH	G	G	G	G	G		G
H	17	H	H		H	GH	G			G		G
I	20	H	H	H	H	GH	G	G	G	G		G
J	39	H	H		H	GH	GH			G		G
K	22	H	H		H	GH	GH			G		G
L	23	H	H		H	GH	H		GH	G		G
M	40	H	H		H	GH		GH	G	G		G
N	52	H	H	H	GH	H		GH	G	G	G	G
O	62	H	H	H	H	H	H	GH	GH	GH	G	G
P	40	H	H	H	H	H	H	GH	GH	GH		G
Q	63	H	H		H	H	H	H		GH		G
R	64	H	H	H	H	H	H	H	GH	GH		G
S	43	H	H		H	H	H	H	G	H		G
T	35	H	H	H	H	H	H	H	GH	H		G
U	41	H	H	H	H	H	H	H	GH	H		H
V	61	H	H		H	H	H	H	GH	H		G
W	54	H	H		H	H	H	H	H	H		G
X	50	H	H	H	H	H	H	H	H	H		G
Y	63	H	H	H	H	H	H	H	H	H	GH	G
Z	61	H	H		H	H	H	H	H	G	GH	G
A1	74	H	H		H	H	H	H	H	H	GH	H
B1	54	H	H		H	H	H	H	H	H	GH	H
C1	63	H	H	H	H	H	H	H	H	H	GH	H
D1	58	G	H		H	H	H	H	H	H		H
E1	64	H	H		H	H	H	H	H	H	H	H
F1	59	H	H	H	H	H	H	H	H	H	H	H

Interlocutors:

1 = to God
2 = grandparents and their generation
3 = bilingual clients in black market services
4 = parents and their generation
5 = friends and age-mate neighbors
6 = brothers and sisters
7 = spouse
8 = children and their generation
9 = bilingual government officials
10 = grandchildren and their generation
11 = doctor

[a]Number of speakers = 32 (both men and women). Blanks indicate inapplicable cells.

questionnaire was near 90% for both men and women, the data in Table 1 may be considered representative of informants' language choices.

In Table 1 the language choices of a particular informant in all situations are indicated in the rows, and the choices of all informants in a particular situation are indicated in the columns. The choices arranged in this way form a nearly perfect implicational scale (scalability 97%). Speakers at the top of the scale use the most German; those at the bottom use the most Hungarian. Those in the middle are the most likely to use both in a single interaction. As in implicational scales generally, the presence of any one of the three linguistic categories in a cell restricts which of the three may occur above, below, and to either side of it. Therefore, when one speaker's choice of a language in a situation is known, it also supplies information about his choices in other situations and about the possibilities open to the speakers higher or lower on the list.

Two factors determine the place of a speaker on the scale, that is, how much H or G he or she is likely to use. The first is age. The rank correlation between speakers' ages and their language use as measured by their rank position in Table 1 is .82 (see Table 2). The younger people are, the less likely they are to use H and the more likely to use G. The older people are, the more likely it is that they will use H with all or most interlocutor types. The second factor is the extent to which the speaker is involved in peasant life. Note that this group of informants was not formally selected as a representative sample of the bilingual community, but rather was chosen to represent a range on the two variables, age and involvement in peasant life.

Given the symbolic meanings of the two languages in Oberwart, it is not surprising that the dimension peasant-to-worker is related to people's habitual language choices. One way to assess informants' position on the peasant-to-worker continuum is via their social network. Social network

TABLE 2

Correlations among Language Choice, Age, Peasantness, and Peasantness of Network for All Informants[a]

Language choice × Age	.82
Language choice × Peasantness of network	.78
Language choice × Peasantness	.67
Age × Peasantness	.45, NS
Age × Peasantness of network	.62
Peasantness × Peasantness of network	.90

[a]Spearman rank-difference correlation coefficients.

was defined as all the people an individual spoke to in a period of time; several encounters with the same person were tallied separately rather than counted as one contact. The average amount of time for all informants was 7 days. In order to relate social networks to the peasant/worker continuum, each of the contacts in a speaker's network was assigned to one of two categories: (a) those who lived in households owning either pigs or cows, or (b) those who lived in households owning neither pigs nor cows. Oberwarters themselves use the ownership of animals as a rough definition of peasant. Therefore, "peasantness" of a person's network, and so his involvement in peasant life, was expressed as the percentage of contacts who owned animals. Speakers were ranked on this measure, and the correlation of this ranking with language choice was .78 (see Table 2), statistically significant at the .01 level.

In addition to this ranking according to social networks, a measure of peasant status was also constructed. Each speaker was ranked along a peasant-to-worker continuum according to how he or she scored on a set of culturally defined criteria of peasant identity such as ownership of animals, cultivation of fields, house features, type of clothing worn, and amount of education. Ranking by these criteria also correlated well with language choice (.67). However, for most individuals (21 out of 32; cf. Gal, 1976, pp. 238–239) the peasantness of their social network was a better predictor of language choice than was their own peasantness. This was the case despite the fact that the measure of peasant status was an elaborate emic scale with 11 criteria distinguishing gradations among peasant, peasant-worker, and worker, while the network measure used only one distinction among contacts.

In sum, with regard to language choice, it matters not only whether a person himself is a peasant but also whether the people he most often talks to are peasants. For most people, the status of their social contacts predicted their language choices better than their own status did. It should be noted that although most other studies of linguistic variation rely on sociological status measures to identify the speakers and the linguistically relevant subgroups, the results described here lend support to the suggestion (cf. Gumperz, 1964; Labov, 1973) that whatever a speaker's social status, his linguistic presentation of self is constrained by his social network.

CHANGE IN LANGUAGE USE

From older informants' reports of language use in their childhood, it is clear that the pattern used today by the oldest peasants, that of speaking

Hungarian to everyone but outsiders and strangers, is also historically the oldest pattern. In addition, several descriptions of Oberwart and the local Hungarian dialect from the 1920s and 1940s make mention in passing of language usage patterns (Imre, 1973; Kovács, 1942, pp. 73–76). They indicate that the oldest pattern was used by everyone in the 1920s. Therefore, the present synchronic differences between informants of different ages are not the product of age-grading in language choice; age or apparent time can serve as a surrogate for repeated sampling over real time (cf. Labov, 1965, for details of this strategy). The synchronic patterns of language use already described can be reinterpreted as reflections of diachronic change, with the oldest usage represented by the oldest informants and the newest represented by the youngest speakers.

In order to illustrate the interaction of time and social network differences in the process of shift, the informants in Table 1 were divided into three generations of 20 years each, and the range of network scores was dichotomized so that speakers scoring at or below the median could be considered to have nonpeasant networks, while those scoring above the median can be considered to have peasant networks. Figure 1 illustrates the differences, in proportion of German used, among generations and among those with peasant and nonpeasant networks within each generation.

In each age group, those with nonpeasant networks use German more than those with peasant networks. Although there is a marked increase in

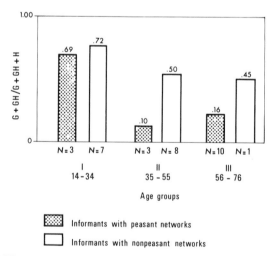

Figure 1. Differences, in proportion of German used, among generations and among those with peasant and nonpeasant networks within each generation.

the use of German by the youngest group as a whole, those young people with peasant networks are still slightly behind the rest of their generation (cf. Gal, 1975, for a discussion of differences between men and women in the youngest group). Translating the generational differences into change over time, we can say that as speakers' networks change and they become less involved in peasant life they use Hungarian in fewer situations and use German correspondingly more. In a parallel but separate process, the new generation since World War II uses Hungarian less and German more, regardless of their social networks.

If Table 1, the summary of synchronic usage, is also reinterpreted as change over time, then it is clear that the shift from the use of Hungarian to the use of German is occurring gradually, situation by situation. For any one interlocutor type, the rule for choice of language is first categorical for the old form (H) and then variable (alternation between German and Hungarian) before it is categorical for the new form (G). In what follows I will argue that in the change from invariable to variable language choice, the purpose for which speakers use the languages undergoes a change. From the point of view of speakers engaged in interaction, the language shift represents a change in the means they use for expressing communicative intent.

When those older peasants who still use the oldest invariant pattern of language choice today were asked why they do not sometimes speak German to their bilingual friends they often replied, "Why should I? He's an Oberwarter, he's one of us." Such remarks, and the association of languages with social groups already discussed, establishes the invariant use of Hungarian as a sign of group membership, a way of expressing social group solidarity. Within this invariant language usage in which choice of language indicates solidarity, communicative intents, such as expression of formality or respect, are accomplished by variation within the chosen language. For example, two tapes of an elderly couple who spoke only Hungarian to each other were compared by counting the values of six phonological variables. One tape was made during a joking dinner conversation, the other during a structured interview. In the interview the frequency of occurrence of standard variants of the phonological variables was significantly higher than during the dinner, when the local variants occurred significantly more often. The same general finding of variation within a language holds true for the young people who use only German for most of their interaction (Gal, 1976, Chapter III).

In short, when choice of language is invariant, then language choice and stylistic shifting within a language are used by speakers for different and complementary functions. Labov (1965) described a similar separation of linguistic means according to functions in his analysis of phonological change in New York. In that case, too, the expression of social status was accomplished by one set of linguistic alternatives (called indicators) the invariant use of which identified a group; expression of what may be called rhetorical or stylistic functions was accomplished with another set (called markers) which evidenced stylistic variation.

When language choice in Oberwart is variable, that is, when both languages may be used by two people in conversational code switching, the associations of each language with a social group remain the same, but, as Blom and Gumperz (1972) and Gumperz (1976) have suggested, speakers build on these connotations for rhetorical effect. The in-group/ out-group contrast which the two languages represent is used to accomplish communicative purposes other than the expression of solidarity.

In Oberwart conversational code switching occurs when, in basically Hungarian dialogues, one of the speakers switches temporarily to German. The interactional effect or meaning of the switched phrases can usually be inferred from the reactions of the participants and a consideration of the whole exchange. Often the German phrase scores as a "topper" in a disagreement; a last word which is not outdone and which serves to win the argument. Switches to German were also used to strengthen commands and to assert expertise and authoritativeness about an issue or about a technical specialty. It is not that German is always used to emphasize the force of a command or to win an argument. Rather the point is that if a speaker wants to, then switching to German at a particular time, for instance, in an argument, can accomplish these communicative purposes.

What is interesting about such code switches is that the use of German appears to carry conversational clout and prestige in much the same way that the worker way of life and its values now carry prestige in the community. Opinions and judgments appear to gain credibility and stature when uttered in German, the language associated by Oberwarters with work, knowledge of the world beyond home, and therefore sophistication.

Returning now to the place of conversational code switching in language shift, note that in conversational code switching language choice is used for rhetorical purposes by retaining and building on each language's role as a symbol of a social group. As in Labov's study of phonological change, it is during the process of change that the functions which had been served by separate linguistic means are both accomplished by the same means.

It is important that conversational code switching is *not* characteristic of the bilingual population as a whole. Its occurrence is sharply restricted (as Table 1 shows) to a subset of speakers in a limited set of interactions.

For those whose networks and status have not changed from what was general in the community perhaps 50 years ago, that is, for the oldest peasants with peasant networks, choice of language is still invariant with most interlocutors (usually all but grandchildren). Language choice continues to serve the function of asserting one's status as an Oberwart peasant. For those whose networks and status are most different from what was general in the community 50 years ago, that is, the young workers with nonpeasant networks, choice of language is just as invariant with most interlocutors (usually all but grandparents) but the choice is German not Hungarian. For both these groups of people, when variable choice of language does occur, it is unreciprocal usage with someone far from them in age. Both groups of people engage in style shifting within the invariably chosen language in order to express a range of meanings other than the peasant/nonpeasant distinction.

Variable choice of language is largely limited to those individuals whose social network, status, and age are not at either extreme. Their values and loyalties with regard to the peasant/worker distinction are often problematic, undecided, manipulable. In nonlinguistic ways they sometimes present themselves as peasants, and sometimes as workers. Such people, in the middle in terms of social change, often have variable choice of language with more than one interlocutor, sometimes with as many as 3 out of 10 (see informants D, O, and P in Table 1). It is only for these people, and only with some interlocutors that conversational code switching is common. For them, the linguistic means are not segregated by function.

In sum, the simultaneous use of language choice for stylistic rhetorical purposes, as well as for signaling social group membership is an indication that language change is in progress: The community is shifting from invariable use of one language to invariable use of another.

REFERENCES

Bauman, R., & Sherzer, J. (Eds.). Introduction. In *Explorations in the ethnography of speaking*. Cambridge, England: Cambridge University Press, 1974.

Bickerton, D. The nature of a creole continuum. *Language,* 1973, *44*(3), 640. (a)

Bickerton, D. Quantitative versus dynamic paradigms: The case of Montreal *que*. In C.-J. Bailey & R. W. Shuy (Eds.), *New ways of analyzing variation in English*. Washington, D.C.: Georgetown University Press, 1973, 23–43. (b)

Blom, J.-P., & J. J. Gumperz. Social meaning in linguistic structures: Code switching in Norway. In J. Gumperz & D. Hymes (Eds.). *Directions in sociolinguistics*. New York: Holt, Rinehart, and Winston, 1972, 407–434.

Fishman, J. Language maintenance and language shift as fields of inquiry. *Linguistics,* 1964, *9*, 32–70.

Gal, S. Peasant men can't get wives: Sex roles and language choice in a bilingual community. Paper presented at the Meeting of the American Anthropological Association, San Francisco, 1975.

Gal, S. Language change and its social determinants in a bilingual community. Unpublished Ph.D. dissertation, University of California, Berkeley, 1976.

Gumperz, J. J. Linguistic and social interaction in two communities. In J. J. Gumperz & D. Hymes (Eds.), *The ethnography of communication. American Anthropologist*, 1964, 66(6)(II), 137–154.

Gumperz, J. J. The sociolinguistic significance of conversational code switching. Unpublished manuscript, 1976.

Imre, S. Az Ausztriai (Burgenlandi) Magyar Szorványok. (The Hungarian ethnic groups in Austria). In *Népi Kultura—Népi Társadolom (Folk culture, folk society)* Budapest: Akadémiai Kiadó, 1973, 119–136.

Kay, P. Synchronic variability and diachronic change in basic color terms. *Language in Society*, 1975, 4(3), 257–270.

Kovács, M. *A Felsőőri Magyar Népsziget (The Oberwart Hungarian folk island)*. Budapest: Sylvester Nyomda, 1942.

Labov, W. On the mechanism of linguistic change. In Charles W. Kriedler (Ed.), *Georgetown University Monograph Series on Languages and Linguistics*, 1965, *18*, 91–114.

Labov, W. On the linguistic consequences of being a lame. *Language in Society*, 1973, 2, 81.

Sankoff, G. Above and beyond phonology in variable rules. In C.-J. Bailey & R. W. Shuy (Eds.), *New ways of analyzing variation in English*. Washington, D.C.: Georgetown University Press, 1973, 44–61.

Sankoff, G., & Laberge, S. On the acquisition of native speakers by a language. *Kivung*, 1972, *5*, 32–47.

Weinreich, U. *Languages in contact*. New York: Linguistic Circle of New York, 1953.

Weinreich, U., Labov, W. & Herzog, M. Empirical foundations for a theory of language change. In W. Lehman (Ed.), *Directions for historical linguistics*. Austin: University of Texas Press, 1968, 97–195.

18

The Linguistic Market and the Statistical Explanation of Variability

David Sankoff / Suzanne Laberge

THE LINGUISTIC MARKET

Though it is well known that the internal differentiation of spoken language is related to social class, the scientific study of this relationship poses a number of very difficult problems. Our experience with the analysis of the Montreal French corpus leads to the realization that directly correlating linguistically variable behavior with social class membership, whether defined stratificationally or dialectically, is not a well-motivated procedure. It ignores established facts such as that teachers, actors, and receptionists tend to speak a more standard variety than other people of similar social or economic position. Adapting the notion of **linguistic market** developed by Bourdieu and Boltanski (1975), we undertook to construct an index which measures specifically how speakers' economic activity, taken in its widest sense, requires or is necessarily associated with, competence in the **legitimized** language (or standard, elite, educated, etc., language).

At first this might seem to be a relatively easy notion to operationalize with a view to an "objective" assignment of index values. Speakers could be grouped according to occupation, and high values could be assigned to those working in educational, literary, political, and administrative fields,

239

and low values to those for whom the mastery of the legitimized speech variety is not a criterion of selection: laborers, manual workers, and so on. This approach, however, is unworkable for a variety of reasons related to the fact that our task is to classify individuals, not occupations. Thus, this method would be inadequate without a good deal of ad hoc "patching up" for housewives, students, the unemployed, and retired persons who make up about half of our sample, and whose occupations are not comparable with those more directly involved in the system of production. In addition, an "objective" classification of speakers according to occupation would tend to be static, taking into account their current situation only. No mechanistic weighting of occupations to arrive at some kind of average score on an occupational history could really do justice to the fact that speakers' roles in the linguistic market (and their patterns of linguistic behavior) change and evolve throughout their lifetime. Thirdly, the notion of an objective classification of occupations, in terms of the linguistic market, is illusory. Construction of such a classification would necessarily depend in many ways on more or less subjective judgments, on the part of experts or laymen, with respect to the nature, the definition, and the measurement of the various criteria used to evaluate a given occupation. Finally, the construction of such a classification, prompted by hopes of cross-language comparisons, would tend to imply that there is some association of a particular occupation with a particular role in the linguistic market, independent of the sociohistorical conjuncture, an assumption we reject. The class structure of different societies at different times is not the same, nor is the situation of a particular occupational category. The methodological dictum that one should standardize such index categories for the sake of comparability trivializes the sociohistorical analysis which is crucial to the understanding of the linguistic market in each case.

The approach we took toward solving this methodological problem was not to try to improve the objectivity of the classification procedure, but inversely, to try to use as fully and as rigorously as possible the richness of the intuitions or subjective reactions of individuals who participate in the daily life of the community. Of course, using this type of data also implies a whole range of methodological problems. The two most important are as follows. First, it is possible that a judge, that is, a person whose assessment is being used as data, is not experienced or informed enough to evaluate adequately the participation of a given individual in the linguistic market. Second, such assessments inevitably reflect the dominant ideology of the society about equality of opportunity for economic success, independent of social background, about relationships between intelligence and linguistic behavior, about the nature of the legitimized language, and so on. These two types of problem can never be totally eliminated from this type of study, but our choice of judges was designed to take into account their effects. We selected eight professional and graduate student sociolinguists who had all observed and worked for several years on sociolinguistic relationships within the francophone community of Montreal. This ensured that all judges were as well-informed as possible. As for the second problem, all the judges had shown in their own work a critical approach vis-à-vis the sociolinguistic situation in Quebec, trying to unmask the ideological prejudices prevalent about questions of language and society. Of course it is impossible to avoid completely the influence of the dominant ideology, but a critical attitude best penetrates the tissue of beliefs and values which disguises the relations of power operating in the linguistic market.

Certain sociolinguists (including one of the authors—S. L.) were not included in the panel because their familiarity with the linguistic behavior and interview content of the speakers in the corpus was too great. Some judges had previously worked on the corpus, but were not familiar enough with the interviews so that this could affect their evaluation.

THE JUDGMENTS

The task assigned to each judge was relatively simple. He or she was presented with 120 slips of paper, on each of which was described the socioeconomic life history of one of the speakers in the corpus. This was accompanied by an instruction sheet containing essentially the material in the first and second sections of this chapter. The task, carried out independently by each judge, consisted of assigning the individuals to ranked groups according to a single criterion, the relative importance of the legitimized language in the socioeconomic life of the speaker. The number of groups as well as the number of speakers in any of the groups were not specified. The judges were instructed to try not to apply objective or explicit criteria fixed a priori (for example, education required to function in a given position, whether a job involves extensive contact with the public, and so on), but to be guided by general knowledge and reactions to the whole of the description to be evaluated.

Clearly, we were not able to make all description slips strictly comparable. This is due in part to the nature of economic activities; when it comes to occupations, for example, it did not seem worthwhile for the purposes of eliciting judges' responses, to elaborate on the specific activities of a nursery school teacher, whereas this would be essential in the case of a foreman or supervisor. Furthermore, we deliberately omitted or left vague explicit reference to age and educational level. This may have resulted in less accuracy and less comparable judgments, but it seemed a desirable methodological choice since we wanted to include age and education as independent variables in subsequent statistical analyses. On the other hand, to take particularities of individual personal histories into account, we often included in the descriptions details about parents or spouses to allow a better perception of the economic context in which speakers are situated. Thus the occupation of the head of the household was given whenever possible in the cases of younger students since this indicates the background from which they come. For housewives, details about their husbands are indicative of their social interaction, with which groups and to what end.

The slips were presented to each judge in a random order and were identified only by a temporary code.

CONSTRUCTION OF THE INDEX AND QUESTIONS OF CONSISTENCY

The classification task carried out by each judge resulted in a number of ranked groups, the rank of each group indicating the importance to it of the legitimized language.

The first step in manipulating these data was to convert each judge's grouping to a numerical scale. To render comparable the scales from different judges, given the variability in the number of groups constructed (ranging between 4 and 12), we simply assigned the value 0 to each member of the group judged most peripheral to the linguistic market, and 1 to the group most central. The remaining groups were spaced at equal intervals between 0 and 1.

The aggregate index for each speaker was thus defined as the mean of the values assigned to him or her by the eight judges. Figure 1 shows the distribution of 120 speakers according to their relationship to the linguistic market. The skewing of the distribution toward low values of the index reflects, of course, a tendency of the judges not to make many distinctions among individuals who do not participate intensively in the market. The simple explanation for this is that the bulk of the speakers participate marginally or only indirectly and that direct participation in the linguistic market is the preserve of a relatively small minority of our sample. And given that our sample greatly overrepresents the upper, upper middle, and extreme lower sectors of the population, based on a scale of annual revenue (cf. Sankoff & Sankoff, 1973), we can conclude that the propor-

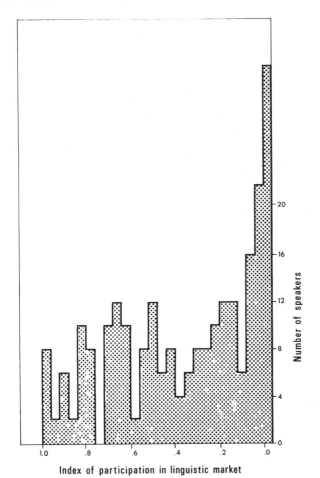

Index of participation in linguistic market

Figure 1. Distribution of speakers according to the relative importance of a mastery of the legitimized language in their economic life. Bars represent number of speakers per interval of .04, except the extreme right-hand bar which represents the seven speakers between 0 and .01, and is hence multiplied 4× for comparability.

tion of the population who participate significantly forms a much smaller minority than indicated in Figure 1.

As our index is an aggregate of several sets of subjective judgments, we felt it important to check whether the different judges showed a high degree of agreement among their ratings. A straightforward numerical comparison was inappropriate because of the incomparability of the number of groups per judge, so we proceeded in terms of the proportion of

disagreements between judges. Suppose one judge ranked speaker A higher than B while another judge ranked B higher than A. We define this as a disagreement between the two judges. If both judges ranked A higher than B or both ranked B higher than A, this constituted an agreement. The remaining cases (about one-quarter to one-third of the 6940 pairs of speakers), where one or both judges classed A or B in the same group, were counted neither as agreements nor disagreements. Then the proportion of disagreements between two judges is simply the number of disagreements divided by the total of agreements and disagreements. Table 1 is then a dissimilarity matrix among judges based on disagreement proportions.

The low rate of disagreement attests to the consistency of our method of operationalizing the notion of linguistic market. We should point out that the apparent systematic differences between judges on overall rates of disagreement are largely the result of different numbers of groups. A judge who makes 12 groups, and hence many more distinctions among pairs of speakers, is relatively more susceptible to disagreement with other judges than one who only makes 4.

Another way of checking the method is to see how consistently individual speakers are classified by different judges. We calculated for each speaker the proportion of disagreement between pairs of judges involving that speaker and all other speakers. The results are presented in Figure 2. Once again, the low rate of disagreement, less than 10% for the vast majority of speakers, is gratifying. It is interesting to examine in more detail the six cases involving rates of disagreement higher than 15%. Four of them are suggestive of some degree of incongruity between present occupation and background, or background and spouse's occupation: an

TABLE 1

Comparison between Pairs of Judges in Terms of Proportion of Disagreements

Judge	1	2	3	4	5	6	7
2	.037						
3	.016	.058					
4	.031	.068	.044				
5	.059	.054	.054	.046			
6	.053	.093	.050	.061	.061		
7	.059	.070	.062	.052	.074	.078	
8	.091	.083	.079	.056	.062	.083	.062

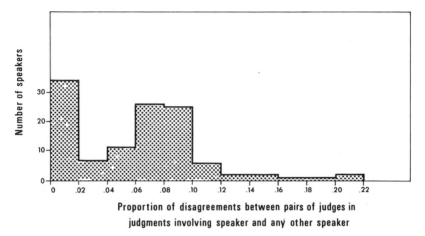

Figure 2. Distribution of speakers according to the amount of disagreement involved in assigning linguistic market index.

accountant's daughter married to a factory worker; a relatively highly educated woman married to a hardware salesman; a student with a rural background; and a woman who worked in a shoe factory before marrying a man who eventually occupied an important bureaucratic position. Of the two remaining cases, one is the wife of an unemployed factory worker, who has worked in the same factory herself, and had occasionally been assigned some responsibility training other workers. The sixth difficult case is an assistant in a nursery for children who does not live at home, and the judges had little other information to work with. In general, then, speakers eliciting many disagreements between judges have conflicting elements within their personal socioeconomic histories, or are simply underdocumented as to their social roles or economic activities. There is no evidence of any systematic differences in subjective perceptions among judges.

THE INDEX AND LINGUISTIC BEHAVIOR

The study of linguistic variation has usually focused on the factors influencing the choice of one of two possible phonological, syntactic, or lexical variants. In our work on the Montreal French corpus, it has been possible to divide these factors into noncontextual (age, sex, education, and some index bearing on the socioeconomic position of the speaker) and contextual, which includes very diverse elements of the linguistic context of a variable, such as its syntactic and phonological environment, the discourse function of the utterance containing the variable, and so on. The contextual/noncontextual distinction is of course particular to the standardized format of our interview. In general sociolinguistic analysis, it is not always possible nor desirable to separate "sociological" from "linguistic" factors.

The data are gathered as for a binomial variable. We record the number of occurrences of each variant in each of its contexts. The effects of the different factors are evaluated in terms of a linear model for the logistic transform of the parameter p of the binomial variable. That is

$$\log\left(\frac{p}{1-p}\right) = \alpha_0 + \sum_{i=1}^{n} \alpha_i x_i$$

where the x_i represent the factors, usually 0–1 variables in the case of contextual factors and real variables for age, education, etc. The α represent the effects.

Because of the nature of the data, we use maximum likelihood methods for estimating the α and log-likelihood differences for testing significance (Rousseau & Sankoff, this volume).

We do not treat the contextual parameters in the same way as the noncontextual parameters. We proceed as in multiple regression, using a stepwise approach to see which noncontextual factors should be included, but forcing the contextual parameters into the regression at all times, once these have been determined to be of linguistic significance. In all of the three examples discussed below (*avoir/être*; *ce que/qu'est-ce que*; and *on/ils*), the index of participation in the linguistic market was by far the most important explanatory variable as measured by the significance of the difference in log likelihood. Education also had a significant effect, but nowhere near as important, and both age and sex had a marginally significant effect on the *avoir/être* variable.

To examine the effect of the linguistic market in more detail, we carried out a second series of analyses where no noncontextual factors were included, but where each of the 120 speakers was assigned an individual parameter to be estimated. We then simply plotted this parameter against the individual's value on the index.

AVOIR/ÊTRE

This variable has been studied in great detail by G. Sankoff and Thibault (1977). The compound tenses, for example, the *passé composé*, of a small number of verbs make use of the auxiliary *être* in variation with *avoir* which is the obligatory auxiliary for all other verbs. The contextual factors consisted of one parameter for each of the 16 verbs in the data set. Figure 3 is a plot of the 119 individual speaker parameters against the linguistic market index. (The remaining speaker had no tokens of this variable.) Despite the scatter, a clear association can be seen between *être* usage and participation in the linguistic market. Of particular interest is the somewhat triangular distribution of points; though some speakers peripheral to the market have a high rate of *être* usage, very few speakers central to the market have a low rate.

CE QUE/QU'EST-CE QUE

The data in this section are drawn from the forthcoming thesis of Kemp (1978). Most of them appear in G. Sankoff, Kemp, and Cedergren (forthcoming). Certain embedded constructions are headed by *qu'est ce que* in variation with the standard form *ce que*. These include headless relative clauses, indirect question forms, and certain equational and cleft constructions. These four syntactic categories provided the contextual factors for our analysis of the 116 speakers showing at least one example of this variable. In Figure 4 we see a pattern similar to Figure 3, except for a greater polarization of the sample between the extremes of *ce que* or *qu'est-ce que* usage.

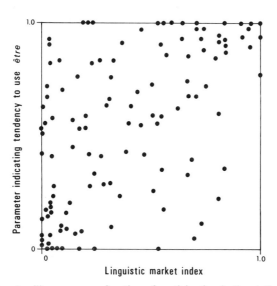

Figure 3. Auxiliary usage as function of participation in linguistic market

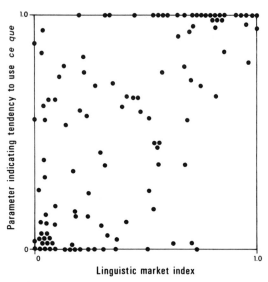

Figure 4. Complement header construction as a function of participation in linguistic market.

ON/ILS

Concomitant with the expanded usage of the indefinite pronoun *on* for the first person plural referent in subject position, the indefinite is expressed by other forms such as *tu* or *vous* (second person singular and plural, respectively) as discussed by Laberge (forthcoming). When the indefinite referent excludes the speaker and hearer, it is often expressed by *ils* rather than *on* (Laberge, 1977). For this latter variable the contextual factors include the presence of various types of disambiguating devices in the context of the variant, and the previous occurrence of one or other of the variants in an immediately preceding clause. Figure 5 indicates that this variable is predicted even better than the previous two; not only do speakers with high values of the index almost all use a great deal of *on*, but speakers with low values almost all use very little.

DISCUSSION

The exercise described in this chapter is part of an attempt to found the sociological aspects of linguistic variation analysis on more satisfying theoretical bases than the "objective" stratificational criteria which have

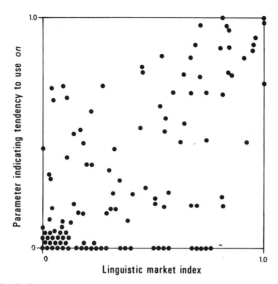

Figure 5. Exclusive indefinite pronoun usage as function of participation in linguistic market.

often been taken for granted. The notion of linguistic market derives directly from a critical and dynamic view of history and society. We have tried to operationalize it without reducing it to an aggregate index of superficial socioeconomic parameters. We would claim that we have done so without sacrificing scientific rigor. The index we have developed effectively captures the "social" component of noncontextual influences on linguistic variation.

ACKNOWLEDGMENTS

This work was stimulated by a series of debates within our group on the sociological characterization of the speakers in the sample, initiated and sustained by Pierrette Thibault. We are grateful to her for her encouragement and collaboration. We also thank Pascale Rousseau, who carried out the parameter estimation, and William Kemp, for making available his data, as well as our judges, who remain anonymous.

REFERENCES

Bourdieu, P., & Boltanski, L. Le fétichisme de la langue. *Actes de la recherche en sciences sociales,* 1975, No. 4, 2–32.

Kemp, W. Description linguistique et sociale de la variation entre *ce que* et *qu'est-ce que* dans le français de Montréal. Unpublished M.A. thesis, Université du Québec à Montréal, 1978.

Laberge, S. Etude de la variation des pronoms sujets définis et indéfinis dans le français parlé à Montréal. Unpublished Ph.D. dissertation, Université de Montréal , 1977.

Laberge, S. The changing distribution of indeterminate pronouns in discourse. In R. W. Shuy & A. Schnukal (Eds.), *Language use and the uses of language*. Washington, D.C.: Georgetown University Press, forthcoming.

Sankoff, D., & Sankoff, G. Sample survey methods and computer-assisted analysis in the study of grammatical variation. In R. Darnell (Ed.), *Canadian languages in their social context,* Edmonton: Linguistic Research, Inc., 1973, 7–63.

Sankoff, G., Kemp, W., & Cedergren, H. The syntax of *ce que/qu'est-ce que* variation and its social correlates. In R. W. Shuy & J. Firsching (Eds.), *Dimensions of variability and competence*. Washington, D.C.: Georgetown University Press, forthcoming.

Sankoff, G., & Thibault, P. L'alternance entre les auxiliaires *avoir* et *être* en français parlé à Montréal. *Langue Française,* 1977, *34*, 81–108.

19

Are the Masses an Inanimate Object?

Michel Pêcheux

INTRODUCTION

What is generally called modern thought is marked by an opposition between person and thing, be it at the juridical level where it appears as a distinction between contract and property; at a philosophical level, between subject and object; or at a moral level, between the intentional and the nonintentional. This opposition has always played an important role in the logico-philosophical analysis of language, and in linguistics today it is central to any discussion of semantics. For example, Chomsky in *Reflections on Language* (1975) treats the various aspects of this theme at some length. In particular he investigates the properties which enter into the definition of the concept of Person, and those which are required to characterize a Thing. We could cite many examples in different currents of modern linguistics to show how this distinction appears semantically self-evident in reflections touching on logic, law, technology, or sociology.

In this chapter, I will illustrate and defend a thesis, which I will state first in a negative form: *The semantic pair person/thing which applies without any obvious problem to utterances of everyday life, is not at all appropriate to politics in the nonbourgeois sense of the term, to the politics of the masses.*

251

To speak of the masses, of political change, and of revolution—in other words of history—in terms of persons and things, subjects and objects, intentions and the state of things, as common sense, transparent distinctions which are necessarily reflected unambiguously in language, is to miss completely the essential ideological nature of discourse and meaning. Lewis Carroll succeeded in describing the world of Alice in Wonderland with its shrinking characters and catless smiles; but no pure logician could do likewise for the Wonderland of politics.

Nevertheless politics indisputably has effects within language, and these are not totally unstructured. I am going to try to characterize some of these effects anecdotally, in terms of an experimental exercise, for which I must first sketch the historical background.

BACKGROUND

During the last 10 years there has gradually emerged in France the possibility of radical social change, based mainly on an alliance between the Socialist and Communist currents, with a common program of government. This alliance is not without its problems and contradictions, due particularly to the persistence of reformism within the socialist component. The experiment described in the next sections focuses on the ideological ambiguity of reformism, as manifested in the **zero growth theory.** This theory which gained currency at the beginning of the 1970s as a general solution to the crises in capitalist countries calls for radical economic and political change, and advocates rigorous economic planning.

In 1972, the socialist Sicco Mansholt published a report espousing this theory. The report circulated in the European Community, provoking a variety of reactions. In France, the ruling bourgeoisie considered the Mansholt report to be courageously realistic. The Communist party denounced it firmly, calling it a trick designed to make the working people pay for the capitalist crisis. The French socialists (and reformist political groups and trade unions in general) hesitated, but evinced a great deal of interest.

In this context a group of research workers at the Centre National de la Recherche Scientifique (Paul Henry, Jean-Pierre Poitou, Claudine Haroche, and myself) undertook the following small experiment.

GENERATING THE DATA

We presented a one-page extract from the Mansholt report to a group of about 50 young executives who were doing a refresher course at a university. They were not told that the text came from the report. Rather, when the first series of 25 students received the text, it was ascribed to a group of left-wing economists. A second series of students received exactly the same text only it was ascribed this time to a completely different source, this time to the right, to a source in the ruling bourgeois government.

Note that the two groups of students differed neither in political attitudes, which were about equally distributed in the two groups, nor in their verbal abilities. They all had similar backgrounds in the French intellectual *petite bourgeoisie,* and comparable scientific university training.

The students were asked to read the text attentively. Then, after it was taken away from them, they were asked to write an objective and complete summary in a dozen lines. There was no possibility of reproducing the entire text mechanically from memory. Rather, each student had to force himself to reconstruct its essential economic and political ideas.

In this way we obtained two groups of summaries from the same original text, which we will refer to as the **right corpus** and the **left corpus.** The question for us was then to see if there were differences or even contradictions between these two corpora.

ANALYSIS

A first examination of these data seemed to lead to negative conclusions: The lexical distribution in one corpus appeared identical to that of the other, and neither was any difference apparent at the syntactic level.

We did not consider these observations conclusive since we had not expected that the differences and contradictions, if differences and contradictions there were between the left corpus and the right corpus, would be found at the syntactic level or at the purely lexical level. The important analytical problem was how the words, expressions, and utterances functioned in each corpus, with different and even contradictory ideological and political referents. In brief, it was the **semantic** and **argumentative** characteristics of each corpus that interested us primarily.

Did this mean that we were reduced to a descriptive interpretation of the **content analysis** type, relying on our intuitions as readers to analyze each family of texts? How could we be sure that such intuitions about referents and arguments would be based solely on our linguistic competence as native French speakers, and that it would not be something completely different showing through, namely, our own ideological and political prejudices? How could we avoid the charge of circularity of reasoning, based on the subjectivity of political readings?

We set out to circumvent these difficulties through the use of a procedure called the **automatic analysis of discourse** (AAD) (Pêcheux, 1969; Pêcheux & Fuchs, 1975), about which a few words will suffice. This is a partly computerized procedure which makes use of the methods elaborated by Harris in his classic, if somewhat dated, "Discourse Analysis" (1952) but which takes into account as much as possible recent developments in linguistics, and which is not so restricted in application.

Harris took for granted a stable text, one that was repetitive and stereotyped, a series of utterances which paraphrased itself. We felt that this condition of stability could be satisfied more generally by the simultaneous treatment of several replicate texts produced in identical conditions, such as is the case for each corpus we collected. In treating each corpus as a single text, we effectively hypothesized the existence of one or several **discursive formations** (Pêcheux, 1975) which dominate in common all the individual texts which make it up.

The discovery of the underlying structure of the discourse is based on the ability to recognize relations of propositional equivalence or implication, expressional synonymy, or contradiction, and so on, between two or more superficially different syntactic forms. This leads to the construction of equivalence classes of forms which can be treated as the basic elements of the discourse. The production of equivalence classes requires an operational definition of what is invariant and what is variable when two sequences are compared. Too general a criterion allows anything to be identified with anything else. Too restrictive a criterion will prevent any equivalences from being recognized.

The outcome of our procedure is a system capable of comparing the component discourses within each corpus, by superimposing one on the other, element by element. Before this comparison can be carried out, the discourses must be linguistically delinearized and transformed into a graph structure with nodes corresponding to utterances and arcs providing the relations of ordering between the utterances.

Discourse analysis requires linguistics, from our point of view, only for the first step of parsing or surface delinearization, insofar as some syntactic theory is a necessary but not sufficient condition for this delinearization. The results of the syntactic analysis serve as input data for the algorithm of the automatic discourse analysis. On the basis of the equivalence criteria just mentioned, taking syntactic and lexical correspondences into account, this algorithm automatically constructs families of strings called **semantic domains.** These are structured bundles of strings extracted from the various discourses in one corpus, whenever these strings are found to be related to each other by relations of synonymy, metonymy, or of paraphrase. In addition, the algorithm calculates relations of intersection, inclusion, and textual dependence involving these domains, enabling us to organize the discourses into their graph representations.

The entire exercise reported here should not be considered a content analysis or a semiological study of the Mansholt report extract, though it involves identifying and analyzing pariphrastic relations. Nor is it simply an analysis of the arguments contained in this text, despite its reduction of each corpus to a directed graph representing the organization of the components of the discourse. The differences not only show up in the nature of the results but are inherent in the way they are arrived at. Though such a text is intended to be understood or analyzed in terms of a single reading as having a single sense, we stress the separation in our analysis of the linguistic task of analyzing the surface structure of the discourse, from the ideological considerations involved in deliberately constructing the double corpus to reveal the interplay of two discursive formations.

At this point it is important to recognize the presuppositions, hypotheses and assumptions entering into this analysis explicitly or implicitly.

In summary:

1. The assembly of the double corpus of summaries according to the procedure just described constitutes in itself a **political and ideological hypothesis** on the part of the researchers. This involves the deliberate juxtaposition of three ambiguities, the inherent ambiguities of the text, the ambiguity of the authorship ascribed to the text, and the ambiguous (*petite bourgeoisie*) class position of the students participating in the exercise. It is postulated that the working out of these three ambiguities will result in a dissociation of the discursive processes entangled in the Mansholt report. We would then be able to distinguish the effects of the different discursive formations as they are selectively filtered and differentially cancelled in the summarizing of the text by the students.

2. The syntactic analysis of the summaries[1] (currently done manually, but which could be at least partially automated) draws on **linguistic hypotheses** concerning the hierarchic structure of sentences, the nature of the basic components of enunciation that they contain, and so on. Thus the analysis inevitably involves **semantic and syntactic presuppositions,** but no semantic presupposition is involved which could appear as such in the end result.

3. The AAD treatment (by computer-implemented algorithm) carries out a series of manipulations on the results of the syntactic analysis and

[1]We would like to thank C. Kervadec and C. Champeaux who contributed greatly to this phase of the project.

results in a set of domains and the relations between these domains, for each corpus of summaries.[2] Inherent in this algorithm as well are **linguistic and mathematical hypotheses,** concerning especially the relationship between the notion of paraphrase and the operation of substituting variable terms within an invariant delinearized context.

4. Finally, as will be illustrated below, the results must be worked through and reinterpreted after the computer analysis. The AAD algorithm brings out and displays certain types of phenomena but does not draw conclusions. This additional treatment of the results and the conclusions we can draw from it puts into question all the underlying hypotheses, of which certain are technical and easily justified by the general principle of the method, and others which have wider theoretical implications and must be evaluated in terms of their confirmation or correction of more general hypotheses.

RESULTS

We will present two sets of results: in the next section the two lists of domains making up the nodes of the **right** and **left discursive graphs,** and in the following section the **structure** itself of these graphs, explaining the procedures step by step. First a word about the format of the results. The algorithm calculates paraphrastic blocks or domains as in the simple example in Figure 1(a). Note that this work was carried out on French materials, but the illustrations presented here have been translated as closely as possible into English.

The results were then manually reorganized by distinguishing nonoriented substitutions (synonymy) from oriented substitutions (nonsynonymy) of an implicative type.

For example, the material in Figure 1(a) would be structured as in Figure 1(b), with the following conventions:

1. Vertical bars bracketing two or more elements indicate that we have identified all these strings, be they words, phrases or sentences as contextually synonymous.
2. Arrows bracketing two elements signify that a relation of implication (or metonymical substitution) holds between them, so that one implies the other but not vice-versa.
3. Double arrows bracket two elements when we recognize a contradiction between them.

---

[2]This work was done on the computer of the *Laboratoire d'Informatique, Sciences Humaines* of the *Maison des Sciences Humaines,* by Jacqueline Léon.

(a)

```
will to maximize the growth per capita
will to maximize the G.N.P. per capita
idea to maximize the G.N.P. per capita
reconsidering the maximization of G.N.P. per capita
```

(b)

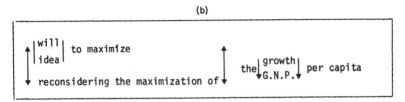

Figure 1. (*a*) Example of paraphrastic block. (*b*) Paraphrastic block after structuring.

4. An X denotes a dummy, or general unspecified term in a string.

Since the complete results of this work will be published elsewhere, I will limit myself to indicating some of the major findings concerning the structure of the domains and the discursive graphs corresponding to each of the two corpora.

THE STRUCTURE OF THE DOMAINS

The two sets of domains calculated separately by the algorithm nevertheless have properties in common, which allow us to classify them under four rubrics, namely:

1. The causes of the crisis
2. Policy about economic reorganization
3. Policy concerning consumption
4. Policy on cultural development.

The Left corpus and the Right corpus are differentiated, however, on two essential points which will be explored briefly.

The Question of Planning

Rubrics 2 and 3 contain connections between the Right corpus and the Left one on the question of planning, through a constellation of elements, including production, consumption, and the pair centralization/ decentralization. But a contradiction runs through this entire interrelation, involving the place of production in planning: Two opposing tendencies are clearly distinguishable in examining Figures 2 and 3.

The Right corpus focuses the debate on the need for **planning of consumption** (domains R35, R36, R41) insisting on its control and surveillance. The Left corpus on the other hand is oriented to the contrary idea of **centralized planning pertaining to production** (L33), implying the need to change economic and political structures (L42).

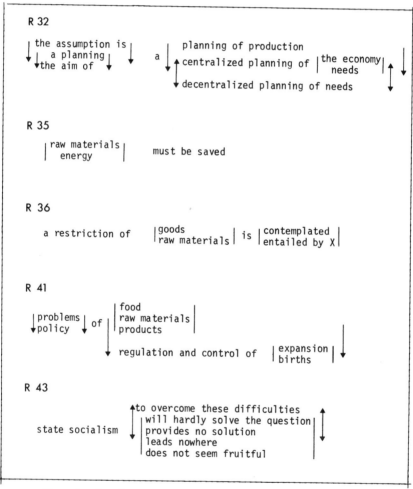

Figure 2. Set of domains from the Right corpus related to planning.

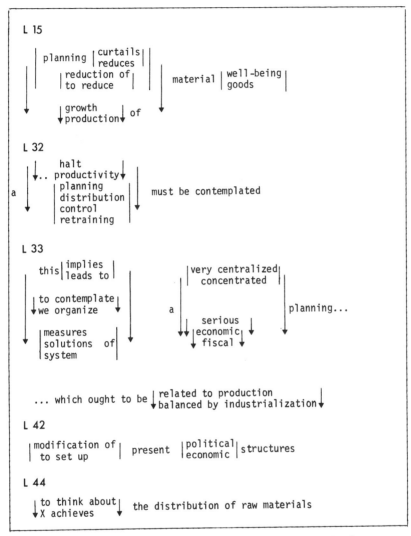

Figure 3. Set of domains from the Left corpus related to planning.

Thus the same term, planning, is a point of differentiation between the two perspectives. The rightist conception of planning is one to which the bourgeoisie in power spontaneously turns whenever the (capitalist) economy goes through a crisis. Ever since the onset of the first major crisis of this nature in 1929, the slogans which announce this authoritarian planning have not really changed. It is always a matter of making the masses accept economies, limitations, and restrictions—all for the common good, naturally!

The opposing concept of planning, that of the Left, focuses on questions of production. Socialist planning can overcome a crisis by developing the economy, while transforming the relations of production from the capitalist to a new, noncapitalist, mode. This conception, clearly rejected by the Right (cf. R43 on state socialism) is clearly present on the Left (cf. L33 cited above), but in a self-contradictory and tangled form: Domain L15 exemplifies this confusion, which stems from the notion that socialist planning involves a sacrifice that must be borne by all.

This illustrates how, in the opposition between the Left corpus and the Right corpus, the discourse of the Right intervenes in that of the Left, to limit it, to distort its form and content. This is the most characteristic sign of reformism in political and ideological struggle.

We will see the effects this **domination** of the Right over the discourse of the Left repeated in the second essential point which differentiates the two corpora: It concerns the question of who should be the political agents for carrying out the envisaged radical reforms.

The Political Agents of the Radical Reforms

The Right discourse and the Left discourse are interrelated on the subject of the so-called radical reforms necessary to overcome the crisis. But they also contradict one another on the same point, insofar as the political agents necessary to effect the proposed transformations are designated on the Right as the government, the authorities, or the state (cf. R51, 52, 53, 61, 63 in Figure 4), whereas these terms do not emerge from the analysis of the Left discourse. We find in their place expressions of the type *it follows that, one should* or the pronoun *we* (cf. L51, 52 in Figure 5). This use of generic terms is symptomatic of the domination of the discourse of the Right over the Left, insofar as the same terminology of radical reform has as referents two opposing processes: On one hand a bourgeois solution which **manages the crisis,** and on the other, the possible beginnings of a revolutionary transformation. We say the Right discourse dominates the Left simply because these two referents can be evoked interchangeably by the same stimulus text, hampers the second perspective, which is a rejection of the first, and induces a reformist illusion in double form, namely:

1. An illusion in which a bourgeois government representing capitalist interests would carry out the same transformations which the working class and the political forces of the Left are fighting for.

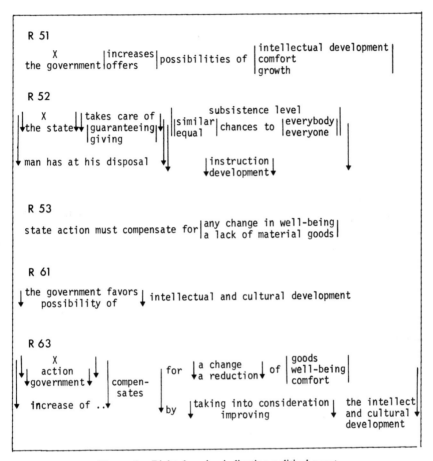

Figure 4. Right domains indicating political agent.

2. An illusion, the obverse of the preceding one, in which these reforms of the Left could be realized without touching the question of state power.

Thus the analysis reveals the relation between conceptions of state power and class position, in particular the class position of the intellectual *petite bourgeoisie*. Our examination of the Right/Left opposition highlights the oscillation between an explicitly reformist conception which conceives of radical transformations within the present political structure, and a conception which places itself above considerations of state power from the start.

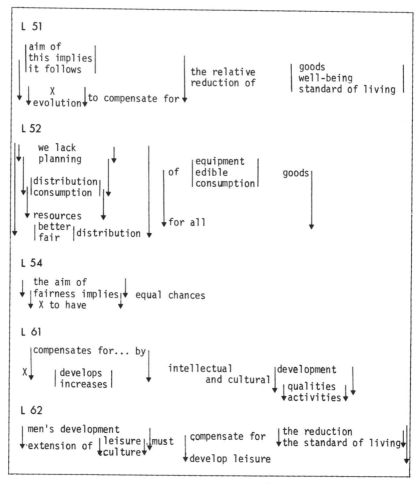

Figure 5. Left domain indicating political agent.

Note that the identity of the political agent or subject in the discourse and undertakings proposed for this subject in the construction of the discourse vary between the Right and the Left, but neither suggests political commitment to a government of the Left to try to transform the nature of state power.

STRUCTURE OF THE RIGHT AND LEFT DISCURSIVE PROCESSES

The second series of results calculated by the AAD algorithm involves the relations between domains. Given two domains, the algorithm determines whether or not one consistently precedes or succeeds the other in the thread of the discourse. The set of these relations permits us to construct two graphs, each containing one **source** (the point of departure for the discourse) and one or more **sinks** (or points of arrival). The source and the sinks are connected by directed paths which indicate the order in which the different domains are reached in the discourse. The existence of several different paths in the same graph attests to the breaking up of the linear nature of the surface structure analyzed. Thus the analysis of each set of continuous and apparently coherent summaries reveals an underlying discursive structure composed of disjointed and even contradictory lines of argumentation.

In Figures 6 and 7, representing the graphs of the Right and Left discourses, each of the main blocks of domains is labeled by number, and is represented by a short phrase for mnemonic purposes.

These schemas suggest many conclusions. I will summarize the essential points.

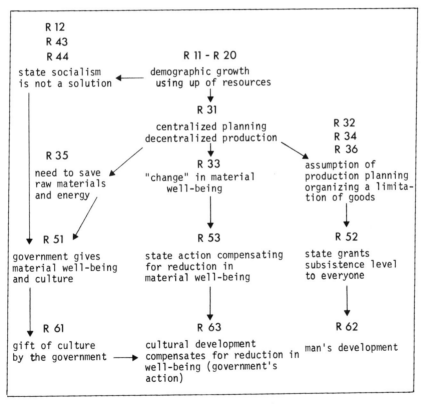

Figure 6. Structure of Right discourse.

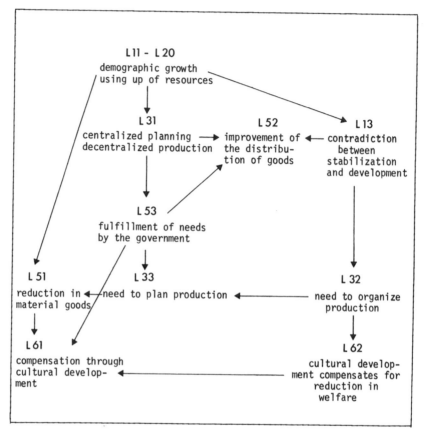

Figure 7. Structure of Left discourse.

1. The number of points having more than one incoming path or more than one outgoing path is greater on the Left than on the Right graph. In this sense the Left graph is more complex than the Right one.

2. Although the source point is the same on the Right and Left (R11, R20; L11, L20 pointing to the cause of the crisis), the sinks differ. R62 and R63 relate to policy rubric 4 on page 257, involving cultural development, and though L61 falls under the same rubric, L52 concerns the policy toward consumption.

3. The trajectories of the Right graph (Figure 6) lead each in its own way to the same destination, the flowering of man in culture (R61, 62, 63). Thus, the path R31 to R62 spells out what we may call **the blackmail of crisis,** a catastrophism which justifies planned measures to restrict consumption. The path R31 to R61 echoes tentatively the age-old promise of

bourgeois happiness (R51: comfort and culture) through a triumphalism which is somewhat restrained, a relative triumphalism explained by the comparison with state socialism, which is seen *a priori* as a nonsolution (R12, R43, R44). And finally the central path R31 to R63 represents the compensatory action of the state and explains the coexistence of the other two paths which may be characterized as catastrophism and timid triumphalism, respectively. This is in no way logically incoherent. It is the very way in which bourgeois political practice functions, ceaselessly juxtaposing demagogic promises and antipopular measures. The contradiction between these two lateral trajectories is therefore purely a matter of outward appearance, and serves to highlight the bourgeois political line of state intervention (central path).

4. The relative complexity of the Left graph (Figure 7) is characterized by the existence of the transverse connection involving L32, L33, and L51, and by the branching from point L53 toward L61 on one hand and toward L52 on the other. Here a contradiction is evident. Everything appears as if the path L32, L33, L53 is expressing the need for a planning of production oriented towards the satisfaction of needs, but it returns nevertheless to the call for egalitarian redistribution (L52), which is an ideological trap, given that no change is envisioned in the relations of production, and which coincides, in fact, with the objective of current bourgeois policy.

5. Once again we see evidence of the limits of autonomy of the Left discourse in relation to the Right: The fundamental blockage here is the idea, taken to be self-evident, that (socialist) planning of production is inevitably accompanied (relation L33–L51) by economic recession. This is the same old idea mentioned earlier (p. 260) that socialism is a burden to be borne.

CONCLUSION

The conclusion to be drawn from this exercise is that there is no objective reading of a political text because there is no common sense understanding in politics. No universal semantics will ever be able to fix what should be understood by **planning, political change, radical reform, government action,** and so on because words, expressions, and utterances change their sense according to the position from which they are uttered. This constitutes the positive form of the thesis I stated in the Introduction.

We are far removed from the transparence of the distinction between person and thing, subject and object, intention and nonintention, precisely because history, that is to say, the class struggle, is neither a person nor a thing; the contradictions of the class struggle run through and organize discourse without ever being clearly resolved.

Based on its class interests, bourgeois thought continually oscillates between two conceptions of society:

1. Society viewed as a thing, a mechanism, a machine which can malfunction, and which must be monitored, controlled, and occasionally repaired.
2. Society viewed as an animate agent, considered as a common project articulated by consensual decision making.

The political ambiguity summarized by the pair economism/humanism, is particularly visible in the effects it provokes within a text like the Mansholt report.

This is not to say that this political ambiguity is limited to the Mansholt report; one could find the same effects elsewhere though perhaps less directly visible, even in certain readings and interpretations of the common program of government of the Left. The latter constitutes a considerable step forward in the struggle of the working class and the proletariat against the bourgeoisie and all its Mansholt plans. Even so the common program is itself the site and stake of an ideological and political class struggle. In order to conceptualize the class struggle, or the struggles of the masses, and in order to orient itself in these struggles, the political practice of the proletariat should divest itself of the categories of economism/humanism and produce its own (e.g., process, contradiction, etc.).

Thus the ideological struggle has nothing whatever to do with so-called semantic misunderstandings giving rise to vacuous problems which will disappear in the light of the formulation of a universal semantics. On the terrain of language, the ideological class struggle is a struggle for the sense of words, expressions and utterances, a vital struggle for each of the two opposing classes which have confronted each other throughout history, right up to the present. This struggle continues today as the unceasing revolutionary struggle against the final stage of capitalism.

REFERENCES

Chomsky, N. *Reflections on language*. New York: Pantheon Books, 1975.
Harris, Z. Discourse analysis. *Language*, 1952, *28*, 1–30.
Mansholt, S. Lettre du 9 février 1972 à Monsieur Franco Mario Malfatti, Président de la Commission européenne. Paris: Editions J.-J. Pauvert, 1972.
Pêcheux, M. *Analyse automatique du discours*. Paris: Dunod, 1969.
Pêcheux, M. *Les vérités de La Palice*. Paris: Maspéro, 1975.
Pêcheux, M., & Fuchs, C. Mises au point et perspectives à propos de l'analyse automatique du discours, *Langages*, 1975, *37*, 7–80.

movements of the head, mimic or following movements occurring after movements by the speaker, and posture shifts, self-grooming movements, and other movements not clearly related to the speech signal. Speaker movements are of much greater variety and include head turns, hand movements, and head nods all of which impressionistically are related (in timing) to the speech stream.

THE DISTRIBUTION OF POSTURE SHIFTS

We will return to the major kinds of body movements which occur when individuals converse, those which are associated in one way or another with speech itself. First, however, we discuss one of the major kinds of movements not associated in any obvious way with speech: posture shifts (body movements involving minimally a change of trunk positioning). Leaving aside for the moment the question of the possible relatedness of posture shifts to speech, the first question to be asked is how posture shifts are related to each other. One way to study this is to see if the distribution of posture shifts fits that of any well-known statistical distribution function. Since posture shifts are relatively rare events (their probability of occurrence within any small interval of time is small) the Poisson distribution is a natural one to try. Table 1 gives the frequency

TABLE 1

Goodness of Fit of Poisson Distribution for Posture Shifts Within 15-Second Intervals

Number of posture shifts	Interactor A Observed	Predicted (λ = .65)
0	32	33.8
1	28	23.6
2	8	8.3
3	0	1.9

Number of posture shifts	Interactor B Observed	Predicted (λ = .45)
0	40	43.3
1	26	19.5
2	2	4.35
3	0	0.68

distribution of posture shifts within 15-second intervals for each of the two Kipsigis interactors in the conversation studied in the previous section over a period of 17 minutes. The parameter lambda is the mean number of posture shifts per interval, and from this parameter the Poisson frequency distribution is determined and compared with the observed frequency distribution. The fit is quite good for each interactor, $\chi_2^2 = 2.33$, $4.37, p > .1$. The meaning of this finding is that, as far as their distribution throughout the time period of an interaction is concerned, posture shifts may be considered random events which are equiprobable within all small, equal intervals. I will suggest a more interesting interpretation of this result in the next section.

THE RELATIONSHIP OF POSTURE SHIFTS TO SPEAKER CHANGE

The occurrence of a posture shift, while not related to the act of speech in any rhythmic way, does seem to be related to one important aspect of speech in conversation: change of speaker. Table 2 presents data (from the same Kipsigis conversation studied above) which are used to test the hypothesis that posture shifts occur independently of speaker changes. The length of the time intervals was 5 seconds. The agreement between the predicted (under the null hypothesis of independence) proportion of co-occurrence of a change of speaker with a posture shift on the part of the new speaker and the probability determined from the observed frequency is tested using a normal approximation to the binomial distribution. A one-tailed test is used since the only alternative to the null hypothesis

TABLE 2

Relationship Between Speaker Change and Posture Shift

	Interactor	
	A	B
Intervals containing speech initiation	48	44
Intervals containing a posture shift	44	30
Observed intervals containing both	30	13
Total	204	

which is considered is that the observed proportion is greater than the predicted. The null hypothesis is rejected for both interactors at the .05 level ($z = 6.4, 2.6$).

If posture shifts are associated with speaker changes of a particular sort (note that not all speaker changes have concomitant posture shifts) then it may be here that an explanation for the Poisson distribution of these is to be found. An examination of the accompanying verbal material suggests that posture shifts are found at major topic shift point or points where speaker–listener roles change. One of the most significant structural aspects of conversation is that topic length and speech or turn length are not predetermined (Sacks, Schegloff, & Jefferson, 1974). Hence posture shifts, as markers of topic changes and major turn changes, may be expected to be distributed in Poisson fashion (assuming that topic/turn length is distributed exponentially).

This of course does not answer the question of why posture shifts are markers of topic changes. I suggest that one possible explanation is that in the course of talk on one topic the physical arena in which a conversation takes place is endowed with aspects of the space which is being talked about as speakers place their scenario and characters in front of and around themselves. A posture shift functions to "clear the stage" and open the way for the creation of a new surrogate space.

PROPORTION OF TIME SPEAKING

In carrying out the research reported in the following three sections, dyads were recorded in three distinct conversations (under slightly different, but randomized, conditions each time). A full break with a brief rest occurred between each conversation, and participants were instructed to begin a new conversation after each break. The interactions were sampled every 10 seconds and the individual speaking was recorded for each sample time (Table 3). The null hypothesis that the proportion of time each individual spoke was constant across all three interactions was tested for six Kipsigis dyads. In no case was the hypothesis rejected, $\chi^2_2 = .9, .41, .39, .73, .67, 1.79, p > .30$.

EFFECTS OF SITTING AND STANDING

This section as well as the next three investigate the effects of varying the physical parameters of interactions (postural position, mutual postural orientation, and distance). Interest in this area is due to Hall (1968). Table

TABLE 3
Relative Proportions of Time Speaking across Three Conversations

Dyad				
1	A	5	4	2
	B	17	24	14
2	A	10	10	14
	B	10	19	19
3	A	16	22	18
	B	8	8	9
4	A	15	17	16
	B	8	8	12
5	A	8	16	13
	B	13	19	13
6	A	14	17	22
	B	13	12	10

4 presents data from three Kipsigis dyads who were recorded in both sitting on chair and standing positions. The numbers represent the total number of body movements (for both interactors) during a 3-minute period (for each dyad in each position). The order of positions was randomized for each dyad, and the location of each 3-minute period within each conversation was determined on a random basis. The null hypothesis of no difference between sitting and standing positions was tested using a t test for the difference of two means and was not rejected at the .05 level, $t_4 = .712$.

EFFECTS OF SITTING AND LYING ON GROUND AND SITTING IN CHAIRS

Table 5 presents data and statistical analysis on the relative frequencies of body movements for three Kipsigis dyads (distinct from those in the preceding section) recorded in each of three positions: sitting on the ground, lying on the ground, and sitting in a chair. The numbers represent the numbers of body movements occurring in 1-minute periods (for each dyad in each position). The order of positions was randomized for each dyad. As in the preceding section there is no evidence that differences in basic posture affect the frequency of interactional behavior $F(2,4) = 6.4$, $.05 < p < .1$ (one-way analysis of variance). There is a significant dyad effect (dyad 3 is systematically more active than 1 or 2), $F(2,4) = 25.2, p < .01$.

TABLE 4
Body Movement Frequencies in Sitting and Standing Positions

Dyad	Sitting	Standing
1	85	121
2	124	133
3	114	101
	323	355
Mean frequency	107.67	118.33

EFFECTS OF DISTANCE

Using the same experimental arrangements as above (with different Kipsigis interactors) the effect of distance on frequencies of body movements was studied (Table 6). As was the case with postural position no significant differences were found for distance, nor were dyad differences significant, $F(2,4) = 1.14, 1.18$.

EFFECTS OF MUTUAL POSTURAL ORIENTATIONS

An attempt was made to study the effects of three different postural configurations—parallel (facing the video camera), facing (facing each other), and angled (facing each other by turning 45° from parallel position). The numbers given in Table 7 were obtained for each dyad by sampling at 5-second intervals and recording the presence or absence of hand movements on the part of the speaker. All numbers were adjusted to reflect frequencies per 50 sample points. Using a two-factor analysis of variance, differences between postural configurations were not significant, $F(2,18) = .78, p = .52$.

TABLE 5
Body Movement Frequencies in Lying, Sitting on Ground and Sitting in Chair Positions

Dyad	Lying	Sitting	Sitting in chair
1	23	26	25
2	23	24	24
3	27	31	28

TABLE 6

Body Movement Frequencies at Three Distances Between Interactors

Dyad	Distance (feet)		
	2	4	7
1	36	26	21
2	26	26	23
3	30	37	31

Note, however, that language differences are significant, $F(2,18)$ = 6.77, $p < .01$. Table 8 shows mean dyad rates for the three languages.

LANGUAGE DIFFERENCES IN AVERAGE TURN LENGTH

Table 9 shows the means for the lengths of speaking time before turn change for three conversations. The interactors were all male elders, but the language used was different in each case. The analysis of variance indicated that the language difference was significant, $F(2,140) = 19.8, p < .01$. There was no attempt to control for individual variation independent of tribal variation and less obviously there was no attempt to control for rate of utterance. Given that languages are spoken at differing rates (again with individual variation at least and possibly also language varia-

TABLE 7

Hand Movement Frequencies for Three Languages and Three Postural Orientations

Language	Dyad	Parallel	Facing	Angled
Luo	1	32	37	42
	2	25	31	23
	3	16	14	18
Kipsigis	1	13	16	22
	2	17	6	19
	3	5	13	10
Gusii	1	35	36	31
	2	26	26	23
	3	12	20	41

TABLE 8 `
Dyad Means Across Postural Orientations

| Language | Dyad means across positions | | |
	Dyad 1	Dyad 2	Dyad 3
Luo	37	26.33	16
Gusii	34	25	24.33
Kipsigis	17	14	9.33

tion present) it is possible that a word or other content measure of turn length would show different results.

OUTLINING MOVEMENTS AND PAUSE GROUPS

In Luo (and in Kipsigis and Gusii to a lesser degree) there is a well-delineated pattern of raising one or both hands (or under some circumstances the head), holding it (them) for a period of time, and then lowering it (them). Impressionistically these movement patterns seem to be associated with pause groups, which are phonetically well marked in Luo by a combination of final stress, distinctive intonation in some cases, and most especially by a pause. Table 10 gives the results of an examination of the occurrence of an outlining movement (or a part of one) with respect to the pause group in one Luo conversation. Four observations may be made: First, although the general tendency is clearly for a pause group to have associated with it an outlining movement, a substantial number of pause groups have no such movement pattern. Second, when it does occur, an upward or downward movement is almost always timed with respect to the beginning and the end of a pause group. Movements not coincident with the onset or offset of a pause group are very rare. The

TABLE 9
Mean Turn Lengths for Three Languages

Language	Mean turn length (sec)
Kipsigis	4.14
Luo	12.21
Gusii	8.17

TABLE 10

Association of Pause Groups and Outlining Movements

Interactor	Pause groups with body movement at beginning and/or end	Pause groups without body movements	Pause groups with body movement other than beginning or end
A	134	53	7
B	98	18	9

general pattern of movement is up at the beginning and down at the end. A very small number of pause groups have an up–hold–further up or down–hold–further down pattern. Fourth, note that some outlining patterns cover more than one pause group (out of a total of 18 such patterns, all but 2 covered two pause groups).

OVERLAPPING AND OUTLINING MOVEMENTS

It should not be thought that simply because the occurrence of outlining movements is tied to pause groups that they have no independent function. They seem to be directly interactional in nature. They signal to the listener that the speaker is engaged in the execution of a piece of his turn.

Indication that this is so is given in Table 11 which shows the results of a careful study of all the overlaps in a conversation between two Luo elders. Overlaps occur in two structurally significant locations in this conversation. The first location is at the beginning of a pause group after the completion of a previous pause group. In this context the presence of an outlining movement does not prevent overlaps. The second location is internal to a pause group and here the data speak quite dramatically to the

TABLE 11

Association of Outlining Movements and Overlaps

Outlining movement pattern	Overlap	
	At beginning of pause group	Internal to pause group
Present	3	0
Absent or complete prior to overlap	3	10

function of the outlining movement. First, note the large number of overlaps which occur internal to a pause group. Clearly, simply being in the middle of the execution of a pause group is no guarantee that a speaker will not be interrupted. Second, note that there are no overlaps which occur internal to an outlining movement pattern. Overlaps occur in just two contexts internal to a pause group: when there is no outlining pattern present or when the lowering movement completing the pattern was executed prior to the completion of the pause group itself. The association of overlap context and outlining movement was significant, p = .036 (Fisher's Exact Test).

HEAD TURNS AND TURN CHANGE

Without exception, all conversations described here involve head movements which bring the speaker and the listener into and out of more or less direct visual contact with one another. The patterns of movement found in the African conversations are extremely complex and undoubtedly multifunctional. Before dealing with those I would like to first consider the pattern of head movements exhibited in a conversation in Eskimo between a native speaker of the language and a nonnative speaker (who was quite fluent in the language).[4] Because of this combination it is not possible to generalize too far about the use of head movements in Eskimo conversation. The conversation was in interview style where the nonnative speaker asked topic-creating questions and the native speaker spoke at length to these (this was a frequently used conversation-generating device in the African conversations as well, where speakers were native speakers of the languages used and were not associated with the researcher). The head turn pattern was extremely consistent throughout the 136-turn conversation. When listening, the Eskimo speaker maintained eye contact with the other speaker, when asking a question, the head was turned toward the listener, and when speaking in declarative fashion, the head was turned away from the listener until just prior to the end of speaking when it was turned toward the listener. Thus at all turn-change points, the Eskimo speaker was visually oriented to the listener.

In the African conversational materials the situation is much more complicated. For example it is no longer true that speakers orient visually to listeners just at turn-change points; although some turn-change points

[4]The research reported here and in the following section was conducted with S. T. Mallon.

are marked by such head turns, many are not so marked, and in addition many instances of head turns occur at points other than turn changes. While it is evident from the large size of the "other" category in Table 12 that there are many instances of head turns which are not easily categorized even in an ad hoc way, it is possible to state a generalization concerning those cases which are categorized. The speaker makes visual reference to the listener just when the listener is involved in some way in the interaction. This involvement can include participation in the content of the discourse, signaled by second person reference, points where it is crucial that the listener understand who a new character in the discourse is, at beginnings of turns and stories where listener attention must first be established before it can be assumed, etc.

In comparison to English-speaking interactors, the African conversants made considerably less use of eye contact, and one common pattern found in English-speaking interactions, where head nodding on the part of the listener replaces a spoken assent, is entirely absent. Further work with the African conversations will therefore have to consider in more detail the interaction between vocal and visual communicational modes.

In Table 12 a small number of head turns appear twice. For instance, a story may occupy several turns or a single turn may contain more than one story, but a story end and a turn end may coincide. The rather large

TABLE 12

Head Turn Contexts

Head turn contexts	Toward	Away
2nd person	11	-
New referent	3	-
Question ask	8	1
Question answer	4	1
Turn		
Beginning	3	5
End	7	3
Topic		
Beginning	2	1
End	6	5
Assent	1	-
Other	21	15
Total	66	31

difference between the number of head turns toward the listener and the number of turns away from the listener is due to the fact that only speakers' head turns are recorded. In many cases the previous speaker remained visually oriented to the other interactor throughout the turn-change period and into the period where his role was that of listener.

HEAD COCKS AND INSERTION SEQUENCES

A highly specialized kind of body movement occurs in Eskimo which does not occur in my African conversations, possibly for the reason that the context which elicited the movement in Eskimo did not occur with any frequency in the African conversations. It is important because it raises the possibility that certain kinds of conversational structures depend typically, if not critically, on extraverbal maneuvers for their execution. In the Eskimo conversation, precisely because the nonnative speaker was less than entirely fluent, there are a total of six insertion sequences (Jefferson, 1972). For our purposes an insertion sequence is a structure where the roles of questioner and answerer are temporarily reversed without a disruption of the primary flow of the conversation. One kind of behavior which is possible with body movement and not possible with speech (except under the condition that what is said be constant as in "uhhh . . . ") is the establishment of a state and the maintenance of that state over a period of time. We have already seen how that possibility is utilized with outlining movements in Luo. With insertion sequences we have the possibility that the inserted sequence be especially marked (with the body) as outside of the main stream of the conversation so that on the cessation of this marking the body is then in the state in which it was prior to the occurrence of the insertion sequence and the mainstream may then be resumed. This is exactly what happened in the Eskimo conversation. For each of the six insertion sequences the Eskimo speaker cocked her head to one side prior to the initiation of a sequence, held the head in the cocked position throughout the sequence and uncocked it immediately on the resumption of the main stream of the conversation. The following example is typical (the location of the head cock is marked with an X):

B: *atiilu,*   *nani*   *inuulauqqit?*
   again+and   wherein   born+past+you+Int
   'Once again then, where were you born?'

A: *Kiŋŋarni*   *inuulauqtuŋa* 1951 *Januaryŋutillugu*
   Cape Dorset+in   born+past+I   1951   January+while being+it
   'I was born in Cape Dorset, in January 1951.'

B: *ai,   iqqaumaviit?*
    aye   remember+you+Int
    'Aye, do you remember?'
A: *ˣiqqaumavuŋa inuugammaa?*
    remember+I   born+when+I
    'Do I remember when I was born?'
B: *ai*
    'aye'
A: *auk   piararuluulauqtuŋali*
    no   child+little+be+Past+but
    'No, for I was just a little child.'

PAUSE GROUPS AND SYNTACTIC STRUCTURE

The pause group in Luo is a phonetically well-demarcated unit characterized by stress on the final word in the pause group, distinctive tonal phenomena, and by a pause between the end of one group and the beginning of another. The extent of coincidence of the pause group with various types of syntactic units was investigated for the conversation studied earlier in the sections on overlapping movements and pause groups, and overlapping and outlining movements (pp. 275–277). In the conversation there are a total of 337 pause groups excluding hesitation pauses and false starts. The total number of words is 1617, and the mean number of words per pause group is 4.8. In characterizing the syntactic structures of the utterances of the conversation, primacy was given to the sentence. Recorded as sentences are all main clause sentences and all embedded sentences except sentence remnants resulting from Equi (infinitival complements) and relative clauses. Recorded as sentences are subject and object complement sentences, and all adverbial dependent clauses. By these criteria there were a total of 261 sentences (excluding incomplete sentences) in the conversation. The mean number of pause groups per sentence is 1.3. Table 13 shows the distribution of pause groups with respect to sentences and primary constituents of sentences (NP,V,Adv). In summary, about 38% of the pause groups were coextensive with a single clause, and 59% were not. Viewed the other way around, there were 261 clauses of which 128, or 49.1%, were coextensive with a single pause group. It is clear that while there is a strong tendency for the sentence to be associated with a pause group, the majority of pause groups are not associated with the (single) sentence, and half of the single sentences are unaccompanied by a pause group. In short a purely syntactic account of the pause group is inadequate.

TABLE 13

Distribution of Pause Groups in Constituent Structure Types

Coextensive with	Number of pause groups	Percentage
More than one sentence	47	13.94
Exactly one sentence	128	37.98
Three or more constituents	31	9.19
Two constituents	35	10.38
One constituent	45	13.35
Less than one constituent	40	11.86
Unclassifiable	11	3.26
Total	337	

It has become clear to psycholinguists (McNeill, 1976) and has been very elegantly demonstrated for conversations in English (Goodwin, 1975) that sentences are not "created" as wholes prior to their utterance, but are made up in pieces as the speaker executes his utterance. At a general level speakers must accomplish two kinds of communicational activities for a conversational "act" to be completed. They must establish the conditions (participants, physical setting, activities) in such a way that they are known and may be understood to be relevant to what follows (with appropriate care taken of the knowledge the listener has), and they must make some kind of speech act—an assertion, a question, an answer, an assent, and so forth. In the case of complex utterances the number of possible opportunities for redoing utterances because of failure to establish the necessary conditions properly is high, and in addition, the syntactic complexity of the utterance is very great. Given these conditions it is not surprising that speakers tend to break their utterances up into pieces with pauses, and it seems very likely to me that these pieces are a reflection of a general principle of establishing only one condition at a time (so that if not understood, an immediate repair may be undertaken) as well as a direct reflection of the way the speaker is composing his utterance as he proceeds. The following sentence from the Luo conversation illustrates this point. Note that its basic structure is copular with a long series of conditions established before the final assertion (pause groups are separated by slashes).

k(a) ιsεɛka·wɔ / pa·rmɛt / mar ti·c /
when you-have-taken permit of   work
ε pɪ·ɲnɔ   mɪ kor(o) ilokori japɪ·ɲnɔ /
in land-that and after you-become man of-land-that
ε k(a) iti·yo
is when you-work
'when you have taken, a permit, for work, now-you become a citizen, is
when you work'

TOPICALIZATION

The final set of results is presented as an illustration of the way in which
actual conversational materials can be used to support (or reject) conclusions about the discourse functions of syntactic rules. I will discuss one
rule only, that of Topicalization, which copies a noun phrase into initial
position in a sentence and then deletes or pronominalizes (depending on
the syntactic environment) the NP in its original position within the
sentence. In many languages rules of this type exist and produce sentences which are not only felt by speakers to be strongly marked in the
sense of being strongly context conditioned, but which are phonetically
marked as well in that the fronted constituent is separated from the rest of
the sentence by a pause (Givón, 1974; Bokamba, 1975). In Luo, sentences
derived by Topicalization are not felt by speakers as marked (that is, they
are not felt to be awkward in isolation), and they are not said to require a
pause break. Table 14 presents the results of an examination of a conversation to test the validity of these claims. There is no tendency for object
NPs which have been fronted to be separated by a comma pause, and
while the frequency of occurrence of object-initial sentences is less than
that of subject-initial sentences, a substantial number of sentences have
fronted objects ($\chi_1^2 = .62, p > .3$).

TABLE 14

Association of Pause Groups with Sentence-Initial Subject NPs and
Sentence-Initial Object NPs

	Subject initial	Object initial
Marked by pause	14	1
Unmarked	64	15

An important lesson may be learned from this example: In the study of discourse functions of syntactic rules, it helps to examine their discourse conditioning across languages and not just in single languages, because what is characteristic for one language may not be the case in another. In English, Topicalization serves only in marked topic changes, particularly ones involving contrast. In Luo,Topicalization is of much more general application, and serves in cases of unmarked topicalization as well. What is common to both languages is the restriction to topic: The rule may not be applied in either language to constituents which are asserted.

SUMMARY

The studies in this paper fall into four groups. Those of the first group (on pp. 268–271) deal with distributional aspects of body movements in interactions. Those of the second group (on pp. 271–275) deal primarily with the effect of varying values of dimensions of the physical setting (such as distance between interactors) on body movement frequency, and secondarily with language and individual differences in body movement frequencies. In general, for the languages and interactors studied, varying the physical dimensions does not appear to affect body movement frequencies, but there exist stable and significant language and individual rate differences. The studies of the third group (on pp. 275–282) deal with the specific interactional functions of body movements in conversation and with the interrelationship between body movements and the speech stream. The final study (Topicalization, pp. 282–283) shows the utility of quantitative data in answering questions of the discourse functions of syntactic rules. In a few cases (principally on pp. 276–280) the results seem interesting and significant in themselves and the other cases all illustrate ways in which quantitative methods can be used in the study of aspects of conversation.

REFERENCES

Bokamba, E. G. Observations on the immediate dominance constraint, topicalization, and relativization. *Studies in African Linguistics,* 1975, 6, 1–22.
Givón, T. Universal grammar, lexical structure and translatability. In M. Guenthner-Reuther & F. Guenthner (Eds.), *Meaning and translation: Philosophical and linguistic approaches.* London: Duckworth, 1975.

Goodwin, C. The interactive construction of the sentence within the turn at talk in natural conversation. Paper presented at the 74th annual meeting of the American Anthropological Association, San Francisco, 1975.

Greenberg, J. H. *Languages of Africa.* Bloomington: Indiana University Press, 1966.

Hall, E. T. Proxemics. *Current Anthropology,* 1968, *9,* 83–108.

Jefferson, G. Side sequences. In D. Sudnow (Ed.), *Studies in social interaction.* New York: Free Press, 1972, 294–338.

McNeill, D. Some effects of context on utterance. In S. Steever, C. Walker, & S. Mufwene (Eds.), *Papers from the parasession on diachronic syntax.* Chicago: Chicago Linguistic Society, 1976, 205–220.

Sacks, H., Schegloff, E. A., & Jefferson, G. A simplest systematics for turn-taking for conversation. *Language,* 1974, *50,* 696–735.

Author Index

Subject Index